Experimental British television

Manchester University Press

Experimental British television

edited by
Laura Mulvey and Jamie Sexton

Manchester University Press

Copyright © Manchester University Press 2007

While copyright in the volume as a whole is vested in Manchester University Press, copyright in individual chapters belongs to their respective authors, and no chapter may be reproduced wholly or in part without the express permission in writing of both author and publisher.

Published by Manchester University Press
Altrincham Street, Manchester M1 7JA, UK
www.manchesteruniversitypress.co.uk

British Library Cataloguing-in-Publication Data is available

Library of Congress Cataloging-in-Publication Data is available

ISBN 978 0 7190 7555 1 *paperback*

First published by Manchester University Press in hardback 2007

This paperback edition first published 2015

The publisher has no responsibility for the persistence or accuracy of URLs for any external or third-party internet websites referred to in this book, and does not guarantee that any content on such websites is, or will remain, accurate or appropriate.

Printed by Lightning Source

We would like to dedicate this book to Catrin Prys Jones, who sadly passed away in 2006.

Contents

	List of illustrations	*page* ix
	List of contributors	xi
	Acknowledgements	xiii
	Introduction: experimental British television – Laura Mulvey	1
1	'Creative in its own right': the Langham Group and the search for a new television drama – John Hill	17
2	'And now for your Sunday night experimental drama …': experimentation and *Armchair Theatre* – Helen Wheatley	31
3	A 'new drama for television'?: *Diary of a Young Man* – John Hill	48
4	'The very new can only come from the very old': Ken Russell, national culture and the possibility of experimental television at the BBC in the 1960s – Kay Dickinson	70
5	From art to avant-garde? Television, formalism and the arts documentary in 1960s Britain – Jamie Sexton	89
6	An experiment in television drama: John McGrath's *The Adventures of Frank* – Lez Cooke	106
7	Don't fence me in: *The Singing Detective* and the synchronicity of indeterminacy – Catrin Prys	120
8	*Visions*: a Channel 4 experiment 1982–85 – John Ellis	136
9	Experimenting on air: UK artists' film on television – A. L. Rees	146
10	Experimental music video and television – K. J. Donnelly	166
11	'Yes, it's war!': Chris Morris and comedy's representational strategies – Brett Mills	180
	Bibliography	195
	Index	205

List of illustrations

1	*The Singing Detective*	*page* 130
2	*The Singing Detective*	130
3	*The Singing Detective*	130
4	*The Singing Detective*	130

List of contributors

Lez Cooke is Research Associate in Television Drama at Manchester Metropolitan University. He is the author of *British Television Drama: A History* (BFI, 2003) and *Troy Kennedy Martin* (Manchester University Press, 2007).

Kay Dickinson is a lecturer in Media and Communications at Goldsmiths College, University of London. She is the author of *Off Key: When Film and Music Won't Work Together* (Oxford University Press, 2008) and the editor of *Movie Music: The Film Reader* (Routledge, 2002) and with Glyn Davis, *Teen TV: Genre, Consumption and Identity* (BFI, 2003).

K.J. Donnelly is Reader in Film at the University of Southampton. He is the author of *British Film Music and Film Musicals* (2007), *The Spectre of Sound* (2005), *Pop Music in British Cinema* (2001) and edited *Film Music: Critical Approaches* (2001).

John Ellis is Professor of Media Arts at Royal Holloway University of London. His books include *Visible Fictions* (1982), *Seeing Things* (2000) and *TV FAQ* (2007), and he has written widely on both television and cinema for journals including *Screen* and *Media, Culture and Society*. Between 1982 and 1999 he ran the independent TV production company Large Door, making programmes on cinema, popular culture and food including Angela Carter's *Holy Family Album* and the award-winning *This Food Business*. His research into the history and forms of TV has produced the AHRC funded database of ITV programmes 1955–85 (TVTiP at the BUFVC website), and from 2006 he joined the EU funded Video Active project aiming to make available online items from historic European TV.

John Hill is Professor of Media at Royal Holloway, University of London. He is the author of *Sex, Class and Realism: British Cinema 1956-63* (1986), *British Cinema in the 1980s* (1999), and *Cinema and Northern Ireland: Film, Culture and Politics* (2006) and co-editor of *The Oxford Guide to Film Studies* (1998).

Brett Mills is a lecturer in Film and Television Studies at the University of East Anglia. He is the author of *Television Sitcom* (BFI: 2005) and co-author with David Barlow of *Reading Media Theory* (Pearson: forthcoming). He has just completed the AHRC-funded research project, 'Funny Business: Interviews with Members of the British Terrestrial Television Comedy Industry'.

Laura Mulvey is Professor of Film and Media Studies at Birbeck College, University of London. Her books include *Visual and Other Pleasures* (Macmillan, 1989), *Fetishism and Curiosity* (BFI, 1996) and *Death 24x a Second: Stillness and the Moving Image* (Reaktion, 2005).

Catrin Prys was a lecturer at the University of Wales, Aberystwyth, teaching through the medium of English and Welsh. She had published on British television drama and had extensively researched the work of Dennis Potter. Her other main research interests revolved around Welsh and European Theatre. She unfortunately passed away in October 2006 and will be sadly missed by all her family, friends and colleagues. This book is dedicated to her memory.

Al Rees is a Research Fellow in the Department of Communication, Art and Design at the Royal College of Art. He is the author of *A History of Experimental Film and Video* (BFI, 1999) and *Fields of View* (BFI, forthcoming).

Jamie Sexton is a lecturer in Film and Media at the University of Wales, Aberystwyth. He is the author of *Alternative Film Culture in Inter-War Britain* (Exeter University Press, forthcoming) and editor of *Music, Sound and Multimedia: From the Live to the Virtual* (Edinburgh University Press, 2007).

Helen Wheatley is Lecturer in Film and Television Studies at the University of Warwick. She has published a range of work on popular genres in television drama in the UK, US and beyond, and is the author of *Gothic Television* (Manchester University Press, 2006). She has also published work on lifestyle television and natural history programming and has ongoing research interests in television historiography, and the idea of 'television for women'. She is currently beginning work on a book on the nature of spectacle and visual pleasure on television.

Acknowledgements

We would like to acknowledge the assistance of the AHRC in this project. It initially emerged out of work undertaken within the AHRB Centre for British Film and Television Studies. We would also like to thank Glen Creeber for encouraging the initial idea.

Introduction: experimental British television

Laura Mulvey

The concept of experimental television might seem an oxymoron to many. However, the essays in this book demonstrate that the aspiration to experiment is present, if not consistent or systematic, as a thread running through the history of British television. The book as a whole is intended to articulate the idea behind the oxymoron and to draw attention to this neglected area of television studies. 'Experimental' is necessarily an evocative rather than a definitive term in the context of television aesthetics, but it enables the designation of ways in which practitioners have pushed at the medium's conventions and boundaries, expanding its vocabulary and investigating its specificity. As some of these aesthetic experiments have taken place on the margins of television, and some have been relegated to oblivion as critical failures, further research is needed (across both the BBC and ITV) to find 'lost' programmes that will fill in gaps and give this fragile tradition a firmer demarcation. *Experimental British television*, which begins with the forgotten work of the Langham Group and ends with the notoriety of Chris Morris's *Brass Eye* (Channel 4, 1997; 2001), has attempted to recover some forgotten examples of experimentation to juxtapose with the better known. Although there have been analyses of experimental work in television studies, the lack of systematic investigation into this area is highlighted by the contrast with the substantial body of work on experimental cinema. This book is thus an attempt to define a hitherto undefined aesthetic field and open up an initial line of approach: to investigate a relatively arid research area and to stimulate further analyses of television in a similar vein. The book's range is, however, necessarily limited, making a gesture towards the issues at stake but only constituting a first step in such a direction.

Experimental British television primarily addresses the aesthetics of television programmes, charting some key examples of experiment and formal or stylistic innovation, drawing mostly on arts documentaries and drama productions. These were the genres for which licence to deviate from the norm was more likely to be granted. Sometimes, synchronously, experimental aesthetics crossed genres (as for instance, with the early use of 16 mm film in the mid-1960s). Even more striking is the diachronic instability of television aesthetics across its history, due to technological and other changes. Whereas experimental film developed, addressed, and over its history returned to, a reasonably consistent set of aesthetic issues, television, over its considerably shorter history, has been beset by change of all kinds: changing institutional or regulatory structures, technological change, or changing contexts and influences. While it is probable that this lack of aesthetic coherence has contributed to the difficulty of articulating the concept 'experimental television', it is still important to try to identify and analyse the aesthetics of this nearly invisible 'radical aspiration' and its varying forms within the changing technologies that condition television aesthetics.[1]

The concept of experimental aesthetics, across the arts, has evolved particularly around the question of medium specificity. In the case of television, 'specificity' is complicated not only by the medium's fluctuating technology but also by its, largely stable, site of reception. Television's intrusive surroundings have been given critical attention that has rarely been given to the site specificity of cinema. Its topography, its place in a domestic setting, came to be a key term defining television specificity, while aesthetics tended to lag behind. These apparently incompatible critical approaches seem to suggest two specificities: one most particularly to do with broadcasting, the material conditions of transmission into domestic space; the other to do with the aesthetics of a particular programme, its textual attributes. Television theory initially developed out of interest in the former type of specificity. Roger Silverstone, for instance, stressed television's place 'in the visible and hidden ordering of everyday life; in its spatial and temporal significance; in its embeddedness in quotidian patterns and habits, as a contributor to our security.'[2] In *Visible Fictions*, John Ellis put the topographical point succinctly: 'Television is a profoundly domestic phenomenon.'[3] He too argues that this significance is necessarily temporal as well as spatial due to the constant availability of the broadcast signal that, once again spatially, emanates from a central point of control. Here the specificity of space conflates with a specificity of time, as the television schedule (in continuity, of course, with radio) articulated the order and sequence of domestic life with appropriate programming.

These spatial and temporal conjunctures had already led Raymond Williams to draw attention to the fact that radio and television are sequential media.[4] Writing in the early 1970s, he said:

> What is being offered is not, in older terms, a programme of discrete units with particular insertions, but a planned flow, in which the true series is not the

published sequence of programme items but this sequence transformed by the inclusion of another kind of sequence, so that these sequences comprise the real flow, the real 'broadcasting'.[5]

Through the use of the word 'real', Williams came close to suggesting an essential specificity for television as a medium. However, unlike radio, television is visual and introduces a particular regime of seeing into its space and time. The combined effect of flow and television's intrusive domestic surroundings led John Ellis to identify the television 'look' as glancing or distracted, unlike the intense cinematic gaze.[6]

From the perspective of this book, these approaches (the domestic space, the glance, the flow) to the specificity of television all bump against an approach that emphasises the aesthetic integrity and televisual qualities of the individual programme. For the concept of experimental television to work, the programme has to detach itself from the surrounding flow. Flow tends to favour an aesthetic of smooth, almost invisible temporal transition, whereas experiment draws attention to itself and to the language of television, catching and then holding the 'distracted glance'. From this perspective, television incorporates a double look: a distracted glance that can become fixed and absorbed. This 'fixed' look has nothing in common with the entranced gaze associated with narrative cinema; it represents a discerning, receptive interaction with a particular programme. But while experimental television challenges the smoothness of flow, there may also be an ideological tension intrinsic to its disruptive nature. If television is domestic, experimental programmes often raise the fraught issue of the family, suitability and shock. Experimental programmes have pushed at the boundaries of acceptability, not only positively through aesthetic innovation but also, in the tradition of negative aesthetics, as a challenge to the complacency of the medium itself. John Ellis puts his finger on this issue:

> Broadcast TV confirms the normality and safety of the viewer's presumed domestic situation. The viewer delegates the activity of an investigatory looking to TV itself. TV returns a particular sense of the outside world to the viewer, against which the normality of the domestic is confirmed.[7]

While the cinematic avant-garde's negative aesthetic has challenged conventions and expectations in its own, by and large, self-contained world, experimental television has actively brought disturbance into the ideological emblem of normality and safety: domestic space. Of course, such a challenge has maximum efficacy when it introduces disturbing, particularly sexual, material into the home. Owing, once again, to its topographical specificity, television became the site of the culture war initiated by Mary Whitehouse in 1963. From Anthony Pelissier's *Torrents of Spring* in 1959, through Ken Russell's *Dance of the Seven Veils* (1970), to Chris Morris's *Brass Eye*, the essays in this book draw attention to the alliance between 'subversive content' and experimentation.

In spite of the emphasis on aesthetics, almost all the case studies recognise the importance of a programme's place in the schedule for its success or even survival. This does not necessarily involve a prime slot, but experimental television needs to find an appropriate location. John Ellis points out that the lack of consistency in scheduling *Visions* (Channel 4, 1982–85) was ultimately responsible for the programme's decline, while Ken Russell's experiments could flourish within the absolute certainty and regularity of *Monitor*'s (BBC, 1958–65) slot, with its established resonance and associations. On the other hand, *New Tempo* (ITV, 1967), contributing to ABC's public service remit quota and, occupying a Sunday afternoon 'graveyard' slot, was able to experiment more radically than most programmes. While the programmes analysed in these essays lead away from the notion of 'flow' and towards a programme's own engagement with the specificity of television aesthetics, their aberrant nature returns them once again to problems of scheduling.

Politics as such and the politics of television necessarily have a bearing on the essays in this book, which broadly traces a history of experiment in British television from its early maturity (the late 1950s to late 1960s) until the arrival of Channel 4 in 1982 (with two later examples). That is, from the time of the BBC/ITV duopoly in which the possibility for experiment depended, almost always, on an informal conjuncture between particular people: those who could make an institutional opening and the creative talent who could fill it.[8]

This situation changed totally with the Broadcasting Act of 1980. While a public service remit had always specified a responsibility 'to inform, educate and entertain', the new channel would have a responsibility, in the now resonant phrase, 'to encourage experiment and innovation in the form and content of programmes'.[9] Furthermore, the new channel would be expected to address 'tastes and interests not catered for by ITV'.[10] Just as the Pilkington Report in 1962 consciously addressed the need for television to respond to and acknowledge changing social and cultural contexts, so did Annan in 1977. This continuity, however, was broken by Channel 4's revolutionary institutional framework: it was the commissioning structure that created the most radical break with the past. Independent production companies, significantly in continuity with 1970s independent film culture (see Chapter 8), were in the forefront of this new era of experimental television. This new industrial pluralism echoed the pluralism represented by the new voices that would be heard on the new channel confirming its initial appeal to a left-liberal nexus. On the other hand, of course, the concept of pluralism was open to opposite interpretations from the right as well as the left. Just as the constitution of Channel 4 in the 1980s quite rightly recognised that the aspiration to a consensual voice for the nation was no longer relevant to British society, Margaret Thatcher, in 1981, announced a similar perception from an opposite political stance:

> To me, consensus seems to be: the process of abandoning all beliefs, principles, values and policies in search of something in which no one believes, but to which no one objects ...[11]

This remark, although it had nothing to do with television, draws attention to a point of rupture in its history. The Prime Minister's dismissive attitude to 'consensus' refers back to the politics of the 1950s and 1960s and can thus conjure up, in the first instance, the ghost of 1950s and 1960s television, when experimental (and other) programmes challenged the traditions of elite culture and class society. But the remark also predicts the destruction, during the 1980s, of the industrial working class (crucial to the 1950s television) and hints at the institutional instability that would overtake the tradition of public service broadcasting during the 1990s. If the public service remit had struggled to keep alive a sense of addressing a nation, it would itself soon be reeling from a carefully calculated series of onslaughts, from those of market forces to the effects of new technologies of delivery. From this perspective, although Channel 4 marks the moment when experiment and innovation were consciously introduced into British television, it also marks the end of the duopoly and the emergence of a politicised policy that would inexorably lead to the Broadcasting Act of 1990.

The tendency for those interested in radical politics also to be interested in radical aesthetics runs through this period of British culture, and is reflected in the different phases of experimental television discussed here. This book has not been able to chart the history of experimental television evenly across the second half of the last century. Most of the essays return to the age of two- and three- channel television. The comparatively well-known impact of Channel 4, and its 'new wave' of experimental television, is charted through two examples of its relation to cinema: the integration and transformation of the independent film sector into a completely new and innovative form of experimental television, and the experimental arts programme dedicated to the cinema, *Visions*. The very rich period of 1980s television, with its anti-Thatcher investigative current affairs programmes and its great anti-Thatcher drama series, is registered only through the important six-part drama *The Singing Detective* (BBC1, 1986). Finally, *Brass Eye* exemplifies, in an extreme form, the self-reflexive satire that characterises some of the most innovative television of the 1990s.

The first two chapters of this book examine two responses to the pressing need for television to respond aesthetically to its new maturity and to reflect its changing social contexts. As Helen Wheatley points out in Chapter 2, *Armchair Theatre* (ITV, 1956–74) represented a conscious attempt to 'democratise' television drama, extending its content to thoughtful and sophisticated reflections on working-class life and culture. Produced by ABC and first aired in 1956, *Armchair Theatre*'s 'tip of the iceberg' experimental plays are both a symptom of, and an intervention in, their surrounding culture. John Caughie has brilliantly described the cluster of political and cultural events in the landmark year 1956 that incidentally and directly affected developments in television. The new voices of working-class writers, symbolised by *Look Back in Anger* (first staged at The Royal Court in 1956) emerged into a radically altered political conjuncture. British television reached maturity as the legacy of the post-war Labour government met the 'affluent society' of the Tory 1950s. This was the moment at which economic, cultural and social factors combined to bring television into British life as, in Brian Winston's term, 'a supervening social necessity'.[12] From the point of view of economics, the 'affluent society' created a working-class able for the first time to acquire commodities, with television an emblem of this new consumer society. From the point of view of culture, public service television gave the working-class access to ideas, drama, political debate, arts and so on in a new extension of the public sphere. From the point of view of society, this was, of course, the 'age of consensus': just as 'Butskillism' encapsulated Conservative continuity with Labour reforms, the television duopoly of the BBC and ITV, by and large, mirrored each other, in spite of the commercial channels' introduction of American programmes and other mass audience pleasers. Both institutions took on board the need to invent a new means of address for a changing audience and a changing concept of the nation while the restriction of channels, the 'era of scarcity' in John Ellis's apt insight, concentrated both address and audience. Television plays dealing with issues of class, education, the everyday, made a key contribution (alongside novels and plays) to that moment in British history when mainstream culture aspired to represent a new concept of the nation and imagine a new unity.

This kind of 'social extension' in television's representation of British life, in itself, would not put the *Armchair Theatre* dramas in the 'experimental' category (nor, as Wheatley emphasises, were most of the plays intended to be). It was the combination of political commitment with aesthetic engagement that is of interest in this history. Through the use of mobile studio (pedestal) cameras, *Armchair Theatre* created a televisual style that was specific to studio recording and live transmission, the conditions under which television operated at the time. Wheatley describes the long takes, using a single moving camera, that transformed the three camera static set-ups that were the norm. These programmes turned the impossibility of editing live broadcasts, and later, after its introduction in 1958, the difficulty of editing videotape, into fascinating experiments with the aesthetics of the new medium. The plays' producers, were, however, wary of 'artiness', never overlooking their place in the flow of ITV's programmes as *Armchair Theatre* followed straight after *Sunday Night at the London Palladium* (ITV, 1955–67; 1973–74). Radicalism of form was echoed in content: the aspiration to put on television images and voices, scenes and dialogues from working-class life combined with the creative struggle to find an appropriate language for the new medium.

In Chapter 1, John Hill turns to the work of the little known Langham Group. In contrast to the populism of *Armchair Theatre*, the group emerged from a BBC initiative (also, revealingly, dating from 1956) to consider 'the problem of experimental television programmes'. Hill points out that, although the group took a range of references from the cinema, including the contemporaneous French New Wave, it aimed to break with theatrical and cinematic tradition to create a televisual language that would be specific to the medium. Whilst the Langham Group also used the mobile pedestal camera, Hill emphasises differences from the *Armchair Theatre* style and approach, and there is a considerable amount of debate about the single camera's aesthetic significance in these and other contexts. However, both chapters together build a picture of early television in which its most skilled and self-conscious practitioners, under benign management, were able to consider and put into practice, in Anthony Pelissier's words, 'something exclusive to the medium'. Hill's description of 'expressionist' devices in *Torrents of Spring* (BBC, 1959) also chimes with Wheatley's discussion of similar devices in *Armchair Mystery Theatre* (ITV, 1960; 1964–65). Furthermore, the use of montage in *Torrents of Spring* prefigures its use in *A Diary of a Young Man* (BBC) in 1964 (see Hill, Chapter 3).

Hill's defence of the Langham Group against accusations of artiness and dependence on literary adaptation once again emphasises the contemporary search for a new reflection of society and a move away from a middle-class milieu. The plays displaced their original settings on to working-class characters and into working-class environments. As Hill points out, the Langham Group's experiments were not taken seriously by Troy Kennedy Martin and others (see Chapter 3). This later antagonism may well be derived from the tension between the new generation of largely non-metropolitan, working-class writers and those they identified with the avant-garde tradition of the London intelligentsia. The founding importance of this period is clear: the aspiration to find expression for working-class stories, accents and environments was as significant in the so-called 'arty' BBC experiments as in the more populist *Armchair Theatre* and would continue to be so during the 1960s. Above all, it was during this period that experiments with form first achieved a televisual 'textuality'. The single, mobile, studio camera not only represents a key stage in establishing the specificity of television but also, as the technology was ephemeral and soon to disappear, it offers an emblem of the essentially changing, unstable, nature of the medium. This condition of almost perpetual change has, needless to say, affected the aesthetics of television, further contributing to difficulties in pinning down a specificity that seems to be characterised by instability.

Chapters 3, 4 and 5 discuss very varied examples of experimental television that flourished during the 1960s. In Chapter 4, Kay Dickinson introduces her discussion of Ken Russell's arts documentaries with the observation that, in the 1960s, culture acquired a new centrality in British society and its economy. This move was, of course, partly due the 'sixties' phenomenon and the successful marketing of British culture both at home and abroad, but it was also, Dickinson points out, an investment in the idea of culture as a new emblem of national life, especially after the collapse of British colonial power. Although this turn towards culture accelerated under the Labour Government (charted illuminatingly by Robert Hewison in the early chapters of *Culture and Consensus*), it was television that played the central part in the extension of culture across the British class system during the 1960s. Furthermore, these chapters reveal a significant shift in radical aesthetics during the period (exemplified by, but not limited to, the programmes discussed). Experiment in television was moving away from the tradition of English realism and new aesthetic influences were apparent in both drama and arts documentaries. In the first instance, there was a sense of exhaustion with 'Englishness' in the 1960s, with the Leavis tradition in literary criticism, as well as the 'Establishment' (as the metropolitan ruling and cultural elite came to be known in the 1950s). From this perspective, it is telling that the most influential challenge to the traditions of English realism came from abroad and from modernism: the influence of Brecht. John Caughie comments on the Berliner Ensemble's landmark visit to London in 1956 and its lasting impact: 'It is hard to conceive of British theatre – or British television drama – without the intervention of Brecht and his challenge to the "natural" and "naturalizing" space of realism.'[13]

The influence of Brecht on British television drama recurs in several essays in the book: particularly in Chapters 3 and 6 but also, if more implicitly, in Catryn Prys's analysis of *The Singing Detective* in Chapter 7. Not only did Brecht consolidate the idea that aesthetic and political radicalism were inextricably linked, but his influence also merged with the quest for televisual specificity to produce a stripped down, self-conscious form of drama. This double tendency can be seen in Troy Kennedy Martin's manifesto 'Nats Go Home', discussed by John Hill in Chapter 3. Hill's discussion of *Diary of a Young Man* draws attention to Kennedy Martin's perception of television as an essentially 'distanciated' medium. The influence of Brecht merges with an aesthetic in which narrative is stripped of naturalistic trappings to find its bare bones and the episodic nature of the story is accentuated by its characteristic 'gestic social encounters'. As a negative aesthetic, the use of montage sequences and stills distance the drama further from the conventions of realism. As a positive aesthetic, these devices, combined with a mixture of location and studio shooting, introduce a heterogeneity that not only echoes television's fragmentation and segmentation but also the episodic, disjunctive nature of the drama's mode of storytelling. *Diary of a Young Man* also dramatises the cultural and social gap between London and the 'provinces' that prevailed at the time. Kennedy Martin and his co-author John McGrath, both Scots, used the opportunity to satirise London as the capital, not so much of Britain, but of Establishment Conservatism. There is something particularly radical, perhaps, in setting a Northern working-class hero in an uncompromisingly modernist drama.

In 1980, McGrath made *The Adventures of Frank*, analysed by Les Cooke in Chapter 6. As the play experiments with the superimpositions and fantastic transformations enabled by the new video-based technology of colour separation, the constantly changing nature of television aesthetics is once again apparent. Cooke draws attention to the strong and persistent influence of Brecht on *The Adventures of Frank*, which is a kind of 'remake' of *Diary of a Young Man* in the completely different political and economic context of early Thatcherism. These two dramas have a resonant relationship across the fifteen years that separates them. *Diary of a Young Man* was transmitted in August 1964, two months before the Labour Party's election victory. *The Adventures of Frank* (BBC1, 1980), on the other hand, as Cooke points out, seems to signal the end of an era, and McGrath's Brechtian aesthetics (although of great importance during the 1970s for his theatre company 7:84) seem to stretch from the 1960s into another world.

During the 1980s, the six-part series became the established form for drama. Out of this response to the specific possibilities offered by television, an innovative form developed that broke with the theatrical legacy of the single play while maintaining the extended parts within a coherent dramatic form. Again, the aesthetics of television drama underwent a radical change not, in this case, due to technology but achieved by collaboration between institutional, production and creative forces. This kind of collaboration characterised the production of *Diary of a Young Man*, the drama that had pioneered the six-part series in 1964, and is further exemplified by the working practices that produced the extremely influential *The Boys from the Blackstuff* (BBC) in 1982.

Dennis Potter's career spans both dramatic forms and, as Catrin Prys points out in Chapter 7, it also exemplifies the crucial contribution of collaboration for the particular demands inherent to the six-part series. Potter also brings back the influence of Brecht, which he had thoroughly absorbed in the 1960s. There is a residual link between the active spectatorship of the Brechtian epic theatre and the deciphering viewer constructed by *The Singing Detective*, analysed by Catrin Prys. She charts the way that the drama is built around enigma, from the detective story to the protagonist's unconscious mind, out of which a particular kind of viewer is constructed, also participating in the struggle to decipher. The drama's complex layering and movement in and out of parallel worlds is only possible within the extended form of the six-part series. Prys demonstrates the way in which the essential heterogeneity of *The Singing Detective*, its fragmentation of a coherent fictional world with memories, fantasies and free association, also produced an aesthetic of repetition and return as themes and motives weave across the six parts.

Another explicit break with the realist aesthetic came from a new generation of artists, equivalent to the 'scholarship boys' evoked by Tony Garnett, who were turning to Pop Art. Art critic John Russell sums up its relevance to contemporary English culture:

> Pop was a resistance movement: a classless commando that was directed against the Establishment in general and the Art Establishment in particular ... Pop in England was a facet of class struggle, real or imagined. It was for the present, and even more for the future: it was not for the past and saw nothing to regret in the changes which had come about in England since 1945.[14]

Ken Russell's first programme for *Monitor*, *Pop Goes the Easel* (BBC, 1962) was a study of four Royal College of Art students who were working with Pop. Huw Wheldon's introduction to the programme vividly illustrates the cultural tensions of the time as he warned the audience that this is 'a world which you can dismiss if you feel so inclined as tawdry and second rate, but a world in which everyone to some degree lives whether they like it or not'. Although Russell's later *Monitor* and *Omnibus* (BBC1, 1967–) biographies study the lives and work of English composers, the nature of 'Englishness' is constantly under question. Furthermore, the programmes are characterised, as Dickinson describes, by an innovative pushing at the boundaries that separated documentary and drama, breaking the taboo against the fusion of the two, gradually introducing, against the grain, character 'impersonation' and eliminating the traditional guiding voice-over. At the same time, of course, in a break with the traditional realist aesthetic, voice-over began to appear in drama, as, for instance, in *Diary of a Young Man*.

Also within these 'benevolent conditions', the arrival of 16mm film and synchronised sound had an immediate affect on television aesthetics. Hill ends his chapter on *Diary of a Young Man* with intimations of future change.

He draws attention to the increasing tension between two diverse aesthetics: that of the studio and that of the location. The introduction of 16 mm film offered liberation into the outside world, displacing the televisual aesthetics and the 'textuality' of the studio. Out of its limitations, the studio aesthetic also had the strength of 'liveness', unlike the cinema and, furthermore, unlike the theatre, owing to the complex studio staging described by Wheatley and Hill.[15] But the spatial constraints of live broadcast were, of course, experienced across television as a whole and current affairs programmes, in particular, grew restless with the limitations of the studio interview and discussion. Exterior scenes introduced without synchronised sound were unsatisfactorily extraneous to both drama and current affairs programmes.

The arrival of 16 mm film complicates an ontological approach to television aesthetics. Jamie Sexton in Chapter 5 traces the use of 16 mm from current affairs (such as *World in Action* [ITV, 1962–98]) as it crossed to the arts documentary and also to drama.[16] For John Caughie the intrusion of film into television represents a 'fall from grace', in an echo of the purist film avant-garde's attitude to the coming of sound to cinema. However, he argues cogently that the 16 mm dramas that appeared in *The Wednesday Play* (BBC, 1964–70) slot transform the material loss of television's ontologically derived 'liveness' and 'immediacy' into an aesthetics in which the term mutates from a literal into a political meaning:

> In general terms, the achievement of the drama documentaries of the 1960s and after is that they built on the specificities of the televisual, on its unique capabilities for the representation of the social real, and introduced a new form to twentieth-century art. They seem to me to have developed an aesthetics of immediacy which was grounded in the technological and historical specificity of television but was articulated as an achieved form rather than a fact of nature, exploiting the illusion of the real for political ends.[17]

He goes on to comment that this incorporation and transcendence of naturalism, when crossed with fragments of montage, achieved a televisual modernism. This book has not covered the very important moment of 16 mm drama as it has been quite thoroughly discussed, and included in Caughie's chapter 'The rush of the real'. Organisational resistance to 16 mm once again draws attention to how individual people have contributed to radical change within the often reluctant institutional settings of television. From Tim Hewett's struggle at Granada's *World in Action* to Tony Garnett's (more difficult) struggle at BBC drama, a clear understanding of the purpose of innovation, and a political motivation, was essential to their success.

Historically, the contribution made by 16 mm film to television is crucial to the experimental aesthetics of the 1960s and, theoretically, film introduces a kind of 'dialectic' to an essential approach to the medium's ontological properties. Television's liveness, unique to the broadcast medium, gives primacy to its temporality: its present tense, its 'nowness', also creates space for direct address, the I/you exchange that is essentially tied to a present moment of time. In this sense, the grammatical form of tense meets the grammatical form of person, that also links the spaces of exchange, the 'here' and the 'there' of each side of the screen. While film liberated television from spatial limitation, it exists inescapably in the past, thus losing the present tense but gaining spatial flexibility. As a number of commentators have pointed out, temporalities have been fused by the conventions of broadcasting, so that even the necessary past-ness of film acquires, on television, a 'psuedo-immediacy', achieved, particularly, by direct address. In this sense, 16mm film on television could exploit two conventions. The hand-held camera could signify the crucial move into the space of reality, of being actually on the spot and in the thick of things; direct address could signify the temporality of television, its immediacy and its ability to cross between 'here' and 'there'.

As television emerged out of the studio, the complicated question of television specificity returned to topography: the recognisable sites and concerns of everyday life could reach the domestic space of reception and the everyday lives and concerns of viewers. This responsibility produced a particular kind of experimental television. While 16mm cinéma vérité had quickly developed an aesthetic that rejected non-synchronous interventions into the recorded sound and image, 16mm television drama absorbed influences from other television forms, particularly the campaigning, issue-driven current affairs programmes such as *World in Action* and *Man Alive* (BBC2, 1965–81). The great experimental plays of the mid-1960s, such as *Up the Junction* (BBC1, 1965) and *Cathy Come Home* (BBC1, 1966), exploited television's flow and its characteristic heterogeneity to create a 16mm drama with a specifically televisual textuality. Although no specific discussion of this particular form of television drama is included here, Jamie Sexton, in Chapter 5, analyses two remarkable, but little-known, arts documentary programmes that consciously worked with the aesthetic potential of 16mm film on television as a specific, although hybrid, form. The portraits in *Who Is?* (BBC2, 1968) are heterogeneous in style, sometimes within a single programme, breaking up internal coherence visually and sonically in order to draw attention to their significance for television aesthetics. In the very dense programmes of *New Tempo*, 16mm loses something of the specificity and consequently the hybridity of film on television. Film, montage, stills, fictional impersonation and, above all, sounds of all kinds, fuse to create an extraordinarily complex experiment with television aesthetics. As the programmes reflect on key issues of society, culture and aesthetics of late 1960s modernity in Britain, the style also sets up an 'echo' in which form and the content also fuse together.

In Chapter 8, John Ellis introduces Channel 4 with an insider's account of a world of utopian hopes and the snares of the schedule. *Visions* was an arts programme dedicated to cinema, thus fulfilling a long-standing cinephile aspiration, introducing the complex and rich development of film culture during the 1970s, both British and international. Ellis describes the aesthetic issues involved in a careful consideration of cross-media aesthetics, particularly the ingenious solution to the presentation of film clips on the small screen. *Visions* also represented the highly developed film consciousness in Channel 4. While the new channel broke with television's ancient cultural investment in drama, concentrating instead on commissioning feature films for Film Four, a new opportunity arose for film experiment on television. In Chapter 9, Al Rees analyses the complex interaction between the independent film movement of the 1970s and the early years of the channel. During this period, the film avant-garde's concept of specificity, more to do with materiality than conditions of reception and production, evolved into a new consciousness of television: a televisual, more video-based, experimental aesthetic began to develop. Although the avant-garde independents were restricted to late-night slots, out of cross-fertilisation with music and the arrival of a new generation of practitioners, a televisual aesthetic developed that could only have grown out of this particular conjuncture. This account leads to Kevin Donnelly's analysis, in Chapter 10, of a parallel cross-fertilisation as aesthetic influences from experimental film affected the development of pop-videos. Donnelly traces the growth of a hybrid space between the music industry and the visual experiments of its more creative talent.

The book closes with Brett Mills's study of Chris Morris, whose career reflects some of the key trajectories of television itself. Morris's origins in radio are a useful reminder of the long-standing history of the transfer of successful radio programmes to television, and his clashes with censorship lead back to those of the 1960s. As Mills points out, Morris's use of the surreal and the fantastic reaches back to *Monty Python's Flying Circus* (BBC1, 1969–74) and his political satire may again be traced back, for instance, to *That Was The Week That Was* (BBC1, 1962–63), which flourished in the last years of the decaying Conservative Government. However, Morris has taken a radical step beyond the very significant tradition of satire in British television, by collapsing the barrier between fiction and fact not by fictionalising fact, but by imposing fiction on well-known, but unsuspecting, public figures. Here, he interferes in reality, creating it rather than representing it, simultaneously pointing out that television, and media more generally, no longer represent or comment on reality but have replaced it.

This book has not been able to address the major institutional developments of 1990s and the aftermath of such 'shake-ups', such as the Peacock Report in 1987, the Broadcasting Act of 1990, the consolidated arrival of Sky satellite broadcasting in 1989–90, the appointment of John Birt as Director General of the BBC in 1993, and the widespread impact of digital technologies. The tradition of experimental television, the continued imperative to innovate and disturb, has tended to shift towards the larger independent production companies, whose consolidation during the late 1980s and 1990s left little space for the smaller companies that had flourished in the early days of Channel 4. Whilst our focus on the more formative years of television preclude in-depth analysis of this era, we have, nevertheless, nodded towards this new, more complex climate with Brett Mills coverage of Chris Morris's professional and aesthetic evolution.

This period has been characterised by a sense of dismay and loss on the part of the supporters of public service television (and those who could still remember *The Wednesday Play*), accompanied by a sense of political disorientation. John Wyver and Carl Gardner summed up these forebodings with great honesty as early as 1983 (and thus even before the overt intervention of Rupert Murdoch):

> This process left critics in the curious position of having to defend and fight to retain a television system which they have spent years attacking for its elitism, paternalism, class-specificity and inaccessibility. In the past two years the debate has become locked in the public service vs. free market dichotomy within which new, more responsive models of television incorporating some of the positive features of the old Reithian set-up, have been precluded. For … there were important impulses and advantages in the Reithian system – in particular an attempt to generalise and popularise a range of dramatic, artistic and musical events and styles for a wider audience. It is this diversity and eclecticism, which occasionally opened up spaces for oppositional voices and contradictory meanings, which is threatened in the current wave of commercial homogenisation.[18]

The quotation eloquently evokes the complexity of public service broadcasting, its representation of a consensus politics that was socially inclusive ('generalise and popularise'), certainly not radical, but broad and confident enough to acknowledge that 'oppositional voices' not only needed to be heard but were also often at the forefront of social change. And it was out of this 'space' that experimental television emerged during the, paradoxical, period of post-war consensus television.

However, one of the greatest changes between the 1950s, the age of experimental television discussed at the beginning of this book, and British television today, is that it is no longer a new medium. The early essays record the excitement that responded to the newness of television and the need to explore the specificity of its language. This sense of excitement seemed to return with the arrival of Channel 4, but the new channel was the first to broadcast old television programmes as 'classics', in an early intimation of the medium's aging. The passing of time has converged with new technologies to transform the landscape of television. Now, of course, the question of flow (whether from programme to programme in a vertical diachronic order or from week to week in a horizontal synchronic order) has been radically altered by the viewer's control over broadcast temporality and the proliferation of channels. Furthermore, once it became possible to buy television programmes on disc, their last umbilical connection with a schedule became severed. The topography of television is no longer confined to the relationship between broadcast and domestic space.

However, the return of live broadcast reasserts television's immediacy and its studio origins: for instance, *Big Brother*'s (Channel 4, 2000–) cameras remaining fixed in real time on a studio object. But more importantly, convergence between media is opening up new possibilities for experiment. This book's examination of British television through its experimental aesthetics has produced a picture of an industry and technologies in a state of constant change. As television regularly faced the need to reinvent itself, experiment might be preserved through this latest, and greatest, era of upheaval in the industry by the very excitement of innovation in a newly configured, globalised media landscape. Throughout this book, the question of television's specificity has been a key but elusive issue. The present conjuncture dissolves all sense of a stable televisual specificity, confirming the sense that, over its history, television's only certainty has been uncertainty.

Notes

1. The phrase 'radical aspiration' is taken from Annette Michelson's essay 'Film and the Radical Aspiration', *Film Culture*, 42 (Fall 1966). While experimental film has been able to occupy alternative screening spaces, with its own culture, publications and movements, the space of radical television has co-existed with the wider 'flow'.
2. Roger Silverstone, *Television and Everyday Life* (London: Routledge, 1994), 19.
3. John Ellis, *Visible Fictions*, revised edn (London: Routledge, 1989), 113.
4. Raymond Williams, *Television: Technology and Cultural Form* (London: Fontana, 1974), 87.
5. Ibid., 90.
6. Ellis, *Visible Fictions*, 24.
7. Ibid., 167.
8. For instance, Michael Barry as Head of BBC encouraged the Experimental Group and the Langham Group in the 1950s; Sydney Newman as Head of Drama at ABC Television encouraged experiment in the *Armchair Theatre* series, later, taking over from Michael Barry at the BBC in 1962, he oversaw the production of *The Wednesday Play* from 1964.
9. Quoted in John Caughie, *Television Drama: Realism, Modernism and British Culture* (Oxford: Oxford University Press, 2000), 190.

10 Ibid.
11 Robert Hewison, *Culture and Consenus: England, Art and Politics since 1940* (London: Methuen, 1995), 209.
12 Brian Winston, *Technologies of Seeing: Photography, Cinematography and Television* (London: BFI, 1996), 6.
13 Caughie, *Television Drama*, 69.
14 John Russell and Suzi Gablik (eds), Introduction, *Pop Art Redefined* (London: Thames & Hudson, 1969), 31–2.
15 See Jason Jacobs, *The Intimate Screen: Early British Television Drama* (Oxford: Oxford University Press, 2000), for a detailed discussion of 'liveness' and 'intimacy'.
16 See Jamie Sexton, '"Televérité" hits Britain: Documentary, Drama and the growth of 16 mm Filmmaking in British Television', *Screen*, 24: 4 (Winter 2003), for an account of these developments
17 Caughie, *Television Drama*, 122.
18 Carl Gardener and John Wyver, 'The Single Play: An Afterword', *Screen*, 24: 4–5 (July–October 1983), 127.

1

'Creative in its own right': the Langham Group and the search for a new television drama

John Hill

The Langham Group, an experimental outfit established within the BBC in 1959, occupies an unusual position in the history of British television drama. While most accounts of the development of TV drama in Britain pay lip-service to the group's efforts, these have mainly been written off as unsuccessful. Such a view appears to have settled into a critical orthodoxy in the early 1960s and has prevailed ever since. In 1964, for example, the producer of David Mercer's first television plays, Don Taylor, declared that the group's work amounted to an 'artistic failure ... based on an aesthetic misconception'.[1] In the same year, Troy Kennedy Martin published his well-known demand for 'experiment and development' in television drama, 'Nats Go Home', but was keen to disassociate himself from the activities of the Langham Group which he denounced as 'an art set-up ... propitiated on the altar of prestige'.[2] Writing at around the same time, Arthur Swinson was slightly better disposed towards the group but still concluded that its work, although 'rich in visual texture', was nonetheless 'lacking in meaning'.[3] Given the scarcity of subsequent writing about the Langham Group, and the lack of opportunities to see what it produced, these accounts have not only remained among the few sources of information about it but have also continued to influence the way in which the value and significance of its work is perceived.

Is it, however, a reputation that is entirely deserved? It is clear, for example, that those critical of the Langham Group's work held allegiances to conceptions of television drama that were unlikely to make them the most sympathetic advocates of the experiments in which the group were engaged. In particular, the group's downplaying of the role of the writer in favour of the producer/director was guaranteed to upset those (such as Swinson) with a vested interest in a traditional form of written script (and the association of 'meaning' with dialogue). However, precisely because of the importance that the Langham Group attached to visualisation (and recorded sound), it has inevitably proved difficult to be sure just what the group was up to. Nevertheless, there is sufficient evidence to indicate that the group's experiments merit more than the usual passing mention and, certainly, amount to more than the artistic 'cul-de-sac' that has often been suggested. On the other hand, in attempting to rescue the group from critical neglect, it would be a mistake to overstate its achievements.

The group itself was short-lived and only three productions – *The Torrents of Spring* (tx. 21 May 1959), *Mario* (tx. 15 December 1959) and *On the Edge* (tx. 16 July 1960) – appear to have been transmitted bearing the title 'a Langham Group production'. Indeed, given the modesty of the group's output, it might even be argued that it is surprising that the group has commanded as much attention as it has. What follows, therefore, is an attempt to identify the group's main aims and activities and, given that only one of the group's productions (*The Torrents of Spring*) has survived, arrive at a tentative conclusion regarding the nature of its achievements. The discussion considers some of the ways in which the group's experiments anticipated subsequent developments in television drama but also suggest how the sense of 'failure' attached to the group was most likely the result of a lack of 'fit' between their experiments and the prevailing mood surrounding television drama at the time.

Origins

The origins of the Langham Group may be traced back to the establishment by the Head of BBC Drama, Michael Barry, of a sub-committee in early 1956 intended 'to chew over the problem of experimental Television programmes'.[4] This evolved into an 'Experimental Group' concerned with 'new methods' of presenting not only 'poetry and the dance' but also 'storytelling and … stories that cannot be told in a conventional form'.[5] This then led to a number of wide-ranging discussions concerning possible forms of television experiment that covered the use of film, the treatment of fantasy and the exploitation of television technology in an unusual manner (including the viewing of 'people from several angles simultaneously').[6] Although it was intended that the discussions should generate ideas for a series of half-hour experimental programmes, these do not appear to have materialised and it was not until the establishment of the Langham Group in 1959 that a specific programme of experimental work was begun. It is, however, clear that the debates of the Experimental Group were to influence what followed.

The name of the group carried no particular significance other than that it was housed in the former Langham Hotel, now occupied by the BBC. Although the group was conceived as 'a floating population of producers, designers, technicians' who would 'change from project to project', the key figure in the group was undoubtedly Anthony Pélissier who was also a founder member of the Experimental Group.[7] Pélissier had worked as both a theatre and film director but moved into television in the mid-1950s when he produced *The Tamer Tamed* (tx. 7 February 1956) and *Mrs Patterson* (tx. 15 June 1956). He became the effective head of the Langham Group and wrote, directed and produced the group's two main productions, *The Torrents of Spring* and *Mario* (billed, in the latter case, as 'A Langham Group Production by Anthony Pélissier').[8] The activities of the group itself were driven by two main concerns. First, the group was conceived of as a kind of research laboratory in which producers should be free 'to study production methods and ideas away from the steady day-to-day demands of regular drama presentations'.[9] Second, it was intended to permit the testing of new techniques that would extend and refine the existing vocabulary of television drama. As Pélissier himself explained, the purpose of the group was 'to explore new techniques ... that break away from the inheritance of the theatre and the cinema, and from which eventually, we hope, will evolve something that is exclusive to the medium'.[10]

New forms of expression

This pursuit of new modes of television presentation led the group in a number of specific directions. From the beginning of the Experimental Group's deliberations, it had been clear that there was a thirst for television to develop new forms of visual expression. In a paper prepared for the group's first meeting, the producer Christian Simpson had stressed the 'visual qualities' of the television medium and called for the use of all 'the tools at our disposal – namely objects known and unknown, shapes, surfaces, in conjunction with lighting, camera movement and accompanying sound'.[11] This emphasis was also reflected in the group's own discussions which included consideration of 'the merits' of 'a 30 minute play without dialogue'.[12] Simpson himself continued to champion the idea of 'Drama Without Dialogue' and, partly under his influence, the Langham Group planned, but did not complete, a production of *Romeo and Juliet*, entitled 'The Time is Now', which it described as 'an essay in Sight and Sound' that would eliminate all studio dialogue.[13] As might be expected, Pélissier also took the view that the television camera was not just 'a recording machine' but was primarily 'a *visual* medium' that should be treated as 'creative in its own right'.[14] As a result, he maintained that the job of the producer-director in television was to provide 'a visual treatment' or 'orchestration' of a subject that would match the way in which 'a composer might ... express an idea in music'.[15]

Thus, while Pélissier's work for the Langham Group is sometimes seen as falling within a well-established tradition of literary adaptation, this was hardly the case. For, although *The Torrents of Spring* and *Mario* are based on works by Ivan Turgenev and Thomas Mann, they are only adaptations in the most general of senses and are almost entirely 'unliterary' in character. Pélissier did not prepare a full dialogue script (or commission a writer to produce one) but concentrated on devising a picture script to which dialogue would be subsequently added following rehearsal with actors. Thus, the 'script' for *Mario* held by the BBC contains barely a word of dialogue but mainly consists of descriptions of what is to be shown and how. Much of the dialogue is also missing from the script prepared for the final rehearsals of *The Torrents of Spring* despite the provision of detailed camera directions to which the finished production largely adheres. This stress upon the visual, rather than the verbal, aspects of television production led, in turn, to two main kinds of visual experiment involving increased camera mobility and the use of montage.

Partly due to his background in cinema, Pelissier was critical of the stylistic functionalism which he believed the multi-camera set-up in the television studio had encouraged. In *The Sleeping Clergyman* (tx. 11 January 1959), co-produced with Michael Barry shortly before the establishment of the Langham Group, and *The Torrents of Spring*, he, therefore, set out to explore the potential of the technique of one camera to each scene. Unlike cinema, the circumstances of live transmission meant that the adoption of this technique involved the elimination of cutting during a scene. As a result, Pélissier's productions contain relatively few shots compared with other dramas of the period. Thus, despite the use of montage, *The Torrents of Spring* still consists of only 43 shots over a running time of 60 minutes. However, while extended shot lengths such as this might be taken to indicate an excessive dependence on stage traditions, this was not so in the Langham productions, which self-consciously sought to break free of 'proscenium presentation' through extended camera movement.[16] It is, therefore, probably more than a coincidence that, in the early 1950s, Pélissier was responsible for directing a mild satire on television entitled *Meet Mr Lucifer* (1953). One of a number of films made in both the USA and Britain to poke fun at the cinema's new rival, the film, as Charles Barr notes, mounts a critique of television's capacity to seduce the 'naive viewer' and identifies this with a televisual aesthetic typified by frontality and direct address.[17] Although Barr is reluctant to attribute any special authorial status to Pélissier, it is tempting to see his productions for the Langham Group challenging the frontality and camera immobility that his earlier film associates with television. Pélissier himself felt that the demonstration of 'the visual potential of how to handle cameras' was one of the group's main achievements and it is indoubtedly the case that the subsequent criticism of the Langham Group's 'aestheticism' has obscured the contribution it made to the freeing up of the television camera.[18] Thus, while ITV's *Armchair Theatre* series (launched by ABC Television in 1956 and headed up by Sidney Newman from 1958) has been rightly celebrated for its encouragement of increased camera mobility, the movement of the camera in the *Armchair* production *Lena, O My Lena* (tx. 25 September 1960), popularly singled out for its innovative camerawork, is much less sustained and systematic than in *The Torrents of Spring*, broadcast some sixteen months earlier.

However, it is not simply the amount of camera movement that distinguishes the two productions but the way that the camera is used. In discussing the famous opening shot of *Lena, O My Lena*, John Caughie indicates how the production succeeds in turning the television studio into 'a full three-dimensional space' but still remains tied to a conception of the studio as 'a space for acting'.[19] While *The Torrents of Spring* could certainly be said to extend the 'performative space' of the studio because of the way in which the camera moves around the sets, the opening out of the studio as 'a space for acting' is hardly its main concern. This is because the production places much greater emphasis than *Lena* upon camera movement as an expressive device 'in its own right', and hence the requirement that actors should not simply 'perform' but also accommodate to the programme's overall visual design.

This kind of 'creative' use of the camera was not, of course, without precedent. In his discussion of camerawork in television drama in the 1950s and early 1960s, Jason Jacobs identifies an 'exhibitionistic' mode in which, he suggests, camera movement is 'not motivated by performance, but *is* the performance'.[20] However, as he also acknowledges, this 'exhibitionistic' element (even in a stylistically flamboyant production such as the *Armchair Theatre* play *Afternoon of a Nymph* made in 1961) represents an extension of an established multi-camera style rather than constituting a fully-fledged style of its own. In the case of Pélissier's productions, however, the multi-camera style is genuinely abandoned for large sections of the drama and it is the moving camera, rather than the actors, that becomes the primary 'performative', or expressive, element. This is particularly evident, for example, in the opening scene of *The Torrents of Spring*, set in a London market, which involves a careful choreography, or 'orchestration', of the actors in relation to the elaborate tracks, pans and tilts of the camera as it moves through a crowded set, temporarily pausing on a succession of characters and significant detail. The subordination of actors to the overall visual design of the production which this entails is particularly evident in the way that the programme employs, as a recurring visual motif, an image of legs, visually abstracted from the rest of the body. Children's legs, for example, are shown at the beginning and end of the production when they are visually linked to an unidentified pair of elegant female legs, dressed in white shoes, walking across their game of hopscotch. Images such as these then become part of a visual pattern whereby a crucial conversation between James (Charles Houston) and Tess (Penelope Horner), concerning the return of Tess's other boyfriend, is conducted while the camera holds not on the faces of the couple but on their legs.

This use of motifs, and the creation of visual rhymes, may be explained in part by an 'impressionist' concern to use visual detail to evoke atmosphere and meaning rather than to advance a story. However, they also indicate an ambition to achieve, through visual means, a certain fusion of 'objective' and 'subjective' states. In a letter to Michael Barry in 1960, when the future of the Langham Group looked at risk, Pélissier pressed for a continuing commitment to experiment on the part of the BBC, without which he despaired that television drama would never be in a position to 'reply' to 'Films like "Hiroshima Mon Amour" or "The Boyar's Plot"'.[21] Although *Hiroshima Mon Amour* would not have opened in UK cinemas in time to influence Pélissier's work for the Langham Group directly, his invocation of the film, nevertheless, suggests how its emphasis upon the subjective perception of actuality chimed with his own concerns. This may be seen, for example, in his very loose 'adaptation' of Thomas Mann's short story, 'Mario and the Magician' (1929).

In Pélissier's hands, a relatively straightforward account of the murder of a hypnotist by a young man, Mario, whom he has publicly humiliated is turned into an explicit meditation upon how the circumstances of the murder are retrospectively pieced together by four journalists as they mull over a collection of photographs and other objects. In this way, the drama seeks to bring together what Pélissier himself refers to as 'the material world of the journalists' and 'the conjectural world' that is brought into being by the journalists' speculations concerning the surviving evidence.[22] While, in *Mario*, Pélissier appears to have made use of shots clearly marked as subjective (such as the superimposition of a still of multiple deckchairs over a picture of Mario), it was more common for him to employ techniques that combined the external observation of actions with the suggestion of interiority. Thus, while *The Torrents of Spring* is much less self-conscious about the process of narration than *Mario*, it is through visualisation (and music), rather than dialogue, that the production aims to intimate the thoughts and impulses underlying the characters' actions. Thus, when James and Tess discover their true feelings for each other, the scene is played without words and it is the combination of camera movement, lighting and music (a song performed by Tess's mother) that carries the main burden of communicating the concatenation of emotional and sexual forces that underpin the visible action.

This particular scene is also followed by one of a number of montages evident in the Langham Group productions. As previously noted, Pélissier was an admirer of Eisenstein and the use of short montage sequences in both *The Torrents of Spring* and *Mario* complements the long takes that were otherwise the productions' main feature. However, although stylistically dissimilar, camera movement and montage are exploited for broadly similar ends. Just as the camera focuses on a specific object or visual detail (such as legs or a reflection) in the course of its movement, so montage is used to link images that are concentrated upon small details or actions. For example, in the montage that follows Tess and James's kiss, the shots include close-ups of a hand trying on wedding rings, a cross around Tessa's neck, a priest's bookmark and a white prayer book. While these images may serve a narrative purpose, indicating the couple's preparations for marriage, the logic of the sequence is nevertheless primarily visual and emotional, establishing a general 'tone' (and set of thematic oppositions) rather than furnishing specific narrative information.

A key component of the montages found in these productions is their use of sound. Although Pélissier emphasised the visual aspects of television and downplayed the importance of dialogue, he still felt that sound was vital to the creation of 'evocative magic'.[23] Just as the production of 'The Time is Now' had been planned to employ an 'elaborate soundtrack' consisting of 'naturalistic sounds', 'special sound orchestration' and 'relevant excerpts' from Shakespeare's original text, so Pélissier's productions supplemented the pared-down dialogue of the actors with previously recorded sounds and specially chosen music.[24] He was influenced in this by the sound experiments of Charles Parker whose work on the 'Radio Ballads', first broadcast in 1958, involved the editing together of field recordings with music and song (performed by Ewan MacColl and Peggy Seeger).[25] Parker was, in fact, recruited to work on the soundtrack for *The Torrents of Spring* which combines special sound effects with children's songs and contemporary popular music. Sound, in this regard, is not only substituted for dialogue but is used to add an extra level of aural montage. Thus, in the 'wedding' montage previously mentioned, the soundtrack consists of a series of transitions from a children's song (previously heard at the play's beginning) to a flute playing the same tune and then church organ music, which proceeds to pick up on the melody. As with certain images (such as those of legs), the song is repeated during the course of the drama and takes on the characteristics of a motif. The sequence involving James's seduction by 'The Princess' (Sandra Dorne), for example, begins with a whistled version of the song before it gives way to an animated jazz number and the sounds of thunder.

Like the earlier montage, the sequence is wordless and sound is used not only to provide an aural link between the couple in Princess's car and Tess at home in bed listening to music on the radio but to invest the events with an added thematic dimension. Thus, the seduction – and subsequent downfall – of the central character is worked through in terms of a contrast (carried over from the 'Radio Ballads') between the 'authentic' culture of the traditional working class (signified by the singing of Tess's mother and the songs and games of the children) and the 'false' world of mass culture (associated with 'the Princess' and the tawdry pop songs she performs).[26] A similar collision of cultures (and emotional forces) may also be found in *Mario* when a group of beatniks attempt to drown out a dance band playing 'a Victor Sylvester type fox-trot' in a hotel ballroom by 'whooping and jiving' to the sound of 'a rock 'n' roll number'.[27]

Success and failure

What this would appear to suggest is that the Langham Group was a more complex phenomenon than is usually recalled. Even its reputation as an avant-garde 'art set-up' requires a degree of revision. For although Troy Kennedy Martin believed the group's ideas could not be applied to 'mass audience viewing', their productions occupied popular mid-evening slots and Pélissier himself considered that the group's experiments should become 'run-of-the-mill'.[28] In this respect, the third of the Langham Group's productions, *On the Edge*, was explicitly intended to demonstrate not only how an innovative approach to 'design and sound' could be applied to 'an ordinary narrative of adventure' but would also prove cheaper than 'conventional methods of production'.[29] It is also the case that many of the elements subsequently championed by critics of the Langham Group, such as Troy Kennedy Martin, may, in fact, be found in the group's productions. As has been seen, the plays involved a deliberate reduction in dialogue, much less emphasis on the close-up and the photographing of faces, considerable freeing-up of the camera as well as the use of techniques designed to give outward expression to internal emotional states. The productions were also distinguished by their use of montage and, in the case of *Mario*, directly anticipate the kind of montage involving stills employed in Troy Kennedy Martin's *Diary of a Young Man* (1964).

Despite such innovations, and the influence that they were to exert (even on their critics), the Langham Group did not last long. Thus, barely eighteen months after its launch, it was incorporated back into the BBC Drama Department and effectively ceased to exist. There appear to be a number of reasons for this. Despite the possible savings to which their experiments might ultimately have led, the group proved costly to sustain. The initial ambition had been that it should complete four to five productions per year but, partly due to the 'research' character of its activities, this did not prove feasible. It was also unclear how much the BBC positively valued rather than simply tolerated the group's activities. No special financial provision was made for the group and Pélissier felt strongly that there was a lack of investment in the technical resources and facilities that he required. This was, by and large, conceded by the Head of Drama, Michael Barry, who defended the group against accusations of 'failure' by highlighting the 'borrowed circumstances' under which it had been forced to operate.[30] Given the economic pressures resulting from competition with ITV (as well as the professional jealousies arising among those enjoying less privileged working conditions), it was perhaps not surprising that BBC management should have opted to close the unit on financial grounds. However, the fact that the group proved so vulnerable to attack also suggests that its activities were partly out of step with the prevailing climate surrounding television drama and that it had failed to win 'hearts and minds'. Thus, while others within television may have shared the group's concern to push back the boundaries of television drama, the 'solution' which the group provided was only ever likely to command limited support.

There are a various aspects to this. First, Pélissier's championing of the producer at the expense of the writer failed to uncover others prepared to follow his lead with the result that the Langham Group quickly came to be regarded as something of a 'one-man band'. However, the apparent absence of aspiring television *auteurs* was less the result of a lack of talent than a deeply-ingrained belief that television drama was pre-eminently a writer's medium. This was certainly the substance of Don Taylor's objections to Pélissier's work. For although Taylor himself was not adverse to technical innovation (coming to advocate the use of 'obsessive close-up', 'unrelated film' and the 'divorcing' of picture from sound), he nevertheless identified the producer-director as the servant of the writer whose task it was 'to direct and shoot the play so as to make the author's meaning clear'.[31] Taylor achieved prominence as the director of David Mercer's plays (the first of which, *Where the Difference Begins*, was produced in 1961), and the experiments of the Langham Group coincided with the emergence of a new generation of television playwrights writing specifically for television. Thus, in the same year that *The Torrents of Spring* and *Mario* were broadcast, John Russell Taylor noted how 'the phrase "adapted by" virtually disappeared from *Armchair Theatre* credits' to be replaced by names such as Alun Owen and Clive Exton.[32] Given this context, the 'writer-less' experiments of the Langham Group would have seemed not only to fly in the face of established tradition but also the very developments responsible for revitalising television drama at this juncture.

This was particularly so given the way in which much of this new writing also signalled a turn towards contemporary subject matter and 'working-class realism'. The relationship of the Langham Group to this movement is, in fact, more complex than is usually granted. While both *The Torrents of Spring* and *Mario* were literary adaptations, they nevertheless departed quite radically from their source material. Turgenev's novel, *Spring Torrents* (1872), for example, concerns the encounters of a minor Russian aristocrat in nineteenth-century Germany. While the bare lineaments of its 'love triangle' are retained in the television production, the social universe that the main characters inhabit is very different. The main character is transformed into an unemployed labourer from Greenock who becomes engaged to the daughter of a working-class Irishman and his Italian wife living in contemporary London (described as 'a Juliet of the street corner' in the advance publicity).[33] The background to their romance is provided by a street market in which the traditional white working class mingle with members of European and Afro-Caribbean migrant groups. As might be expected, given the involvement of Charles Parker, there is also a concern to give expression to the 'ordinary' sounds and accents associated with a working-class district. So, despite the confinement of the production to the studio, the use of recorded sound signals a departure from 'literary' language that is reinforced by the partly improvised speech of the actors. Moreover, just as the novelty of working-class realism was commonly associated with increasing sexual explicitness, so *The Torrents of Spring* goes much further than a working-class drama such as *Lena, O My Lena* in testing the boundaries of permissible representation.[34] Indeed, the main controversy that the play generated was not the result of its experimentalism but its allegedly salacious content.

As was to become increasingly the case, BBC plays had been the subject of attack for their inclusion of 'unnecessary' and 'unsavoury' sex scenes.[35] The Deputy Director of Television Broadcasting Cecil McGivern was, therefore, particularly outraged by the way in which the programme presented the seduction of James by 'The Princess', which he claimed 'must have offended and shocked many normal, decent people'. 'The so-called "Langham Group"', he continued, was 'formed to achieve new techniques and new thought, not to indulge in license which results in licentiousness'.[36] However, while even the programme's defenders felt the scene may have been too 'realistic', the focus on the power and destructiveness of sexual desire in both *The Torrents of Spring* and *Mario* also suggests that neither production was primarily interested in the observation of surface realities.[37] One of Pélissier's most interesting film projects had been *The Rocking Horse Winner* (1949) based on a short story by D. H. Lawrence in which the film's critique of materialism is shot through with suggestions of unconscious sexual impulses and metaphysical coincidences. In the same way, for all their delineation of social and economic distinctions, both *The Torrents of Spring* and *Mario* depart from the class concerns of working-realism in the 'romantic' –

rather than 'materialist' – emphasis that they place upon, as Thomas Mann's narrator puts it, 'powers stronger than reason or virtue'.[38] While this may have encouraged comparisons with German expressionism, it inevitably distanced the plays from the emerging wave of social realism and no doubt added to the perception that they were aesthetic experiments with little to say about contemporary social issues.[39]

The drive towards social realism in television drama affected the impact of the group in another way. As has been noted, it was one of Pélissier's aims to move towards an aesthetic that was distinct from theatre and film, and specific to television. This meant that, despite his cinema background, he avoided film inserts that had already become a common feature of much television drama. His conception of television specificity, therefore, involved the restriction of the drama to the studio and the use of the electronic camera (although, as has been seen, this aesthetic did, perhaps somewhat contradictorily, permit the use of pre-recorded sound). However, given the growing demand for 'authenticity' and 'realism', television drama began to abandon the studio in favour of increased location shooting on film. While the move towards film may have proved slow and uneven, the pursuit of a television aesthetic confined to the TV studio (and 'live' transmission) came, nevertheless, to seem increasingly anomalous (and even a director such as Don Taylor, who considered the 'continuous performance' to be the core of television drama, began to experiment with film inserts in productions such as *A Suitable Case for Treatment* (tx. 21 October 1962)).

Conclusion

Apparently shocked by its sexual explicitness, Cecil McGivern declared that *The Torrents of Spring* 'was not suitable for a public service broadcasting corporation'.[40] Michael Barry, on the other hand, defended the importance of 'a place in television for experiment' and insisted that the BBC should 'lead any such endeavour'.[41] Although, as Head of BBC Drama, Barry has often been criticised for presiding over a regime of television drama that was excessively dependent on the stage, he was, in fact, a consistent supporter of experiment and even collaborated with Anthony Pélissier on *The Sleeping Clergyman* just prior to the establishment of the Langham Group. Indeed, it may well have been a feeling that his own enthusiasm for experiment had been underestimated that led him to respond to Troy Kennedy Martin's call for a 'New Drama' in 1964 by suggesting that it was bit 'late in the day'.[42] However, whatever his own role in the development of drama at the BBC, his instincts were surely right. It was necessary for television to encourage experiment and it was right that the BBC, as a public-service broadcaster, should take a lead in this. What Barry also made clear was that his support was for experiment per se rather than any particular style or approach. As he observed with regard to Pélissier, it was never intended that 'the "gospels"' should 'be written by one apostle'.[43] It is probably in this light that the Langham Group should now be regarded. Under Pélissier, the Langham Group headed in a particular direction. And while neither Barry nor Pélissier intended that this should exhaust the BBC's interest in television 'experiment', it was sometimes perceived as doing so. This was a burden it was unable to carry and probably encouraged many of the criticisms directed at it. However, understood as a preliminary skirmish rather than a fully fledged campaign, the efforts of the Langham Group to encourage experimental television drama undoubtedly acquire an interest that previous accounts have only partly acknowledged.

Notes

1. Don Taylor, 'David Mercer and Television Drama', Appendix to David Mercer, *Collected TV Plays: Volume 1* (London: John Calder, 1981 [1964]), 240.
2. Troy Kennedy Martin, 'Nats Go Home: First Statement of a New Television Drama', *Encore* (March–April 1964), 21. See also my discussion of Troy Kennedy Martin's article elsewhere in this volume.
3. Arthur Swinson, *Writing for Television Today* (London: Adam and Charles Black, 1965), 180.
4. Letter from Ian Atkins to Anthony Pélissier, 22 February 1956, BBC Written Archives Centre (WAC), T31/292. My thanks to Trish Hayes and Jeff Walden at the BBC Written Archives Centre for their assistance.
5. Minutes of the Meeting of the Experimental Group, 30 May 1956, BBC WAC T5/2147/1.
6. Minutes of the Meetings of the Experimental Group on 27 June 1956 and 11 July 1956, BBC WAC T5/2147/1.
7. Memo from Elwyn Jones, Documentary Assistant to Head of Drama, Television, May 1959, BBC WAC T5/2409/1.
8. *Radio Times* (11 December 1959), 11. It is worth recalling that at this stage the BBC did not distinguish between producers and directors and that Pélissier, like other television directors, combined both roles (as well as, in the case of his Langham productions, taking credit for the 'script').
9. *Radio Times* (15 May 1959), 4.
10. *Radio Times* (11 December 1959), 4.
11. Memo from Christian Simpson to Mrs Adams, 11 May 1956, BBC WAC T5/2147/1.
12. Minutes of the Meeting of the Experimental Group, 11 July 1956, BBC WAC T5/2147/1.
13. Memo from Christian Simpson to Michael Barry, Head of Drama, Television, 14 August 1959; Memo from Michael Barry to Controller of Programmes, Television, 25 February 1960, BBC WAC T5/2147/1.

The Langham Group and the search for new drama

14 'Anthony Pélissier in discussion with Roger Manvell', *Society of Film and Television Arts Journal*, 7 (Spring 1962), 11–12.
15 Anthony Pélissier, *Radio Times* (11 December 1959), 4.
16 *Radio Times* (11 December 1959), 4. Although he queries the simplistic equation of 'one-scene/one-camera' with the 'static relay of performance', Jason Jacobs nevertheless indicates how the 'one-camera technique' of Fred O'Donovan in the post-war period was widely regarded as 'theatrical' in *The Intimate Screen: Early British Television Drama* (Oxford: Oxford University Press, 2000), 61–2.
17 Charles Barr, 'Broadcasting and Cinema 2: Screens within Screens', in Barr (ed.), *All Our Yesterdays: 90 Years of British Cinema* (London: BFI, 1986), 211.
18 Letter from Anthony Pélissier to Michael Barry, 22 February 1960, BBC WAC T31/292.
19 John Caughie, *Television Drama: Realism, Modernism and British Culture* (Oxford: Oxford University Press, 2000), 77.
20 Jacobs, *The Intimate Screen*, 144.
21 Letter from Pélissier to Barry, 22 February 1960, BBC WAC T31/292.
22 Appendix to script for *Mario* held by BBC WAC.
23 Letter from Pélissier to Barry, 22 February 1960, BBC WAC T31/292.
24 Memo from Michael Barry to Controller of Programmes, Television, 25 February 1960, BBC WAC T5/2147/1. There was, of course, a benefit in using recorded sound in so far as it not only permitted greater concentration on the use of the camera during the broadcast but also reduced some of the technical problems generated by the extensive movement of the camera.
25 The methods of the 'Radio Ballads' group are discussed by Stuart Hall and Paddy Whannel in *The Popular Arts* (London: Hutchinson, 1964), 259–60.
26 In his defence of the play, David Gretton, the Assistant Head in the Midlands Region (where Charles Parker was a senior features producer), argued that Parker explicitly used 'beat music' to signal the dangers of 'lust'. Memo from David Gretton, Assistant Head of Midland Region Programmes, to Deputy Director, Television Broadcastng (DDTelB), 29 May 1959, BBC WAC T5/2409/1.
27 Script for *Mario*, BBC WAC. There is, in this respect, a curious echo of Troy Kennedy Martin's complaint in 'Nats Go Home' that television drama of the time was reminiscent of 'Victor Silvester [sic] fox-trots being danced in the world of the Beatles' ('Nats Go Home', 32). However, whereas Kennedy Martin was clearly on the side of The Beatles, *Mario* is much more ambivalent about the virtues of rock 'n' roll.
28 Letter from Pélissier to Barry, 22 February 1960, BBC WAC T31/292.
29 Michael Barry to Controller Programmes, Television (CPTel), 17 August 1960, BBC WAC T31/292. The 'one-camera technique', in this respect, had the virtue of restricting the number of sets, many of which were themselves kept simple.
30 Memo from Head of Drama, Television, to Controller of Programmes, Television, 17 August 1960, BBC WAC T31/292.
31 Don Taylor, 'The Gorboduc Stage', *Contrast*, 3: 3 (1964), 206; 'David Mercer and Television Drama', 248.
32 John Russell Taylor, 'Armchair Theatre', in *Anatomy of a Television Play*

(London: Weidenfeld & Nicolson, 1962), 10.
33. Memo from Documentary Assistant to Head of Drama, 21 May 1959, BBC WAC T5/2409/1.
34. The BBC appeared to accept a link between '"kitchen-sink" plays' and the 'sordid and sleazy' in its evidence to the Pilkington Committee on Broadcasting. See *Report of the Committee on Broadcasting, 1960* (London: HMSO, 1962), Cmnd. 1753, 40.
35. Just three months prior to the programme's transmission, the Head of Drama, Michael Barry, had circulated a memo dealing with criticisms of 'Sexiness in BBC Television Plays', 2 February 1959, BBC WAC T16/62/3.
36. Memo from Deputy Director of Television Broadcasting to CPTel, 25 May 1959, BBC WAC T5/2409/1.
37. Memo from David Gretton, Assistant Head of Midland Region Programmes, to DDTelB, 29 May 1959, BBC WAC T5/2409/1. Gretton argued that the characters were, in fact, symbolic and that the realism of the seduction scene was at odds with the play's basic moralism.
38. Thomas Mann, *Mario and the Magician and Other Stories* (London: Minerva, 1996), 148.
39. In his defence of *The Torrents of Spring*, the Controller of the Midland Region, John Unkerley, claimed in a telegram that 'the production had something of the quality that made the early German films so memorable' and bore comparison with Josef von Sternberg's *The Blue Angel* (1930), 22 May 1959, BBC WAC T5/2409/1. The emphasis on the power of the hypnotist in *Mario* also contains echoes of *The Cabinet of Dr Caligari* (1919) (albeit that the element of political allegory to be found in both this film and Mann's story is largely missing).
40. Memo from Deputy Director of Television Broadcasting to CPTel, 25 May 1959, BBC WAC T5/2409/1.
41. Memo from Head of Drama, Television, to CPTel, 17 August 1960, BBC WAC T31/292.
42. Michael Barry, 'Reaction: replies to Troy Kennedy Martin's attack on naturalistic television drama', *Encore*, 49 (May–June 1964), 39.
43. Memo from Head of Drama, Television, to CPTel, 17 August 1960, BBC WAC T31/292.

2

'And now for your Sunday night experimental drama ...': experimentation and *Armchair Theatre*

Helen Wheatley

> There was something different about ABC's *Armchair Theatre*... There was an excitement ... a bravery, an experimentation, a daring about it.[1]

Made in a transitional moment in the history of British television drama, *Armchair Theatre* (ABC, 1956–68; Thames, 1968–74)[2] can be seen as an example of an anthology series which pushed the boundaries of television drama production, bringing together an acute sense of social awareness with the technical skill and creative ambition of a team of innovative programme makers. *Armchair Theatre* was an aspirant drama series which held its sizeable audience in high regard, challenging its viewers with ideas and settings which directly related to their own lives and social contexts; it was also experimental in the imaginative and formally inventive ways in which it negotiated studio production. The term 'experimental' needs to be treated as a relative term within the history of British television drama, however. What was cutting edge and experimental in the early 1960s may well have become absorbed into easily recognisable forms and styles in the twenty-first century. On the other hand, experimental drama which has not been replicated or partially absorbed into the formal conventions of television drama *in general* may very easily slip out of sight, given the well-documented difficulties with the historical study of television. The sheer extensiveness of television's textual history obscures a good deal of innovation and experimentation in television drama: thus, in order to deal with the 'unmanageable' past of British television drama, historians have tended to focus on the development of particular dramatic forms and trends. This brings about a certain tendency toward the production of linear historical narratives that cannot possibly take into account the heterogeneity of television's formal experimentations: the most dominant of these linear historical narratives is the development of social realism as television's presiding dramatic form.

This chapter, which looks in detail at *Armchair Theatre* as a canonical text in the history of experimental television drama, seeks to both acknowledge the series' significant development of a social realist style, and to look beyond this towards the programme's other formal experimentations. It is not uncontroversial, however, to label *Armchair Theatre* as experimental drama. Historically, discussions of television drama in general, and *Armchair Theatre* in particular, have resisted the high cultural associations of experimentalism, given that television drama has simultaneously been understood in relation to the popular, the generic, the ordinary and the everyday. For example, Leonard White, third series producer of *Armchair Theatre*, was very wary of applying the term to his productions. In a recent interview, however, he conceded that '[*Armchair Theatre*] was innovative in the sense that television itself was the new invention, so for a long, long while each new drama was still relating to the new invention and [it] was certainly *different* for the simple reason that our story editors were finding different writers, and different writers that wanted to say something different'.[3] This wariness, and White's rejection of the term 'experimental' in favour of 'innovation' and 'difference', is understandable given the institutional context of the programme's production. As ABC wished to provide a viable and attractive alternative to the 'high-brow' elitism of the BBC, the notion of experimentalism, with its associations with elite culture, would not have been openly embraced by the production team at ABC. However, this chapter seeks to challenge this unwillingness to view *Armchair Theatre* and its generic off-shoot series, *Armchair Mystery Theatre* (ABC, 1960–65), as experimental television drama. A good deal of experimentation with the formal possibilities of television drama is seen in these series, even while the series producers steadfastly insisted on a populist address to the 'ordinary viewer'. Just as John Caughie has argued, in relation to art television, that television drama's 'relationship to the territory of the popular is almost always a negotiated one',[4] so notions of generic populism and challenging experimentalism are balanced and negotiated throughout *Armchair Theatre*'s history. The makers of *Armchair Theatre* produced experimental drama that could sit within the flow of popular television, following on, in the schedules, from *Sunday Night at the London Palladium* (ATV, 1955–67; 1973–74), retaining the viewers of the preceding variety show for what was often challenging, and formally experimental, drama.

'The new breed': ABC television and the industrialisation of British television drama

Carl Gardner and John Wyver's description of the conventional dramatic productions on television which pre-dated *Armchair Theatre* provides a useful starting point for an understanding of *Armchair Theatre*'s innovations:[5]

In its early days TV drama picked up the predominant patterns, concerns and style of both repertory theatre and radio drama (as well as many of their personnel, with their distinctive training and working practices) and consisted of televised stage plays, 'faithfully' and tediously broadcast from the theatre, or reconstructed in the studio, even down to intervals, prosceniums and curtains. Such an approach, which takes the television process itself as transparent, almost by definition precluded any innovation of TV style or any attempt to develop a specifically televisual form for small-screen drama.[6]

This description bluntly characterises early television drama as decidedly un-televisual, borrowing from other dramatic media (theatre and radio), and failing to develop a medium-specific form of its own. Whilst Gardner and Wyver's description does not account for many significant earlier dramas,[7] it does establish the debt that many early BBC dramas owed to the theatre. This was the context in which the producers of *Armchair Theatre* understood its experimentation and in which the series expanded the possibilities of drama production on television. By the early 1960s, which is the period frequently viewed as the series' creative zenith, ABC's drama department was producing outstanding anthologised teleplays in a range of styles and genres. In a climate of financial confidence for the commercial companies in the UK, this kind of experimentation flourished particularly at ABC Television, where series' producers, directors, writers and designers were given the opportunity to try out ideas and to make mistakes without fear of cuts in their budget or programme cancellation.[8] In these circumstances, *Armchair Theatre*'s conditions of production both facilitated and, in fact, necessitated, experimentation with the forms of television drama, further encouraged by the programme's anthology format.

The drive to locate a single author as the originator of creativity and artistic expression has produced a rather distorted view of *Armchair Theatre* within critical histories of television drama.[9] A 'great man' narrative has figured producer Sydney Newman as possessing the sole creative vision behind the series, obscuring the achievements of his predecessor, Dennis Vance, and Leonard White, who took over from Newman as producer, as well as the scores of directors, writers and other creative personnel who worked on the series. To revise a Newman-centric history of *Armchair Theatre* would be to draw attention to the *combined work* of production personnel, who produced the sense of experimentation and innovation in the series. From this perspective the industrial conditions of the series' production and some of the working practices of ABC Television's drama department illuminate the context in which popular experimental drama was created.

As Leonard White has argued,[10] the fact that there were at least three episodes of *Armchair Theatre* in production at any one time meant that there was always a variety of personnel working on the series, which in turn led to a sense of variety in the dramas produced. Whilst it has been previously proposed that the series was formally homogeneous (under the watchful eye of Newman), producing a series of social realist dramas in the kitchen-sink style, the variety of people within the production teams, and the sheer number of people working simultaneously on different *Armchair Theatre* episodes, meant that experimentation with form and content was far more heterogeneous than most histories of the series acknowledge. This pattern of production on *Armchair Theatre* produced 'non-classical' television drama in John Caughie's terms,[11] and its complex systems of authorship often resulted in a productive dialogue between producer, writer and director, as well as drawing on the creative input of personnel who had not previously been considered part of the 'creative team'. For example, White describes the creative input offered by the technical/engineering department at ABC: 'We had marvellous engineers ... who were actually pressing us, and that was a lovely thing of that time of Teddington, of ABC Television: the engineering department were always with us. They were not separate, they were all inventing things themselves and trying to get us to take it up. They were pushing *us* technically.'

Most of the retrospective accounts of the production of *Armchair Theatre*[12] also convey a sense of production teams (particularly those new to television production) 'making things up as they went along' or 'training on the job', and thus experimenting with what was or was not possible within the financial and temporal constraints of television drama production during this era. Writing in 1959, Sydney Newman described this 'pioneering spirit' in relation to the directors working on *Armchair Theatre*:

> As new as the medium itself is the breed of men who make fine television drama directors ... Unlike the films or the theatre, this medium is not kind to the solitary genius, the uncompromising idealist, the vain ass ... The new breed are tough as commandos, disciplined like Jesuits and think and act with the speed of lightning. Consider: they interpret a play they have never seen produced before; spend thousands of pounds; argue, cajole, charm and co-ordinate the efforts of hundreds of technicians, actors, artists; satisfy playwrights, treasurers, unions, producers, story editors – and do all this within five weeks ... No formalistic traditionalists, these.[13]

Newman's description depicts the television director working on the series as a creative negotiator who operated inside an industrial setting and outside of convention or tradition. Drawing on the image of the 'the solitary genius, the uncompromising idealist, the vain ass', Newman pointedly eschews the notion of the singular authorial figure within *Armchair Theatre*. This is not to suggest that Vance, Newman or White's role as producer was insignificant in the aesthetic or technological development of *Armchair Theatre*, but that patterns of authorship on the series are more complex than has been traditionally acknowledged.

John Caughie has argued that the professionalisation of drama production at ABC Television marked a 'shift from television drama as a reproduction of theatre or literature to television drama as a production of television in which creativity and technology were realigned'.[14] This is a rather different narrative of industrialised production than that of the film industry, particularly the Hollywood studio system. The industrialisation or professionalisation of the ABC drama department produced a plurality of visual styles and ways of working, rather than a formal unity across the company's output. Discussing this industrialisation Leonard White offered the following astute analogy:

> We were absolutely opposed to the Hollywood system ... I always thought that we were [like] a factory producing a daily newspaper; in the newspaper you had the news, of course, and a short story which was the little bit of drama in the newspaper ... All these things were being churned out by the television company, and therefore the programme controllers ... were producing shows day by day, like the daily newspaper. Because we were [under] that pressure, that challenge, we hardly ever had any time: I mean even when we made mistakes, and we made them, it didn't rock the boat. We didn't have any real time to think about yesterday's [episode], last weekend's [episode]. If one [episode] was not doing its job, or whatever, there were three others at least in production at the same time in production. So I always used to think it is factory-like, but ABC ... I just regarded as being the *best* factory that there was in television at that time in this country.

In White's terms and in the context of a factory-like mode of production, the volume and frequency of the output of an anthology series like *Armchair Theatre* meant that mistakes could be made without garnering much attention, arguably allowing the creative teams working on individual teleplays to try out new techniques and approaches.

White's comparison of the television production company to a newspaper points toward the fact that the weekly (or sometimes bi-weekly) anthology format of *Armchair Theatre* was fundamental in providing a space in which unconventional styles and 'difficult' subject matter could be tried out. While not every episode in the series' eighteen-year run was formally innovative or challenging in some way, it is clear that the series' producers sought to find a *balance* between experimental and more conservative teleplays. While I have argued elsewhere that a sense of generic balance was sought within the series, eschewing the notion of formal coherence and 'kitchen-sink realism' of *Armchair Theatre*,[15] there was also an intended balance between 'conventional' and 'experimental' teleplays within the series. Howard Thomas, then managing director of ABC Television, remembers an agreement with Sydney Newman that only one in four of the *Armchair Theatre* plays should be experimental.[16] Later, Leonard White recalled that at the end of November

1964, Brian Tesler, ABC's Controller of Programmes, stipulated that there had to be five accessible scripts for every 'difficult' one.[17] White acknowledges that the term 'experimental' was 'not exactly a word to entice viewers',[18] arguing that Tesler's question to the makers of individual *Armchair Theatre* episodes was usually 'Is it accessible?'[19] However, this emphasis on viewer appeal makes the programme makers' willingness to experiment with 20 to 25 per cent of the individual teleplays all the more striking, and seems to confirm John Corner's suggestion that the 1950s and early to mid-1960s was a time in television production which saw an 'often subtly interactive relationship between "official" and "popular" discourses, an unparalleled mixing of "high" and "low" forms'.[20]

To illustrate this point, two of the most significantly experimental strands in *Armchair Theatre*'s history are discussed here: firstly the 'kitchen sink' dramas which have come to represent the whole of the series' output within critical histories of television drama, and secondly, the less famous, though no less innovative, impressionistic mystery thrillers of *Armchair Mystery Theatre*. In relation to these strands, it is argued that while realism is key to understanding the experimental drama produced at ABC, the notion needs to be broadened to encompass subjective or psychological realism, as well as social realism. Subsequently, it is concluded that, in the context of British television in the 1950s and 1960s, experimental drama was marked by its experiments with 'the real'.

Studio realism and the 'kitchen-sink'

Experimentation in this period of British television drama's history was often concerned with the search for medium-specific form, an exploration of what would become 'typically televisual' as the medium matured. In the UK, particularly for those writing for *Armchair Theatre*, there were lessons to be learned from similar, contemporaneous explorations in the United States, typified by the work of tele-playwrights such as Paddy Chayevsky, Tad Mosel and Rod Serling. Ted Willis, author of *Armchair Theatre* episodes 'Hot Summer Night' (tx. 1 February 1959) and 'The Scent of Fear' (tx. 13 August 1959), remembers that,

> As I read the plays of Chayevsky [1955] and his introductory words I felt as though someone had kicked open a door. I had been struggling to get television into focus in my mind, trying to define how writing for this small screen differed from writing for the stage or the cinema. Paddy Chayevsky suddenly supplied most, if not all, of the answers.[21]

The American and Canadian influence on the series is well documented,[22] suggesting that Newman's appointment signalled an influx of Canadian and

American émigrés to ABC, that a lack of home-grown material was filled by strong teleplays from the USA and Canada in the early days of the programme,[23] and that these influences subsequently brought about a certain sense of professionalism and a 'slickness' which had not been seen on British television before. However, whilst the grittiness of the kitchen-sink dramas for which *Armchair Theatre* became so famous might be seen as quintessentially British, understood as part of broader new wave in post-war British culture, as John Caughie has argued,[24] there was also a strong link between the social realism of *Armchair Theatre* and anthology series in the USA like NBC's *Goodyear Television Playhouse* or CBS's *Playhouse 90*. The series borrowed a certain intimate mode of address from these dramas, and a deep concern with the colloquial and the everyday.

Importantly, the kitchen-sink dramas of *Armchair Theatre* offered what might be understood as the 'democratisation' of British television drama, producing dramas of social extension that represented the lives of Britons beyond the upper middle-class drawing rooms of the capital. These 'writer-led experiments'[25] were scripted by playwrights such as Harold Pinter, Ray Rigby and Ted Willis, and, most prominently, Alun Owen. Owen's teleplays for *Armchair Theatre* depicted the lives of ordinary people in or from Liverpool (*No Trams to Lime Street* (tx. 18 October 1959); *Lena O My Lena* (tx. 25 September 1960); *The Hard Knock* (tx. 8 July 1962)) and Wales (*After the Funeral* (tx. 3 April 1960); *The Ways of Love* (tx. 9 April 1961)). The Canadian émigré director William 'Ted' Kotcheff directed all of these teleplays, among others for *Armchair Theatre*, and together Owen and Kotcheff took the viewer (and the camera) closer to the intimate detail of their characters' everyday lives and relationships within a regional setting.

To take a striking example of this work, Owen and Kotcheff's *After the Funeral* is deeply concerned with the search for regional and familial identity, set at the wake of the wife of Captain John Roberts (Charles Carson). As the family and villagers gather to pay their final respects, grandson Morgan (Hugh David), a well-respected academic and expert in Welsh culture and language, clashes with Dave (William Lucas), his older brother who has returned from sea, arguing simultaneously about the care of their elderly grandfather and their national identity. The use of regional accents and the Welsh language (which is untranslated throughout the drama), are the most striking markers of the teleplay's search for national identity.

Like other Owen teleplays (such as *Lena, O My Lena*), the conflict in *After the Funeral* centres around the notions of national identity, class and education, as characters struggle to find and accept their place in contemporary society. The teleplay is essentially a chamber drama set in the family home and draws a noticeable parallel between the intimate narrative concerns of the drama (the issues of family, paternity, inheritance and identity) and the intimacy of the setting, conveyed through the enforced close proximity of the actors to the cameras within the studio/room set. Relatively short focal distances accentuate an almost uncomfortable sense of closeness, as with the close-up track which reopens the episode after the first advertising break. The camera tracks across the decimated tea table in close-up to the sound of conversational chatter about the dead woman which occurs off screen, lingering over chipped teacups and half-picked ham bones and underlining the very 'ordinariness' of the drama taking place. The slow, close-up track is then repeated as the camera follows the line of faces gossiping around the tea table, again stressing a sense of detail to be read in the quotidian activities of this Welsh funeral.

Whilst an emphasis on intimacy and the representation of everyday life might not appear to be experimental in the context of television drama's current vogue for gritty social realism, from soap opera to the serial dramas of writers like Paul Abbott and Russell T. Davies, at the turn of the 1960s it was remarkable enough to earn the series the epithet 'armpit theatre' and a reputation for producing dramas which were strikingly different from the norm. Although 'After the Funeral' is fairly conservative in its shooting and editing techniques, and might be considered to be formally conventional in relation to other studio-based dramas, its innovations lie in its representation of the everyday.

It is well documented that the makers of *Armchair Theatre*'s social realist teleplays experimented with the form, as well as the content, of television drama. As early as 1961 the series was being praised for innovation in shooting techniques and set design:

> Almost from the beginning there was a three-dimensional quality to *Armchair Theatre* productions which was ahead of rival efforts. Sets were adventurous and elaborate and the geography was convincing – the camera followed people through doors and along corridors and into the next location instead of switching arbitrarily from scene to scene.[26]

Writing in the television journal *Contrast*, Purser's description points towards the studio realism of *Armchair Theatre*. This prefigured the verisimilitude that location filming would offer later in the 1960s, transforming the studio space into a flexible dramatic setting which moved beyond proscenium framing and 'theatrical' set design. In the ABC studios at Didsbury (and later Teddington), cameras moved fluidly around three-dimensional sets, allowing actors to direct the movement and stasis of the cameras, as opposed to the setting dictating a relatively small number of camera set-ups and compositions. Outlining the series' experimentation in setting and shooting, John Caughie proposes:

The objective was quite explicit: to use the camera as a way of breaking free from the stasis of theatrical space to the mobility of cinematic space. Viewed in retrospect, however, what is striking is not that the space has become 'real' in the Bazinian sense, but that the studio has become fluid and expressive, freeing the actors within the space. There is a sense that the actors inhabit a space, rather than being constricted within a frame ... Crucially for notions of realism in television, what is created in plays like *Lena, O My Lena* is a performative space – a space for acting – rather than a narrative space – a space for action. The studio remains a studio, but the actors invest it with meaning.[27]

Caughie argues that realism can be located in the dynamic relationship created between actor, setting and camera, illustrating this point with an example from the opening of *Lena, O My Lena*, in which an extended tracking shot moves the viewer from the outside of a wholesaler's packing yard through the studio space to the introduction of several of the drama's key characters. In this teleplay, as in many other episodes of *Armchair Theatre*, the innovative articulation of televisual space as social space within the studio setting is most striking. As a coda to this discussion, however, it is important to note that these experiments with a 'free flowing' shooting style and long average shot length were not technologically determined: the pedestal cameras employed in the production of *Armchair Theatre* were in use at the BBC before the establishment of the drama department at ABC. In relation to his earlier suggestion that the technicians working on the series pushed the available technology, working closely with their directors and designers, Leonard White has argued that pedestal cameras were operated quite differently in different institutional contexts:

> The BBC always regarded the pedestal camera in those days as a fixed camera. I'd acted on television, I'd seen pedestals, and the guy operating that particular camera... had a chair behind the camera. He would set it up and sit down. That was nowhere near the concept that guys like Ted Kotcheff and Philip Saville [had of it] ... they regarded that as a handheld camera, and my God, that was hard work for the cable bashers!

It would, therefore, seem that a later extended tracking shot in *Lena, O My Lena* might be seen as even more iconic of this moment in television drama's formal history than the opening shot. As student and 'new boy' Tom (Peter McEnery) walks back from a lunch break at the rear of the wholesalers with Lena (Billie Whitelaw), a girl from the neighbouring factory, the viewer is given a sense of the dynamic movement of the camera operator and cable bashers working on *Armchair Theatre*. Following Tom and Lena's conversation about meeting up after work, in which Lena leads Tom and the camera in a girlish stride around the space, the camera works furiously hard to keep up with the two actors (indeed, at one point in the sequence, a pair of hands accidentally appears from behind a piece of set, frantically pushing out more cable to allow the mobile pedestal camera to keep up with the actors). Whilst the set design here is rough, in places little more than painted flats depicting the scenery beyond the wholesaler's yard, the mobile camera allows the viewer to focus on the nuanced performances of Whitelaw's gum-chewing local lass and McEnery's awkward student, out of place in his present environment. Subsequently, a sense of social realism is created through action and dialogue, gesture and intonation in *Armchair Theatre*, and conveyed through a dynamic relationship between actor and camera.

Armchair Mystery Theatre: experiments in tele-impressionism

This discussion of *Armchair Theatre* as experimental drama, concludes with another branch of the series: *Armchair Mystery Theatre*. In an earlier article, I offered an extended discussion of this offshoot of *Armchair Theatre* which was initially conceived as a stop-gap to fill the summer months whilst Newman was on holiday, arguing that its non-naturalistic teleplays offered something akin to the Hollywood B-Picture in terms of their experimentation with form and style.[28] I proposed that episodes such as *The Blackmailing of Mr S* (tx. 26 July 1964) could be understood as expressionist in their use of avant-garde shooting and editing techniques. However, I wish to counter my earlier analysis of *Armchair Mystery Theatre* to a certain extent here, by arguing that the teleplays in this series can be more accurately understood as impressionist in style. As a representation of extreme, often paranoid, subjective states, many of the teleplays in this series offered innovative and creative approaches to the rendition of psychological, subjective realism.

The most famous explorations of impressionist form and style in relation to an audio-visual medium can be found in the French Impressionist cinema of the late teens and early 1920s. Filmmakers such as Abel Gance, Louis Delluc, Germaine Dulac, Marcel L'Herbier, Jean Epstein, and others had,

> [an] interest in making narrative form represent as fully as possible the play of a character's consciousness ... To intensify the subjectivity, the Impressionists' cinematography and editing [presented] characters' perceptual experience, their optical 'impressions' ... The Impressionists also experimented with pronounced rhythmic editing to suggest the pace of an experience as a character feels it, moment by moment.[29]

Susan Hayward also points us toward the relationship between the avant-garde, impressionist filmmaking, and melodrama:

> Melodrama as a sentimental narrative was perceived by the avant-garde as a perfect vehicle for the psychological expression of subjectivity. Subjectivity now became not just a question of point of view, but also included the implicit

notion of voyeurism and speculation (of the other) as well as the issue of desire, and the functioning of the conscious and the unconscious mind.[30]

Impressionism in film has thus been closely associated with formal experimentation and avant-garde practice, particularly the possibilities of representing subjective states and inner consciousness using cinematographic devices (for example, irises, masks and superimpositions) and innovative editing techniques (such as rhythmic or montage editing).

Within that branch of French Impressionist cinema that Ian Christie identifies as the 'modernist/reflexive' mode,[31] memories, flashbacks, dream sequences, optical and psychical points of view, and montage sequences all serve to represent the thoughts and feelings of the central protagonist/s. These techniques can also be clearly seen in many of the teleplays of *Armchair Mystery Theatre*, suggesting a comparable moment of experimentation with *televisual* form in Britain in the early 1960s. Whilst the producers of these teleplays did not identify themselves as avant-garde practitioners, or demonstrate the proclivities for self-theorisation of the French Impressionists, *Armchair Mystery Theatre* employed video effects and vision mixing to produce a similar focus on emotion, psychology, subjectivity and the exploration of mood and sensation. Similarly, the makers of the series employed irises and masks, superimposition, extreme changes in colour and contrast, shots taken at very close range or from unusual angles and, most strikingly, a heavy use of montage editing, to facilitate the representation of extreme subjective states, such as dreams and nightmares, flashbacks and premonitions, madness, paranoia, anxiety, amnesia, desire, and so on. All of this was also coupled with frequent extreme amplification of sound and the use of voice-over.

Of the episodes of *Armchair Theatre* that are still available to view, the tele-impressionist style is most clearly evident in *Time out of Mind* (tx. 19 July 1964),[32] *The Blackmailing of Mr S*, and *Man and Mirror* (tx. 13 June 1965),[33] though archival research suggests that other teleplays in the series shared these stylistic tendencies. For example, the actress Diana Wyngard who appeared in an episode entitled *Eye Witness* (tx. 5 June 1960), told from the point of view of a woman found paralysed and speechless at the scene of a murder, told the *TV Times* in 1960: 'I'm fascinated by [this play] ... It's so rare to find a play, even one written specially for television like this, that really couldn't be done on the stage'.[34] This was clearly due to the teleplay's specifically televisual techniques of representing character subjectivity.

Recalling the production of *Armchair Mystery Theatre*, series producer Leonard White comments:

> How risky it was to experiment with changing the style of conventional television drama production. While still harnessed in the live method of recording

productions, we were pushing all the time for the fast-moving style of film cutting (editing) with many and shorter scenes in the format – especially in [*Armchair Mystery Theatre*]. All of which constantly challenged the dexterity of the cameramen (and cable bashers), the boom operators and the 'switcher', and crew in the control room ... Within the constraints of live recording we were living dangerously.[35]

White's memory of *Armchair Mystery Theatre* as fast-paced and edgy is confirmed by close analysis of the available episodes of the series, and particularly the teleplay *Man and Mirror* written by Robert Muller and directed by Patrick Dromgoole, a Victorian domestic psychodrama. This episode called on the vision mixer or 'switcher' to create striking extended montages of superimposed images in order to produce an impressionist representation of the spiralling madness of one of its central characters. In line with Susan Hayward's characterisation of cinematic impressionism's interest in the melodrama, this teleplay saw the alignment of this genre (or rather the melodramatic sub-categories of the mystery-thriller or psychodrama) and an impressionist style, through its explorations of a disturbed human subjectivity.

Man and Mirror follows the story of Mrs Isabel Manners (Sybil Thorndike) who lives with her two disturbed sons, Edward (Richard Pasco), a recently divorced composer, and Geoffrey (Denholm Elliott), a general practitioner with an interest in psychoanalysis. The lady of the house, an overbearing mother with an iron grip on both her sons, believes that someone is trying to kill her. Meanwhile, it is suggested that Geoffrey Manners is treating his brother for a split-personality disorder and a 'lack of sexual restraint'. However, in the dénouement of the drama it is revealed that the doctor himself is the one who is losing his mind, as he appears in his mother's bedroom, dressed as a marionette and ready to kill her. At this point the viewer also discovers that Geoffrey is the mysterious man in the top hat and opera cape who has been terrorising the local women, and not his brother who, nevertheless, is infatuated with their housemaid (Anne Cunningham). During this scene, Geoffrey's horrific appearance (his rouged face and 'baby' voice) articulates the tension between surface appearance and inner mental state which has developed as a key theme in the teleplay, as well as reliving the suggested childhood trauma of his abuse. 'Man and Mirror' is thus permeated with Oedipal horror and a sense of domestic claustrophobia, representing the family home as an interior space of confinement in which two over-mothered men slowly lose their minds. As Mrs Manners complains, 'At times, I am made to feel a prisoner in this house', her son, Geoffrey, replies, 'I dare say we all suffer from that feeling from time to time, Mama.'

The impressionistic devices employed in this episode centre on the use of montage to visualise the madness of Dr Manners. The first of these is a montage sequence, showing Manners's pet chameleon, in extreme close-up, standing on a glass surface and accompanied by the following voice-over: 'How old are you, I wonder? You do not look happy. An absence of freedom? Does it count for so much as it does without it?' At this point in the narrative, the meaning of this sequence is unclear; the viewer later understands the chameleon as a rather obvious metaphor for Manners's split personality. Without the full knowledge of its significance however, the montage of the chameleon serves to break the flow of the narrative, expressing this character's emotional state rather than offering exposition. The second montage sequence is even further removed from the narrative, acting as a separate scene and not obviously tied to any of the central characters, although the viewer later understands it as another visualisation of Geoffrey Manners's madness.

Building an impression of a disturbed mental state, the following images are dissolved on top of one another, framed by exterior shots of the house at night: a close-up of the chameleon; an image of gloved hands; a close-up of a pile of coins; a shot of a hand picking up an egg; a close-up of a shining top hat; a shot of an antique clock face; a shot through a keyhole of a woman undressing, which racks in and out of focus; a repeat shot of the chameleon; a shot of a blank picture frame which then zooms into the centre of the image to reveal a roaring fire; and finally a close-up of flames. Classic impressionist devices such as the use of the masked shot and racking focus, extreme angles of vision, and repetitive, rhythmic, montage editing are accompanied by the increasingly distorted sound of a ticking clock, representing the disturbed psyche of Geoffrey Manners in a non-naturalistic way. Whilst this might be identified as an impressionistic moment within an otherwise conventional drama, it conforms to Robert Ray's suggestion that the impressionistic text is often identified by 'intermittent intensities that break free from the sometimes indifferent narratives which contain them'.[36] This shows that experiments with the form of television drama in Britain in the 1960s extended beyond the social realist paradigm, and that a movement of tele-impressionism during this period can validly be identified. Clearly these modes of non-naturalistic representation did not have the same impact on the future of British television drama as the social realist episodes of *Armchair Theatre* proper, nor did the use of montage editing change the predominant aesthetic of British television drama in the same way that the mobile camera did. This is perhaps partly why these episodes are less well known and infrequently discussed by television historians up until this point. However, they did establish creative and innovative ways to represent extremes of emotion and feeling and explored television drama's potential for presenting subjective realism, techniques which are worthy of further consideration.

Experiments beyond naturalism and social realism within the ABC drama department were not only confined to *Armchair Mystery Theatre*, however. Within *Armchair Theatre* proper there were several striking examples of teleplays which were dramatically different from their kitchen-sink counterparts. *The Rose Affair* (tx. 8 October 1961), for example, was '[t]he most discussed drama production [of 1961]'[37] according to *Contrast* magazine, employing masked actors and a self-conscious, gestural performance style to retell the story of 'Beauty and the Beast'. The designer on this teleplay, Voytek, also produced a minimalist set design for Charles Wood's *Prisoner and Escort* (t.x. 5 April 1964), directed by Philip Saville, which told the story of a military prisoner being transported for a court marshal. As another creative, non-naturalistic response to the restrictions of the studio space, Voytek designed a performance area in which lighting rigs and scaffolding were freely seen, and in which 'prop men' were shown moving walls up and down to create new sets within the studio, destroying the illusion of reality but creating 'a performative space – a space for acting – rather than a narrative space – a space for action'.[38]

In concluding this discussion of *Armchair Theatre* and *Armchair Mystery Theatre*, it is important to note that the production of experimental drama in this period was reliant on a conception of the average television viewer as engaged and thoughtful. Alongside more populist offerings, it was assumed that the episodes discussed in this chapter would be watched and enjoyed by a mass audience. This attitude to the audience is reflected in television critic Peter Black's introduction to the television journal *Contrast*, in 1961. Black asks: 'Is *Wagon Train*, for example, watched in drowsy, habit-formed indifference, which has to be broken into by a burst of hoof beats or a menacing phrase from the background music? Or is the audience conscious, appreciative, critical? It is neither, all the time. On the other hand, it is both, some of the time.'[39] The perception of a conscious, appreciative, critical audience is of paramount importance when understanding the production of experimental drama within *Armchair Theatre*. Contemporaneously, the Pilkington Report called for 'the new and the challenging, because individual listeners and viewers should not be denied the opportunity of responding to them'[40]. In this report, ABC received special mention for its attitude toward viewer appeal: 'ABC Television Ltd told us ... that people who claimed that they know what the public wanted rarely did, but always underestimated'.[41] However, in contrast to the Pilkington Report's findings, the ITA's own consultation into the state of television drama told a different story. The *Report of the ITA Consultation on Television Drama* (23/24 June 1965, ITA File 225/2), produced by Sir Robert Fraser, concluded that 'in 1960 the great majority of plays had been intelligible to the great majority of viewers, but by 1965 many of them were not', arguing that 'most viewers could not endure obscurity'.[42] This shift in attitude toward the place of experimental drama in the schedule was significant. According to Leonard White, it signalled a more general demise in the production of the anthologised single play:

> I think [the Consultation] was one of these things where more likely ... it was because they did not want the single play. They thought they ought to rely on soaps and series, and other sorts of continuing series ... That sort of thing was tickling somebody's fancy at the time and the single play got in the way. A great, great pity that anybody should ever think that because [the single play] is the basis of it all.

With the BBC announcing the return of the anthology drama series in Spring 2006, one might wish to view the history outlined in this chapter as evidence of the potential compatibility between the industrial production practices of television and the production of experimental and innovative drama. This analysis of *Armchair Theatre* and *Armchair Mystery Theatre* has shown that it was possible to produce experimental drama in the context of a nascent production company (ABC) working under tight financial and temporal constraints. Furthermore, these programmes prove that large numbers of television viewers were open and receptive to experimental drama produced within and outside of the social realist paradigm. Viewer appeal during this period did not simply mean crowd-pleasing, formulaic television drama. Given the sheer volume of original teleplays produced by ABC in the 1950s and 1960s, and given the well-documented problems with the preservation and archiving of British television drama, it is perhaps all the more striking that several key examples of teleplays of such a high calibre are left in the archives, which testify to a moment of heterogeneous experimentalism on commercial television.

Notes

I gratefully acknowledge the support of the Arts & Humanities Research Board which funded the research project 'Cultures of British Television Drama, 1960–82' at the University of Reading. This article is one of the outcomes of the research.

1   Billie Whitelaw interviewed in *And Now For Your Sunday Night Dramatic Entertainment* (Microcraze Productions for Channel 4, tx. 8 February 1987).
2   Please note that this chapter discusses the *Armchair Theatre* episodes produced by ABC Television. After ABC's merger with Associated-Rediffusion, the programme was produced by Thames from 1968.
3   Unless otherwise indicated, all quotes from Leonard White have been taken from my interview with him at the symposium 'Producing Popular Television Drama, 1960–82', University of Reading, 16 October 2004.

4 John Caughie, *Television Drama: Realism, Modernism and British Culture* (Oxford: Oxford University Press, 2000), 127.
5 As Jason Jacobs has argued, however, Gardner and Wyver's description of early television drama ignores some significant exceptions in the production of pre-ITV drama in Britain. Jason Jacobs, *The Intimate Screen: Early British Television Drama* (Oxford: Oxford University Press, 2000), 3.
6 Carl Gardner and John Wyver, 'The Single Play from Reithian Reverence to Cost-Accounting and Censorship', *Screen*, 24: 4–5 (1983), 115.
7 See Jacobs, *The Intimate Screen*.
8 The ITA's repayment of its £500,000 government start-up loan five years early is indicative of the financial security which was being enjoyed by the commercial companies at this moment in British broadcasting.
9 See, for example, George Brandt, *Television Drama* (Cambridge: Cambridge University Press, 1981), or Andrew Crisell, *An Introductory History of British Broadcasting* (2nd edn) (London and New York: Routledge, 2002).
10 At the symposium 'Producing Popular Television Drama, 1960–82', University of Reading, October 2004.
11 Caughie, *Television Drama*, 125–8.
12 For example, Irene Shubik, *Play for Today: The Evolution of Television Drama* (2nd edn) (Manchester: Manchester University Press, 2000); Shubik, 'Television Drama Series: A Producer's View', in Jonathan Bignell, Stephen Lacey and Madeleine MacMurraugh Kavanagh (eds), *British Television Drama: Past, Present and Future* (London: Palgrave, 2000), 42–7; and Leonard White, *Armchair Theatre: The Lost Years* (Tiverton: Kelly Publications, 2003). Also see the television documentary *And Now For Your Sunday Night Dramatic Entertainment* (Microcraze Productions for Channel 4, tx. 8 February 1987).
13 Sydney Newman, 'Producing a Television Play', in ABC Television Ltd, *The Armchair Theatre: How to Write, Design, Direct, Act and Enjoy Television Plays* (London: Weidenfeld & Nicolson, 1959), 20.
14 Caughie, *Television Drama*, 77.
15 See Helen Wheatley, 'Putting the *Mystery* back into *Armchair Theatre*', *Journal of British Cinema and Television*, 1: 2 (2004), 199.
16 Howard Thomas, *With an Independent Air* (London: Weidenfeld & Nicolson, 1977), 169.
17 White, *Armchair Theatre*, 128.
18 Ibid., 114.
19 Ibid.
20 John Corner (ed.), *Popular Television in Britain: Studies in Cultural History* (London: BFI Publishing, 1991), 2.
21 Ted Willis, *Evening All: Fifty Years Over a Hot Typewriter* (London: Macmillan, 1991), 137–8.
22 See, among others, Caughie, *Television Drama*, 72–5; Shubik, *Play for Today*, 9; and Wheatley, 'Putting the *Mystery* back into *Armchair Theatre*', 200.
23 For example, the 1958 season of *Armchair Theatre* was bolstered by American teleplays such as 'Tragedy in a Temporary Town' (Reginald Rose), 'The Five Dollar Bill' (Tad Mosel), 'Paid in Full' (Mordecai Richler), 'Noon on Doomsday'

(Rod Serling), 'The Travelling Lady' (Horton Foote), 'The Greatest Man in the World' (James Thurber, ad. Reuben Ship), 'Please Murder Me' (Gore Vidal), 'The Emperor Jones' (Eugene O'Neill), and 'The Time of Your Life' (William Saroyan).

24 Caughie, *Television Drama*, 61–9.
25 John Ellis, *Seeing Things: Television in the Age of Uncertainty*, (London: I.B. Tauris, 2000), 149.
26 Philip Purser, 'Landscape of TV Drama', *Contrast*, 1: 1 (Autumn 1961), 18.
27 Caughie, *Television Drama*, 75.
28 See Wheatley, 'Putting the *Mystery* back into *Armchair Theatre*'.
29 David Bordwell and Kristin Thompson, *Film Art: An Introduction* (4th edn) (New York: McGraw-Hill, 1993), 463–4
30 Susan Hayward, *French National Cinema* (London and New York: Routledge, 2005), 115.
31 Ian Christie, 'Forms 1890–1930: the shifting boundaries of art and industry', in Michael Temple and Michael Witt (eds), *The French Cinema Book* (London: BFI Publishing, 2004), 124.
32 Available to view through the National Film and Television Archive at the British Film Institute.
33 'Time Out of Mind' and 'Man and Mirror' are available to view through the Canal+ film library.
34 *TV Times*, 1960, 16.
35 White, *Armchair Theatre*, 146.
36 Robert Ray, 'Impressionism, surrealism, and film theory: path dependence, or how a tradition in film theory gets lost', in John Hill and Pamela Church Gibson (eds), *The Oxford Guide to Film Studies* (Oxford: Oxford University Press, 1998), 69.
37 *Contrast*, 1965, 108.
38 Caughie, *Television Drama*, 75.
39 Peter Black, 'Foreword', *Contrast*, 1:1 (Autumn, 1961), 2.
40 The Pilkington Report (HMSO, 1962), 285.
41 Ibid., 19.
42 Bernard Sendall, *Independent Television in Britain, Volume One: Origin and Foundation, 1946–62* (London and Basingstoke: Macmillan, 1982), 334–5.

3

A 'new drama for television'?: *Diary of a Young Man*[1]

John Hill

Diary of a Young Man was a six-part series broadcast on BBC1 in August and September 1964. Billed in the *Radio Times* as an example of 'a new kind of writing for television', it was a self-consciously 'experimental' work, intended to extend the boundaries of television drama through the employment of new techniques.[2] Written by Troy Kennedy Martin and John McGrath, produced by James MacTaggart and directed by Ken Loach and Peter Duguid, it also represented a significant coming together of personnel within the BBC with an interest in changing the direction of television drama. The series also had the benefit of being accompanied by a manifesto, 'Nats Go Home', written by Troy Kennedy Martin and published in spring 1964. Described as a 'first statement of a new drama for television', this proposed 'a working philosophy' containing 'a new idea of form, with new language, new punctuation and new style.'[3]

First published in the theatre magazine *Encore*, 'Nats Go Home' was followed in the next issue by a series of responses from a variety of figures including the Head of BBC Television Drama, Sydney Newman, the former Head of BBC TV Drama, Michael Barry, the then critic but later distinguished television writer Dennis Potter, the actor Tony Garnett (just about to embark upon a career as a BBC story editor and producer) and the Granada producer Philip Mackie.[4] The article was then reprinted in *Screenwriter* along with a further set of comments by a number of practising television writers.[5] The fact that so many were prepared to contribute to the debate it stirred suggests not only the importance that was attached to the article when it first appeared but also its success on touching on matters of shared concern. 'Nats Go Home', in this regard, clearly amounted to something more than just a 'pitch' for Kennedy Martin's new series but successfully tapped into, and helped to crystallise, ideas and arguments that were already in circulation within both television and the culture more generally.[6] In particular, the essay may be seen to draw upon and articulate a growing sense of discontent during this period with the established approach of the television play. The discussion that follows, therefore, begins with an overview of the context from which the manifesto, and the accompanying series, emerged. It then moves on to consider the ideas within the manifesto and analyse how these were exemplified in the series itself. The chapter concludes with an assessment of some of the issues and questions to which the manifesto and series give rise.

Towards 'a new kind of dramatic communication'

A number of factors contributed to the development of the ideas contained in Kennedy Martin's essay and put into practice in the *Diary of a Young Man* series. The essay itself was published by *Encore*, a theatre magazine strongly associated with the emergence of a new theatre in Britain, in the wake of John Osborne's *Look Back in Anger* (1956). The British cinema had also enjoyed its own 'new wave' and new kinds of formally innovative filmmaking from across Europe had been entering the country. Although ABC's *Armchair Theatre*, under Sydney Newman, had introduced new kinds of subject matter into television drama at the end of the 1950s and early 1960s (see Chapter 2), there was still a strong sense that television had failed to find the new forms of expression equivalent to those found in the theatre and cinema. This was due in part to technological constraints but was also the result of aesthetic choices.

In the early 1960s, the bulk of television drama was still shot in the studio, employing a limited number of sets and often transmitted live. Although the introduction of videotape in 1958 had allowed drama to be pre-recorded, it remained expensive and cumbersome to use and extensive editing was discouraged. As a result the recording of television drama remained very close to the live broadcast, normally consisting of a continuous recording following a few days of studio rehearsal. Thus, while John Caughie detects an increase in camera mobility in the recording of television drama during the 1950s and early 1960s, he also suggests how the dominant aesthetic of television remained wedded to the idea of theatrical performance and the use of the studio as a 'performative space'.[7]

Although this aesthetic was seen by its defenders as well-suited to the specific characteristics of the television medium, there was also a growing sense that it was inhibiting the advance of television drama. The Langham Group (discussed in Chapter 1) had sought to break free of 'proscenium presentation' through the development of new production methods but was, nonetheless, attacked by Troy Kennedy Martin as 'an art set-up ... propitiated on the altar of prestige'.[8] In contrast to what he perceived as the aestheticism of their experiments, Kennedy Martin called instead for an approach to television drama that could be 'applied to mass audience viewing'.[9] In doing so, he identified an emerging form of television drama that not only sought, as in the case of the Langham Group, to experiment with visual language but also to do so within a strong narrative framework.

Two series, in particular, are worth noting. *Storyboard* ran from July to September 1961 and consisted primarily of adaptations of short stories by different authors, including John Dickson Carr, Bernard Malamud and John Wyndham. The series was significant in bringing together Kennedy Martin (as one of the co-writers of the series) with the director and writer John McGrath and the young Scottish producer, director and actor, James MacTaggart, who had recently moved from Glasgow to London to join the BBC Drama Department. Although the series, as others before it, involved literary adaptations, it was nonetheless flagged as an innovative attempt to tell – in 'visual terms' – stories with a 'strong narrative thread'.[10] What this meant in practice was described by John McGrath who recalls how the team sought 'to get away from ... the whole pseudo-theatrical approach to television' in order 'to create narrative drama' that, in the case of one episode of the series, involved the use of 36 locations in 30 minutes (in spite of the live conditions of broadcast).[11] This emphasis on increased pace, reduced shot lengths and multiple sets was then carried over into Kennedy Martin and McGrath's work on *Z Cars* which began broadcasting early the following year.[12]

Meanwhile MacTaggart went on to produce a follow-up to *Storyboard*, *Studio 4*, which ran intermittently from January to September 1962, as well as the more openly experimental series *Teletales*, launched in 1963. Originally entitled 'Nursery Slopes', the series was conceived as a training ground for new directors recruited in anticipation of the launch of BBC2 in 1964. Based primarily on adaptations from short stories, the series was written by Roger Smith and Christopher Williams who had previously worked on the *Studio 4* series and had impressed MacTaggart with their prowess in 'distilling the printed narrative into a visual story'.[13] It was also Smith and Williams who provided the series with its rationale:

> The stories will be told with maximum economy and condensation. The juxtaposition of scenes and the cutting between them will be crucial to the narrative. The style of narration will be fluid, using and exploring the resources of framing, camera mobility and studio space. Narrative and camera will select the relevant "information" in each scene. We hope that this method will allow us to liberate the action from the accepted necessities of naturalism, while not detracting from the interest of the story.[14]

One example of this method was provided by Smith's original play *Catherine* (tx. 24 January 1964), concerning a young woman who has recently left her husband. Described by MacTaggart as 'breaking most of the accepted rules of television', the production was directed by Ken (then Kenneth) Loach and featured Tony Garnett in the role of the young woman's husband.[15] The play itself was shot in a bare studio with no conventional sets. In order to achieve maximum narrative 'fluidity', the production employed a narrator, used lighting to signal changes in scene and cut extensively, employing over 120 shots in less than 30 minutes. This also included short montage sequences such as when Catherine is seen to dine with a succession of unappealing men.[16]

Although experiments such as these were not high profile, their influence did begin to spread. At the beginning of 1964, BBC drama was faced with a degree of crisis. Audiences for the single play were in decline and the two main single-play drama series, *First Night* and *Festival*, had been the subject of criticism for their poor quality and 'low moral standard'.[17] In an effort to improve the BBC's position in the ratings, the Chief of Programmes BBC1, Donald Baverstock, proposed a reduction in single plays in order to divert resources towards popular series and serials such as *Z Cars* and *Dr Finlay's Casebook* (which had, in fact, taken over the *First Night* Sunday-evening slot in January 1964).[18] These proposals were bitterly opposed by the Head of the Drama Group, Sydney Newman, who had appointed MacTaggart as the series producer of *First Night* in the belief that things could be turned around.[19]

Although *First Night* did not in the end survive (eventually mutating into *The Wednesday Play*), Newman's appointment of MacTaggart did, as John Cook suggests, mark the beginning of a 'strategic alliance' between 'the Canadian outsider', Sydney Newman, and 'the band of youngish, dissident experimenters led by MacTaggart' who, following Newman's arrival at the BBC in 1963, 'sensed they might be on the ascendancy'.[20] Indeed, if evidence of this alliance was needed, it could be found in Newman's own 'manifesto' published more or less simultaneously (in Spring 1964) with that of Kennedy Martin, in which Newman made his own spirited defence of the purpose of television drama, arguing that series such as *First Night* which 'reach out for new writing' are 'on the side of the angels'. He then proceeded to propose the two new directions that television plays should take: a move towards 'greater realism' through an increase of location shooting as well as a move towards 'a new kind of dramatic communication' shorn of 'naturalistic trappings'. In the latter case, he suggested how this might involve stories in which 'all irrelevancies are eliminated' as well as the use of 'stills, graphics [and] the bold and unafraid use of "off-camera" narration'.[21] In doing so, he was not only echoing a number of Troy Kennedy Martin's own formulations in *Encore* but also, like Kennedy Martin, describing many of the aesthetic techniques that were to become a feature of *Diary of a Young Man*.

Ironically, due to the uncertainty surrounding BBC drama policy at the beginning of 1964, *Diary of a Young Man* almost did not get made. However, in so far as it employed a 'new kind of dramatic communication' within the series format, the programme appeared to satisfy the aspirations of both camps within the BBC and entered production in June 1964.

Articulating the issues: 'Nats Go Home'

As this review of the context of television production in the early 1960s would suggest, Kennedy Martin's essay articulated and brought into sharper focus many of the ideas about narrative and visualisation that had been germinating over the preceding few years. As his title suggests, the main focus of his critique is 'naturalism' which he insists is 'the wrong form for drama for the medium'.[22] From a contemporary point of view, the choice of the term 'naturalism' seems to be an odd one given that it is not the features normally associated with naturalism (such as the representation of contemporary realities) that seem to be the object of attack. Indeed, from an alternative perspective, it might be argued that it had been a naturalistic impulse towards social extension and contemporary observation that had been responsible for much of the most innovative television work of the period, including Troy Kennedy Martin's own *Z Cars* (the purpose of which he had described previously as holding 'a mirror up to English life').[23] However, as has been seen, at the time that Kennedy Martin's essay appeared, the term 'naturalism' had gained a wide currency within television drama circles (and beyond) and had acquired fairly specific (if not always fully agreed) associations. What, above all, the reference to 'naturalism' seemed to designate was the 'theatrical' approach to television drama that prevailed at the time and it is certainly this that Kennedy Martin picks up on when he declares that '[a]ll drama which owes its form or substance to theatre plays is OUT'.[24] For Kennedy Martin, this approach to television drama displayed a number of key features. '"Nat" plays', he argues, involve the telling of 'a story by means of dialogue' rather than other means; they work within 'a strict form of natural time' in which 'studio-time equals drama-time equals Greenwich Mean Time', and they rely heavily upon the use of close-ups – the photographing of 'faces talking and faces reacting' – which it was assumed would act 'subjectively upon the viewer' to generate emotional involvement in 'a character's predicament'. Kennedy Martin believed that the strategy of 'the new drama' had to challenge these conventions and 'free the camera from photographing dialogue … free the structure from natural time' and abandon the pursuit of subjective identification with characters through the exploitation of 'the total and absolute objectivity of the television camera'.[25]

In order to do so, Kennedy Martin proposed (as had been the case with

Storyboard) a 'narrative form of drama' that would reduce the dependence upon dialogue and permit a freer time structure.[26] Although for Kennedy Martin the main virtue of a narrative approach is that it permitted the presentation of action in 'a condensed form', he also took earlier calls for greater narrative pace one step further by advocating a particular model of narrative which he referred to as 'based on story rather than plot'.[27] This does not, however, rest upon a formalist distinction of the kind that characterises plot (or 'syuzhet') as the arrangement that the telling of a story (or 'fabula') actually takes. Rather, Kennedy Martin appeared to be drawing upon Bertolt Brecht's distinction between 'dramatic theatre', which Brecht associated with 'plot, and 'epic theatre', which he linked to 'narrative' and 'story'.[28] Kennedy Martin's demand, therefore, was that the new television drama should reject the carefully plotted forms of narrative (characteristic, in this case, of both 'dramatic theatre' and Hollywood cinema) in favour of 'non-Aristotelian' forms of episodic narration similar to the eighteenth-century picaresque novel. In particular, he recommended the use of a narrator, already experimented with in the *Storyboard* and *Teletales* series, as a way of both eliminating dialogue and achieving the fluidity of action that naturalism's apparent subordination to 'natural time' prevents. However, Kennedy Martin was also conscious of the need for a new visual vocabulary to match the new forms of temporality involved in this approach to storytelling. He, therefore, called for an increased use of editing in order to condense dramatic action and excise the 'dead time' involved in the 'real time' of naturalistic drama.[29]

He was also concerned that television drama should liberate itself from the strict linearity of 'naturalism' and develop the capacity to move backwards and forwards in time (as well as exercise the right to extend and not just condense time). In order to be able to do so, he followed Sergei Eisenstein in advocating the use of montage which, he argued, would not only permit the construction of new temporal relationships but also the creation of new meanings through a juxtaposition of shots, including stills. The advantage of montage of this last kind, Kennedy Martin explained, is that it also provided the means of achieving the emotional involvement that the naturalist concentration on the photographing of dialogue failed to deliver. Why this should be so was accounted for in terms of his analysis of the apparent 'objectivity' of the television camera.

According to Kennedy Martin, television drama sought – through its commitment to the close-up – to involve the television viewer in forms of identification with characters similar to those solicited by the classic Hollywood film. Kennedy Martin believed, however, that the cultivation of this kind of subjective involvement was fruitless for television. This, he argued, was not due to television's different conditions of viewing ('watching the telly in family groups') nor deficiencies of acting, design and direction; rather it was 'the very use of the camera' that keeps the viewer '"one step removed" from the drama'.[30] In this regard, Kennedy Martin's argument appeared to be that it was not simply a particular camera style ('naturalist' or otherwise) that was responsible for this effect but the very qualities of the television image itself. In his original essay, Kennedy Martin presents this as if it were almost some kind of 'essential' feature of television. In a later account of his position, however, he suggests that it may also have been a product of the technology then available. Thus, while he continues to argue that a 'distancing effect' is 'built into the medium', he also concedes that this was 'more apparent during those days of black-and-white television, when the lighting and the limited focus of the electronic cameras produced images which stood out in an exceptional way'.[31]

The argument that television is ill-equipped to sustain audience identification with characters led Kennedy Martin in a number of directions. Although he mainly used the term 'naturalism' as a synonym for televised theatre, he also followed Brecht in identifying naturalism with the theatrical tradition associated with the work of the Russian director Konstantin Stanislavsky at the Moscow Art Theatre. Stanislavsky's ideas had, of course, been taken up by the Actors' Studio in New York, founded by Lee Strasberg in 1947, and had entered television through the plays of Paddy Chayefsky (the author of the famous 1953 television play *Marty* starring Actors' Studio alumnus Rod Steiger). For Kennedy Martin, however, the 'Method's' enthusiasm for a dramaturgy of psychological motivation and vulgarised Freudianism simply reinforced the performance-driven theatricality of television and failed to provide the kind of access to 'interior thought' that he believed non-naturalistic forms could.[32]

His argument, in this respect, is quite complex. For while Kennedy Martin's debt to Brecht is clear, his stance on television involves a degree of reversal of Brecht's original position. Thus, whereas Brecht's theatrical practice is associated with 'alienation' or 'distancing' effects designed to disrupt the emotional spell of 'illusionist' drama and inhibit the spectator's identification with characters, Kennedy Martin's analysis suggests that television drama is already, in effect, in possession of these features. As a result, his concern is less with how to achieve the 'distanciation' of the viewer than with how to generate the emotional involvement that the apparent 'distancing' effects of the television camera prevent. Thus, while he distinguishes between two kinds of viewer involvement – 'objective involvement which stimulates mind and imagination' and 'emotional' involvement that 'directly disturb[s] the senses' – it is the latter form of involvement that he believes it is most difficult for television drama to achieve.[33] It is for this reason that Kennedy Martin was drawn towards the use of montage which he suggests is capable of cutting across the 'unblinking' view of the television camera and provoking (in a manner similar to Eisenstein's cinema) 'total involvement of an emotional kind'.[34] In this respect, Kennedy Martin's appeal for the exploitation of 'objectivity' of the television camera is only partly understood as a self-conscious – 'anti-illusionist' – strategy intended to stimulate critical reflection on the part of the viewer for it is also clearly identified with the arousal of strong emotional engagement on the part of the television audience as well.

Thus, while the broad sweep of Kennedy Martin's call for a new television drama is apparent, it is also quite complex in detail, bringing together divergent and even potentially conflicting strands (that are often 'ironed out' by later accounts of his position). His emphasis upon freeing television from dialogue builds upon a growing call for television to evolve a visual aesthetic that extends beyond the showing of 'talking heads'. However, it also entails a privileged position for the spoken voice-over which, in some respects, makes his prescribed form of drama even more 'wordy' than its predecessors.[35] His emphasis upon freeing drama from natural time involves a growing emphasis upon a 'narrativisation' of events, and a use of continuity editing that eliminates time in the interests of narrative economy. However, he also lays stress on a form of narration and use of montage that will enable movement through time and space and permit discursive rather than simply narrative forms of exposition. Furthermore, while his reflections on 'objectivity' may appear to rest upon Brechtian principles, it is also linked to a demand for the expression of subjective states (as in the films of Alain Resnais which – despite their dream-like qualities – are observed to have achieved 'new kinds of objectiveness'), as well as a call for the emotional stimulation of the television viewer that draws on the ideas of Eisenstein.

From theory to practice: *Diary of a Young Man*

Although the series had still to enter production when 'Nats Go Home' was published, the two were nevertheless conceived together – to the extent that one critic complained that the programme appeared 'to have been written and directed as an illustration of a thesis rather than as an independent work'.[36] Due to the difficulty of actually seeing them, the programmes have, however, received much less attention than the essay with which the series was linked. For a long time, only one episode (Episode 1) was known to have survived while two more (Episodes 5 and 6) have only recently been 'discovered'. Inevitably, this has made it impossible for the series to achieve the same kind of afterlife as the essay which has, as a result, been discussed largely in isolation.

The episodes that have survived, however, do provide a fair indication of how Troy Kennedy Martin's ideas concerning narrative, character and visual techniques were put into practice and also allow us to arrive at some kind of assessment of them. The story concerns the escapades of two northerners, Joe (Victor Henry) and Ginger (Richard Moore), who arrive in London at the start of Episode 1 in pursuit of 'a bird, a pad and some money'. Partly modelled on the picaresque novel, the story consists of a series of loosely connected episodes in which the central character Joe (a character of 'low estate') undergoes a series of encounters with those in a more economically and socially advantaged position. Thus, in Episode 2 Joe experiences the difficulties involved in opening a bank account and, in an ironic reference to *The Times* of the day, takes up charring as a way of making contact with the 'top people'. In Episode 4, Joe obtains a job in a shipping department which exposes him to the ruthless double-dealing and backstabbing of the company board, while in Episode 5 he is faced with the commercialised world of PR and advertising. As this might suggest, the series contains a strong satirical impulse (undoubtedly influenced by the iconoclasm of programmes such as *That Was the Week That Was*) that pokes fun at the 'Establishment' and seeks to expose the greed and hypocrisy with which it is associated. Thus, Episode 1 features a montage of the London 'rat race' consisting of shots of MPs (including actual footage of the then Conservative Prime Minister Sir Alec Douglas Home), military personnel, policemen, and bankers leaving work. The sequence then concludes with some of the same 'generals, admirals and detectives' being welcomed by a 'model' as they enter a Soho doorway (this, it will be recalled, was only one year after the Profumo affair).

The loose, episodic approach to narrative that the series employs is combined with a particular attitude towards characterisation. Although Joe develops as a character during the course of the series, the emphasis of the drama is less on his personal and psychological growth than the situations into which his character is propelled and the meanings to be extracted from them. Accordingly, the people that Joe meets are less 'rounded' characters than types who exemplify particular social positions or roles such as clerk, constable or businessman. Indeed, as if to reinforce the lack of interest in psychological realism, certain actors – such as Frank Williams – play more than one part or – as in the case of Glynn Edwards who plays both a variety of policemen and a prison officer – variations on the same part. Joe is invested with rather more psychological depth but is himself a social type fashioned along the lines of the sexually aggressive northern working-class hero derived from the social-realist literature and films of the period. In doing so the series also inherits the 'masculinism' of this tradition, organising the story in terms of male experience and linking Joe's progress with the sexual conquest of women of higher social status (Rosie in Episode 1, Fred in Episode 5).[37]

In line with Kennedy Martin's call for the removal of dialogue, Joe is also employed as a narrator, telling the story in the style of a diary entry. While, for Brecht, the employment of forms of direct commentary (including the use of a narrator) encourages the expression, as Raymond Williams puts it, of 'alternative points of view' which contribute to a mode of 'complex seeing', Joe's first-person narration tends to reinforce the organisation of the story around a male point of view.[38] However, the use of voice-over is not always consistent (verging at times on recitation) and also creates a degree of disjunction with the way that Joe's character is otherwise shown.[39] Much of Joe's narration, for example, is told in a faux naif style suggestive of his deprived background (in an orphanage) and poor education. However, at various points within the series Joe acquires an articulacy and intelligence at odds with the simple persona suggested by the voice-over. Thus, in the first episode when Joe and Ginger end up in Covent Garden after a night's drinking, their encounter with Uncle Arthur (Will Stampe) provides the pretext for a debate about the Blitz in which Joe demonstrates sufficient knowledge of the Second World War (including a grasp of relevant statistics) for Uncle Arthur to suspect he is 'a student, a reader of books, an intellectual'. In this way, Joe emerges less as a fully coherent character governed by the norms of psychological realism, than a character capable of adapting to his surroundings in line with the need of the drama to place him in a variety of 'gestic' social encounters that will highlight prevailing attitudes and dispositions.

As this might suggest, *Diary of a Young Man* is more a drama of ideas than it is of actions. In his account of television naturalism, Kennedy Martin had argued that:

> When it deals with people's personal relationship with God, or with nature, or with themselves it does by refraction through some dialogue style. When it deals with any of the abstracts – fear, impotence, hunger, hate, love or hope it does so indirectly through symbols or again through dialogue with other people – wife, colleague or even a stranger.[40]

In many respects, it is a concern to deal with 'abstracts', and to find a new televisual vocabulary in which to do so, that informs *Diary of a Young Man*'s aesthetic choices. This may be seen in Episode 5, 'Life or a Girl called Fred' which deals explicitly, if somewhat ironically, with the question of 'the meaning of life'. In this Joe meets a beautiful older woman, Fred (Jean Marsh) at his new place of work, a public relations firm. After they have slept together, Joe reveals that he is in fact married and Fred threatens to commit suicide. In order to prevent Fred from taking her own life, Joe then embarks upon a pursuit of 'the meaning of life' that involves a wide-ranging tour or people who might assist him, including a psychiatrist, a biologist, a priest, the Chief of the British Beats, a philosopher, the Chief Lord Justice, a Chelsea pensioner, the 'man in the street' and a Buddhist. As this might suggest, Joe's quest is presented less as a dramatically probable set of meetings than a series of emblematic encounters, shot through with elements of absurdism (the Chief Lord Justice, for example, is found in a supermarket where he is subsequently arrested for shoplifting). These encounters are also engineered with a degree of disregard for the norms of verisimilitude. Hence, there are cuts from place to place – such as the biology lab to the home of the priest – with little sense of how Joe got there or explanation of how he knew where to go.

In a memo to Sydney Newman about breaks during the recording of the series (written at a time when the expectation was that these should not exceed five), James MacTaggart observed that the programme derived from 'the gospel according to Troy Kennedy Martin' and was 'taut, condensed and utterly devoid of flabby realistic fill in stuff'.[41] This description of the absence of 'realistic fill in stuff' usefully brings together two key aspects of the *Diary of a Young Man's* approach to editing, identifying not only the temporal compression but also the violation of the conventions of 'realism' involved in the presentation of Joe's journey through contemporary London.

This attitude towards narrative is further reinforced by *Diary of a Young Man's* use of stills. As in the 'photo-roman' of Chris Marker, whose film *La Jetée* was released in 1962, combinations of still images are used to achieve a quickened form of movement through time and space (and partly to capture something of the tempo of modern city life).[42] Thus, in Episode 1 a montage, consisting of over fifty stills, shows Joe and Ginger spending a night 'on the tiles' in the company of various hangers-on and false friends. In a sequence such as this, the action (occurring over several hours and across various London locations) is presented through a series of core images which, in Kennedy Martin's terms, 'distil' – rather than 'restate' – narrative information.[43] However, while such montages may, through the compression of time and space, provide a distillation of narrative action, they also permit a degree of departure from narrative linearity. In Episode 1, for example, one of the series of stills deals with Joe and Ginger's difficulties in obtaining a hotel. However, as this proceeds, the pace of cutting is increased and a number of stills are then repeated in a rearranged non-chronological order.

What this seems to signal is a move towards more rhetorical forms of exposition within the series. Thus, while the programme borrows the use of a narrator from the novel, it is also indebted to the documentary voice-over and the more discursive forms of exposition and explanation with which the documentary is associated.[44] Furthermore, in the hotels montage, the combination of Joe's voice-over and out-of-sequence stills not only shows us what has happened to Joe and Ginger but also presents an attitude towards, and a comment upon, the events that are being shown. This alternation between narrative and rhetorical modes of exposition becomes a feature of the series more generally and involves the use of both stills and moving images. Thus, in Episode 5, there is a sequence in which Joe is shown sitting at the foot of Nelson's Column in Trafalgar Square. As he meditates upon the meaning of life, the series of shots that follows mixes moving images of Trafalgar Square and other locations (such as a church and a railway station) with still images of both people (the Chief of the British Beats and the philosopher) and places (Buckingham Palace, the National Gallery, the law courts) relevant to Joe's quest. In this way, the combination of voice-over and montage assumes the characteristics of a short 'essay' in which the images are organised according to Joe's reflections (and his contemplation of 'abstracts') rather than his physical movements or dramatic actions.

In this way, such montages also provide the access to interior thought which Kennedy Martin had sought to achieve by breaking with extended dialogue sequences. However, it is also a significant feature of the programme to include explicitly subjective sequences. This may be seen, for example, in Episode 1 when Joe and Ginger, having failed to find a place to stay, fall asleep at the foot of the Albert Memorial. A brief montage of both stills and camera shots of the memorial then follows in which Joe imagines, in a style indebted to photomontage and Pop Art, the heads of members of the Beatles and Sir Alec Douglas Home to have been superimposed upon different statues. A more extended dream sequence occurs in Episode 5. In this, Fred, dressed only in her underwear, inspects a band of grenadier guards as well as the many people (such as the biologist, priest and Chelsea pensioner) whom Joe has consulted in the course of the episode. In a scene containing visual allusions to *The Seventh Seal*, these characters then pursue her across open land where she falls down a well-like hole. The faces of the gathered crowd are then seen, from her point-of-view, while a tele-printer at the bottom of the screen reports, in a manner reminiscent of the football results, the human voice's admission that it does not know the meaning of life. Fred then places the rope thrown down to her around her neck while the group proceeds to pull her to her death.

As this would suggest, the satirical social comment of the series is also combined with the logic of the absurd, enacting not only the 'absurdity' (and meaninglessness) of a godless universe but the 'surreality' of dreams and unconscious states. This is manifest not only in the introduction of dream sequences into the drama but also in the blurring of the boundaries between 'reality' and 'unreality' in other sequences. Thus, in Episode 5, following his breakfast with the priest, Joe is shown sitting on the upper deck of a bus. Looking out of the window, he sees Fred standing on Cleopatra's Needle on the Embankment, apparently preparing to throw herself into the River

Thames. This is an ambiguous scene. Within the film's off-kilter dramatic world, it seems to be taking place, with Fred having grown impatient with Joe's failure to find an answer to the meaning of life. However, it is also realised in a way that confuses the distinctions between 'objective' and 'subjective' reality. A crowd gathers round to enjoy Fred and Joe's argument with little apparent regard for Fred's safety. A comic policeman (of a type familiar from previous episodes) arrives to warn Fred that suicide is in violation of the Port of London's regulations and moves the crowd along. This includes Joe and Fred whom the policeman then fails to recognise, as if they are not, in fact, the same couple that he has only just encountered. This kind of event of indeterminate status – part-reality and part-dream – then provides the basis for a large section of Episode 6 dealing with 'relationships'.

In this episode, Joe is released from prison (having failed to pay maintenance for his and Rosie's child). Discovering that Rosie is now living with Ginger, Joe suggests that the three of them retreat to the country to take stock of their situation. Upending notions of rural tranquility, however, the drama then plunges them into an apparently insane world of unlikely encounters. They are picked up by rally drivers who take them to Wales where they encounter Italian cowmen blocking the road. Taking shelter for the night with the cowmen they are then confronted by 'Scotch beatniks' ('with their och aye and their Ginsberg') whom the local mayor is seeking to fumigate. Finding what they believe to be a quiet spot the next day, they then get caught up in military manoeuvres involving both British and German soldiers (who appear to be reliving the Second World War). No clear explanation of these events is provided and they shed little light on the predicaments of the central characters. As such, they function mainly as an exemplar of the apparently irrational (and incomprehensible) world with which the characters are struggling to come to terms. Thus, while Joe's final speech to camera informs us that 'even in a civilised country power and money are the most important things', the social commentary that earlier episodes may have provided has long since been overtaken by a more generalised sense of the absurdity of existence and the impossibility of making rational sense of it.

The legacy

There is no doubt that *Diary of a Young Man* was regarded as a success for the BBC. As previously noted, Sydney Newman had joined the call for new forms of dramatic expression and was suitably enthused by the production. Writing to James MacTaggart following the transmission of the first episode, he described the programme as 'a major breakthrough in television story telling'. '[F]or sheer variety', he continued, 'in the total use made of live action, film and stills combined with the highly original and imaginative use of words, music and sound effects, this is television of the first order'.[45] Despite its record of concern regarding the sexual content of BBC plays, the play was also appreciated by the Board of Governors. As a result of the Board's complaints earlier in the year, Newman had been forced to call for 'the total elimination of scenes of men and women in bed with sex in mind'.[46] Given the programme's fairly explicit treatment of Joe's sexual exploits, *Diary of a Young Man* was certainly in breach of Newman's instruction and unsurprisingly attracted criticism. A Nottinghamshire vicar, in particular, gained widespread publicity for his attack on the show's 'filth and depravity'.[47] Nevertheless, while the Chairman of the Board of Governors, Lord Normanbrook, agreed that some of the programme's 'themes were open to objection' he also considered it 'a success d'estime as an experiment'. Even Dame Anne Godwin, who had previously led the charge against BBC drama's apparent preoccupation with sex, admitted she had enjoyed the series which she felt had shown 'evidence of new ideas'.[48] In this respect, the programme's formal invention and obvious seriousness of intention was seen as sufficient to immunise it against the mounting 'clean-up' campaign then being directed at the sexual content of BBC drama.

However, there is also evidence that this very same experimentalism gave rise to certain problems for the audience. It will be recalled that Kennedy Martin believed that his 'philosophy' should apply to the 'mass audience' and, as if to put him to the test, the series was broadcast on a prime slot on BBC1: mid-evening Saturday, immediately after the popular US legal series, *Perry Mason* and at the same time as the hugely popular comedy series, *The Larkins*, on ITV. This may not necessarily have worked to the programme's advantage, however. The audience for *The Larkins* was estimated to be nearly three times that for *Diary of a Young Man* while the BBC's 'reaction index' for the first episode dropped below the average for televised plays during that quarter. Ironically, given Kennedy Martin's disparagement of their work, it even fell below that for the Langham Group's production, *The Torrents of Spring* (tx. 21 May 1959).[49] The responses of viewers to the first episode also highlight some of the ways in which the aesthetic approach of the programme did not always achieve the intended effects. Thus, while a number of viewers were excited by the programme's freshness and originality, others were disconcerted by its techniques. Joe's 'expressionless' narration was identified as 'annoyingly monotonous' while the story itself was regarded as 'full of improbabilities' and, at times, 'like a farce'. Even the use of stills, intended to speed up the action and encourage the viewer's involvement, was regarded by some as 'disconcerting and detrimental to the continuity of the story'.

While such comments undoubtedly reflect the programme's departure from the audience's normal 'horizon of expectations', they also suggest some of the tensions involved in the programme's approach (and Kennedy Martin's theorisation of it). It will be recalled how Kennedy Martin's analysis of the 'objectivity' of the television medium led him to reject psychological realism and the pursuit of viewer identification with characters. As John McGrath, the co-author of *Diary of a Young Man*, subsequently explained, the 'involvement of the viewer' derived from 'seeing what happens, rather than being drawn into the emotions of the characters to whom it is happening'.[50] In practice, however, this balancing of detachment and involvement was difficult to sustain. As the reactions to the programmes indicate, the devices designed to maintain a distance between viewers and characters could also lead to viewers failing to care sufficiently about the situations these characters confronted. As one of the BBC's respondents – a schoolmaster – observed, the lack of a genuine 'feeling of identity' surrounding characters could detract from 'real communication' with the viewer 'not initially disposed to find touch with such material'. Thus, while Kennedy Martin was surely right to suggest that television was ill-suited to securing the forms of subjective identification associated with Hollywood, his proposals also appeared to underestimate the other ways in which the television viewer might engage with characters. As Kennedy Martin's own experience of *Z Cars* – which, he explains, had 'started with character' – might suggest, this is particularly so in the case of the series form in which it is the characters, and the familiarity with them that viewers develop, that provide the continuing thread across a number of episodes.[51]

The issue of television 'objectivity' also connects to another emergent tension within the series. One aspect of Kennedy Martin's analysis of the 'objectivity' of the television camera, and its 'unblinking' gaze, was what he identified as the 'non-selectivity' of the television image. The 'nature of the TV camera', he suggests, 'is to seize on a visual object and to state it *per se*' with the result that the focus of an image is diluted through the intrusion of 'obtrusive detailed phenomena'.[52] While Kennedy Martin identifies this characteristic with the TV studio play, the odd aspect of his formulation is that in a series such as *Diary of a Young Man*, in which material shot in the studio is combined with material shot on film, it is the film image rather than the studio image to which this argument seems to apply the most. While the use of film inserts, shot on 35 mm, was not uncommon at this time, *Diary of a Young Man* was unusual in the amount of film material it contained, and the way in which it is intercut throughout – rather than just at the beginning of – each episode. Kennedy Martin's essay, moreover, does not specifically argue for the use of film in this way. Indeed, in a subsequent article, he suggests that it is the telerecording of studio action (rather than discontinuous filming) that provides the proper basis for subsequent editing.[53] However, given his emphasis on the break-up of continuous time and demands for forms of editing to match, it was more or less inevitable that film should be seen to offer the means for achieving these goals. Thus, in his response to Kennedy Martin's manifesto, Tony Garnett argued that once 'absolute continuity' is abandoned in favour of 'editing after the event', then 'most people would contend that you were making films'.[54]

However, the use of film alongside material recorded in the studio also generated a degree of disjunction in the kinds of image presented. While Kennedy Martin fretted about the way in which the electronic image fell under the thrall of 'obtrusive detailed phenomena', it is actually the depth and density of the film image, in comparison to the studio image, that is most striking in *Diary of a Young Man*. In Episode 1, for example, the visual density and 'effect of the real' provided by location footage of Joe and Ginger staggering up St Martin's Lane behind a street-cleaning lorry inevitably throws into relief the flatness and stylisation of the subsequent studio sequence set in Covent Garden. In this respect, the visual regime may be seen to be an unstable one, straddled between film and studio drama. Certainly, Ken Loach, the director of three of the episodes (including Episodes 1 and 5), was to come to the conclusion that the use of cinematic inserts into studio recordings was 'a hopeless venture' due to the basic incompatibility between 'discontinuous shooting and continuous recording'. 'The change of gear', he observed, was always 'apparent', exposing 'the mechanics of both'.[55]

In this way the incorporation of film into television drama, as a response to problems of editing, may be seen to have reinforced the very 'objectivity' (and 'non-selectivity') that montage had been intended to overcome. The movement towards film also threw into relief some of the ambiguities surrounding the idea of 'naturalism'. As has been seen, while Kennedy Martin's account of 'naturalism' drew on the 'common-sense' usage of the time, it was also a fairly restricted understanding of the term that referred primarily to the theatricalism of the television play. This meant that 'naturalism' conceived in other ways – such as a move towards social extension and observational accuracy – could actually be seen to offer the means of escape from the theatrical conventions of the studio-bound play. This is clearly evident, for example, in Tony Garnett's reply to 'Nats Go Home' in which the leading exponent of literary naturalism, Emile Zola, is recruited by him to the anti-naturalist cause in television.[56] In this respect, Troy Kennedy Martin's somewhat confusing call for 'new kinds of objectiveness' may be seen to have sown the seeds of two divergent approaches: the cultivation of the detached, intellectual 'objectivity' provided by Brechtian and other modernist devices and the observational 'objectivity' (or naturalism) that the use of film (and particularly shooting on location) could provide.

While, in *Diary of a Young Man*, the 'observational' aspects of the drama remain subordinate to the programme's dominant modes of self-conscious narration and montage, this begins to change in Loach's subsequent work (especially that made with Garnett). Thus, while voice-over and montage survive in *Up the Junction* (1965) and *Cathy Come Home* (1966), their use becomes more documentary in character, paving the way for the gradual elimination of formally obtrusive devices in the work that follows.

This should not be understood, however, as simply a technical matter dictated by the increasing use of 16 mm film and the opportunities for documentary-style shooting that this provided. For what also underpinned this shift was an increasingly political conception of the role of television drama. As Garnett himself has said of the move away from 'the traditional studio play' to 'location filming': 'We wanted to go out into the world where we could capture the conditions of people's lives, how people actually lived, and bring that material back to create a dramatic document. The drive was political as much as aesthetic.'[57] In comparison, what now appears peculiar about Kennedy Martin's call for a 'revolutionary' new drama is how little he was interested in what this new drama might express. There is a general sense that the 'new drama' should be more in sync with the 'now', with 'the world of the Beatles', as he puts it, rather than the world of 'Victor Silvester's foxtrots'.[58] There is also an expectation that the new drama will furnish access to the world of dreams and the unconscious. However, in spite of the connotations of anti-colonial struggle contained in the manifesto's injunction to 'go home', there is little sense of how the demand for formal innovation might possess a social or political purpose. This is evident, for example, in the way that aesthetic devices associated with both Brecht and Eisenstein are invoked, but without any reference to their original political underpinnings.[59] As a result, Kennedy Martin is happy to praise a variety of television plays that he sees as fulfilling his demand for formal innovation, including adaptations of Saki, but is generally oblivious to their actual content.

It may not be surprising, therefore, that John Russell Taylor complained shortly after its transmission that *Diary of a Young Man* was 'all dressed up with nowhere to go' – 'lots of technical invention but ... no apparent motive except to prove a case about television's need of a new language'.[60] While this is certainly overstated, it is also hard to avoid the conclusion that the pressure to say things in a new way weighs heavier than the pressure to say new things. There is, perhaps, a degree of irony here. Ten years later, the 'rediscovery' of Brecht within British film theory led to the dismissal of the kind of 'progressive' realism associated with Loach and Garnett, such as *Cathy Come Home*, in favour of a 'revolutionary' modernism.[61] However, as we have seen, Ken Loach's work had itself emerged from an earlier engagement with Brechtian ideas. The twist, of course, was that these ideas had entered television debate in a peculiarly apolitical form that led Loach to abandon them once his work became more overtly political in character. The legacy of *Diary of a Young Man* is, therefore, a mixed one. While it successfully demonstrated the feasibility of new techniques in television drama, it did so in a way that appeared to imply that these were *only* techniques detached from any particular cultural or political project beyond the overthrow of televisual theatricalism. Thus, while John Cook argues that the 'importance' of Troy Kennedy Martin's manifesto for *The Wednesday Play*, including the plays of Dennis Potter, 'cannot be overstated', its main achievement was to offer a general rallying point for those interested in new forms of television drama rather than to provide a workable aesthetic model that others actually followed.[62] As a result, while *Diary of a Young Man* remains an important milestone in the history of television drama, its influence on subsequent plays was probably much less than might have been expected.

Notes

1 I should like to acknowledge the financial support of the Arts and Humanities Research Board (now Council) in the research for this article. I am also indebted to Jeff Walden and Trish Hayes at the BBC Written Archives Centre (WAC) and Kathleen Dickson and Steve Tollervey at the British Film Institute (BFI).
2 *Radio Times*, 6 August 1964, 5.
3 Troy Kennedy Martin, 'Nats Go Home: First Statement of a New Television Drama', *Encore* (March–April 1964), 21.
4 'Reaction', *Encore* (May–June 1964), 39–48.
5 'Television Drama – Is This the Way Ahead?', *Screenwriter*, 15 (Spring 1964), 18–28, 35.
6 Philip Mackie suggested rather unkindly that Kennedy Martin's article was 'a prospectus for his new series which he wants someone to put on', in 'Reaction', *Encore* (May–June 1964), 44. In fact, the BBC had already accepted the series for broadcast but was involved in protracted negotiations over the fee.
7 John Caughie, *Television Drama: Realism, Modernism and British Culture* (Oxford: Oxford University Press, 2000), 77.
8 Kennedy Martin, 'Nats Go Home', 21. Although Kennedy Martin was not alone in his criticisms of the Langham Group, my suspicion is that his denunciation has contributed to an underestimation of some of its ideas which, at least in conception, were far more formally radical than Kennedy Martin's own.
9 Kennedy Martin, 'Nats Go Home', 21.
10 *Radio Times* (20 July 1961), 51.
11 John McGrath, 'TV Drama: The Case against Naturalism', *Sight and Sound* (Spring 1977), 103. Lez Cooke provides a description of the third programme in the series *The Middle Men* (tx. 11 August 1961) which he indicates not only involved extensive cross-cutting but also a rapid montage sequence of twenty shots. See *British Television Drama: A History* (London: BFI, 2003), 54.

12 See Stuart Laing, 'Banging in Some Reality: The Original "Z Cars"', in John Corner (ed.), *Popular Television in Britain: Studies in Cultural History* (London: BFI, 1991), 125–44. Kennedy Martin wrote and McGrath directed the first episode of *Z Cars*, 'Four of a Kind' (tx. 2 January 1962).
13 *Radio Times* (24 October 1963), 51.
14 Memo from Roger Smith and Christopher Williams to Elwyn Jones, BBC WAC T5/2399/1.
15 *Radio Times* (16 January 1964), 45.
16 As a copy of *Catherine* has not survived, I am relying on the shooting script and contemporary descriptions of the production for information.
17 Memo from Sydney Newman, Head of Drama Group (with reference to the comments of the Midland Region Advisory Council) to Stuart Hood, Controller Programmes, Television, 1 May 1964, BBC WAC T16/62/3. Although it is usually *First Night* that is seen to have led to complaints about the sexual content of plays at this time, it was in fact a *Festival* production, *Say Nothing* (tx. 19 February 1964) that most angered the BBC Board of Governors when it reviewed drama policy in February 1964.
18 M. K. Macmurraugh-Kavanagh portrays this as part of 'a campaign to eradicate the single play from BBC schedules' in her essay 'The BBC and the Birth of "The Wednesday Play", 1962–66: institutional containment versus "agitational contemporaneity"', *Historical Journal of Film, Radio, and Television*, 17:3 (1997), 374. This seems, however, to overstate the case. While both the Director of Television, Kenneth Adam, and the Controller of Programmes, Stuart Hood, called for changes to the format of both *First Night* and its companion series *Festival*, the preference of both was for a single-play format that would permit a greater mix of plays rather than the abolition of the single play per se. Similarly, Baverstock's proposal was to reduce the single play to one weekly series on BBC1, rather than to end single-play production altogether.
19 Roger Smith and Tony Garnett also became story editors for the series, which Garnett described as consisting of plays 'dealing with contemporary themes ... which break through the conventional barriers of naturalistic form'. Memo from Tony Garnett to Peter Aylen, 30 April 1964, BBC WAC T5/2081/1.
20 John R. Cook, '"Between Grierson and Barnum": Sydney Newman and the Development of the Single Television Play at the BBC, 1963–7', *Journal of British Cinema and Television*, 1: 2 (2004), 221.
21 Sydney Newman, 'Drama', *Journal of the Society for Film and Television Arts*, 15 (Spring 1964), 4.
22 Kennedy Martin, 'Nats Go Home', 21.
23 Peter Lewis, '*Z Cars*', *Contrast* (Summer 1962), 311.
24 Kennedy Martin, 'Nats Go Home', 23.
25 Ibid., 25.
26 Ibid.
27 Ibid., 31.
28 See 'The Modern Theatre is Epic Theatre', in *Brecht on Theatre*, trans. John Willett (London: Eyre Methuen, 1964), 37.

29 Kennedy Martin's equation of drama time with real time is, nevertheless, overstated. As George W. Brandt points out, while there were definite constraints upon the manipulation of time, it was still possible, even in live drama, to imply time lapses between scenes. See 'Introduction, in George W. Brandt (ed.), *British Television Drama* (Cambridge: Cambridge University Press, 1981), 13.
30 Kennedy Martin, 'Nats Go Home', 30.
31 Troy Kennedy Martin, 'Sharpening the Edge of TV Drama', *The Listener* (28 August 1986), 9. John Caughie, however, suggests that the explanation of this apparent 'objectivity' may lie in 'the three-camera set-up of the "live" studio drama' which permitted 'a variety of views of a scene' but made 'it difficult to cut into the middle of it and identify the look of the spectator with the look of the character'. See *Television Drama*, 122.
32 Kennedy Martin, 'Nats Go Home', 31.
33 Ibid., 30.
34 Ibid., 31. In *The Film Sense* (London: Faber & Faber, 1970 [1943]), Eisenstein suggests how montage is capable of generating 'inner creative excitement in the spectator which distinguishes an emotionally exciting work from one that stops without going further than giving information or recording events' (p. 37). It is the creation of this same kind of creative and emotional excitement through montage to which Kennedy Martin appears to aspire.
35 Raymond Williams criticises Kennedy Martin's claim that the 'common denominator' of naturalist plays is that 'they tell a story by means of dialogue'. As he points out, this is true of 'all written plays from Aeschylus onwards' and, therefore, the issue at stake is not the use of dialogue per se but rather the 'the relation between speech and other forms of signification'. See 'Realism, Naturalism and their Alternatives', *Ciné-Tracts*, 1: 3 (1977–78), 5.
36 John Russell Taylor, 'Television of the Month: Drama', *The Listener* (13 August 1964), 247.
37 This characteristic of working-class realism is discussed in John Hill, *Sex, Class and Realism: British Cinema 1956–1963* (London: BFI, 1986), chap. 7. In Episode 1 of *Diary of a Young Man*, Joe's growing resentment of Rosie (Nerys Hughes), and her supposed humiliation of him, leads effectively to him forcing his way into her flat and then into her bed. Although, as indicated below, the series acquired a reputation for sexual explicitness, the 'virility' of the working-class hero had become such a familiar landmark that Joe's misogynistic outbursts ('All I wanted to do was to strip her and take her like the empty thing she was, a doll, a useless object who humiliated Ginger and me') passed without comment.
38 Raymond Williams, *Drama from Ibsen to Brecht* (Harmondsworth: Pelican Books, 1973), 318.
39 The lack of 'fit' between Joe's voice-over and his character is evident in the opening recitation heard in Episode 1. According to John McGrath, this was originally written for an entirely different piece, a musical entitled 'Jack'. See John McGrath, *Naked Thoughts That Roam About: Reflections on Theatre 1958–2001* (London: Nick Hern Books, 2002), 18–19.

40 Kennedy Martin, 'Nats Go Home', 24.
41 Memo from James MacTaggart to Head of Drama Group, Television (HDGTel), 2 July 1964, BBC WAC T5/630/1.
42 Don Taylor also indicates that stills had been used by the Langham Group. See 'David Mercer and Television Drama', Appendix to David Mercer, *Three Generations: A Trilogy of Plays* (London: John Calder, 1964), 241. This seems to have been so of *Mario* (1959) in particular.
43 Kennedy Martin, 'Nats Go Home', 27.
44 Indeed, Jamie Sexton suggests that John Boorman's television documentary *Barry Langford* (tx. 28 August 1963) which makes use of stills montage may have been a direct influence on *Diary of a Young Man*. See '"Televerite" hits Britain: documentary, drama, and the growth of 16 mm filmmaking in British Television', *Screen*, 44: 4 (Winter 2003), 441.
45 Memo from Head of Drama Group to James MacTaggart, 13 August 1964, BBC WAC T5/630/1.
46 Memo from Head of Drama Group, Television to Peter Luke, James MacTaggart, Cedric Messina and Eric Tayler, 25 March 1964, BBC WAC T5/2239/7.
47 'Vicar raps the BBC's "filthy" young man', *Daily Herald*, 8 September 1964. The vicar was particularly upset by the 'carrying-on' between Joe and Fred in Episode 5.
48 Minutes of the meeting of the Board of Governors, 24 September 1964, BBC WAC R1/32/2.
49 '*Diary of a Young Man*', BBC Audience Research Department, 31 August 1964, BBC WAC T5/630/1. Subsequent quotes of viewer comments are also derived from this report.
50 John McGrath, 'TV Drama: The Case against Naturalism', 102.
51 Peter Lewis '*Z Cars*', 313.
52 Kennedy Martin, 'Nats Go Home', 29–30.
53 Troy Kennedy Martin, '*Up the Junction* and after', *Contrast* (Spring 1966), 139–40. In a later interview, Kennedy Martin actually expressed his 'disappointment' that Loach and Garnett had moved in the direction of film. See Lez Cooke, 'Interview with Troy Kennedy Martin', *Movie*, 33 (Winter 1989), 36.
54 'Reaction', *Encore* (May–June 1964), 45.
55 Kenneth Loach, 'Film versus Tape in Television Drama', *Journal of the Society for Film and Television Arts*, 23 (Spring 1966), 12.
56 'Reaction', *Encore* (May–June 1964), 44.
57 'Contexts', in Jonathan Bignell, Stephen Lacey and Madeleine Macmurraugh-Kavanagh (eds), *British Television Drama: Past, Present and Future* (Basingstoke: Palgrave, 2000), 17–18.
58 Kennedy Martin, 'Nats Go Home', 32.
59 Pete Mathers suggests that this was a more general feature of writing in *Encore* in which references to Brecht were primarily of a technical kind. See 'Brecht in Britain: From the Theatre to Television', *Screen*, 16: 4 (Winter 1975/6), 81–2.
60 John Russell Taylor, 'The Quarter: BBC Drama', *Contrast* (Autumn 1964), 250.
61 Colin MacCabe makes this argument in a special issue of *Screen* devoted to

Brecht. See 'Realism and the Cinema: Notes on some Brechtian theses', *Screen*, 15: 2 (Summer 1974), 7–27. For a review of the subsequent debate in relation to television drama, see John Caughie, *Television Drama*, chap. 4.

62 John R. Cook, *Dennis Potter: A Life on Screen*, 2nd edn (Manchester: Manchester University Press, 1998), 27.

4

'The very new can only come from the very old': Ken Russell, national culture and the possibility of experimental television at the BBC in the 1960s

Kay Dickinson

Huw Wheldon, one-time Managing Director of BBC TV and, later, its Deputy Director General once declared: 'Television, a conviction no less strong for eluding us so often in practice, resides in the imagination.'[1] Between 1958 and 1964, Wheldon was both the Commissioning Editor and the dependable anchorman for *Monitor*, a well-respected fortnightly Sunday evening arts magazine programme where Ken Russell first made his name. Wheldon's insistence on the centrality of imagination later prompted Russell to profess, '*Monitor* was and still remains the one and only English experimental film school ever, and Huw Wheldon was its guiding genius.'[2] By pointing out television's encouragement of creativity, rather than any of its other capabilities, Wheldon's remark also invokes an important shift that was taking place in Britain at the time: manufacturing and colonial economies were increasingly giving way to creative and cultural ones throughout the second half of the twentieth century. His statement is thus emblematic of a shift in 'Britishness' that had great bearing on what experimentation could be and what the imagination could achieve.

Correspondingly, the popularity of Russell's innovations appears to have rested on his smooth bridging of a seeming chasm between a quickly eroding (but utterly central) imperial sensibility and the contemporary insistence on the value and purpose of Britain's *cultural* achievements as the way forward for the country. His film 'Elgar' (first broadcast on 11 November 1962) melded these sometimes ostracised notions so successfully that it was, as John Gardiner notes, 'repeated four times during the 1960s, won a higher audience reaction index than any other 'Monitor' documentary yet made, and was voted Britain's second most popular television program of the decade'.[3] Significantly, it was Russell's insistent overlapping of 'old' and 'new' that brought about his most inspirational contributions to 1960s television.

Yet, only eight years later, Russell abruptly fell from televisual grace with

Ken Russell, national culture and experimental TV 71

the transmission of 'Dance of the Seven Veils' (15 February 1970). This vilifying interpretation of the life of the composer Richard Strauss provoked much controversy amongst, most damagingly, MPs and the Strauss family, starkly highlighting the contours of what the interaction between cultural production, national self-perception and artistic experimentation could be during this period.

'Getting out the dressing-up basket': cultural biography and the questioning of 'history'

At the heart of Russell's inquiries into the formation of British identity lay an urgent examination of what history and culture might mean to each other. This amounted to bold formal re-evaluations of how creative figures from the past could be represented on television. For the purposes of brevity and precision, I concentrate here almost exclusively on five of his celebrated portraits of composers: 'Elgar', 'Béla Bartók' (broadcast on 24 May 1964) and 'The Debussy Film' (18 May 1965) for *Monitor* and, later, 'Delius – The Song of Summer' (15 September 1968) and 'Dance of Seven Veils', which both went out as part of the Omnibus series.

The most contentious characteristic of Russell's productions during this period, and the one which Wheldon most abhorred and attempted to curb, was his insistence on using actors within the arts documentary format. Whilst Russell and Wheldon's disagreements could simply be registered as a struggle between two creative personalities, they also paint an incredibly detailed picture of an experimental project in progress, aided and abetted by the unique traditions and practices of British public broadcasting and post-war politics. On the whole, *Monitor* was comfortably studio-bound and typically comprised two different segments, usually interviews. In contrast, Russell's most striking contributions to the show were lengthy dramatised profiles of individual artists that often swallowed up the whole *Monitor* slot. Little by little, Russell edged impersonation into the material he provided for the series in an attempt to dismantle the barriers blocking theatrical modes of expression from attaining the status of the historical document.

Wheldon's first concession to imitation was a close-up of an impersonator's hands conducting in 'Prokofiev' (also known as 'Portrait of a Soviet Composer') (broadcast on 18 June 1961). Russell had wanted 'Elgar' to be acted, but Wheldon conceded only the 'figures in a landscape' approach (for which the film is so beloved), forbidding, above all, the use of dialogue, an absence that also distinguishes 'Béla Bartók'. The impersonation occurring within 'The Debussy Film' is pushed further by its intricate narrative: the story of an ensemble making a film about the life of the composer, where 'fictionalisation' is already inbuilt. By the time he made 'Song of Summer' and 'Dance of the Seven Veils', Russell had nudged 'factual' television into the realms of the fully fledged biopic, albeit by basing the former on Fenby's account of his sojourn with Delius, and allegedly constructing Strauss's dialogue out of verifiable quotations. To what extent might this outwardly simple stylistic tinkering relate to greater concerns about new developments in the national economy? How might Russell have then re-routed all these negotiations into an understanding of 'the past'? Could the objections of Wheldon (an otherwise liberal and nurturing producer) have belied a somewhat defensive stance to the enormity of various socio-historical changes? At the very least, Russell and Wheldon's quarrels reveal the close connection between formal experimentation, politics and ethics.

The 're-corporealisation' of a dead subject, as far as Wheldon was concerned, added significant confusion to *Monitor*'s delivery of information. He maintained that the audience's confidence in the genre would be broken by upsetting the hierarchy separating artistic playfulness and abstraction from historical recounting.[4] In doing this, it could be argued, Wheldon refused to truly honour the documentary subjects' own more elusive modes of expression. The following exchange about the filming of 'Prokofiev' (admittedly delivered from Russell's autobiographical perspective) gives some sense of the issues at stake:

> [Wheldon commences] 'I gather we're planning to get out the dressing-up basket again,' he said.
> 'This time I've got better actors,' I said.
> 'Assuming you have, how do you propose to integrate them with old archive material?'
> 'By degrading the material I shoot myself so that it looks as grainy and contrasty as the real thing,' I said.
> 'That's immoral,' he said. 'You *are* deliberately setting out to deceive the public ... I'm going to forbid you to have an actor impersonating Prokofiev and pass him off as a real man.'[5]

On one level, Wheldon's remonstrations position him as a gatekeeper for a particular notion of integrity that was specific to a surprisingly short period of time[6] and suggest Russell as just another contributor to a broader 1960s trend of exploiting fictional tools to delve into problems that, although not definitively real, were certainly realist.[7] These types of debates were pushed still further on television by the expressly politicised and de-mythologising work of Peter Watkins. His re-enactment work *Culloden* aired after both 'Elgar' and 'Béla Bartók', perhaps paved the way for the more experimental rendition of fact and fiction in 'The Debussy Film'.

However, the precise political auspices that powered Watkins's work were not those driving Russell, nor was Russell concerned with proselytising against false consciousness, as was Watkins. Drama and fact do not disrupt each other in Russell's programmes in quite this manner: actuality is allowed a careful measure of a certain kind of drama, one which, ultimately, entertains and reaffirms something larger than the documentary economy. Thus titbits of mundane everyday life (ones that Russell swears to be recorded traits of the great figures he is depicting) enter the films, stressing a democratic take on history over the approaches of more exclusively staid and ennobling biographies. We see Elgar flying kites and Debussy's entourage playing with balloons. Within 'Elgar', these insertions are encircled by multiple rostrum shots of photos of the composer, as if to both weigh down this alternative agenda of truth and to question, through juxtaposition, our ordering of such records. The overlapping of the structures of history writing and media narrative reshape the semantics of each sphere of production. History is invited to absorb some of the particular, creative flexibility of the increasingly prominent (mass) cultural industries, perhaps an inevitable outcome of a certain hegemonic shift within the country. Hayden White argues that, 'Demands for a verisimilitude in film that is impossible in any medium of representation, including that of written history, stem from the confusion of historical individuals with the kinds of "characterisation" of them required for discursive purposes, whether in verbal or in visual media.'[8] Russell embraces this idea as the very matter of history, as licence rather than limitation.

Strategically, such excursions from the Wheldon format were, to some extent, evocative of the practices of the music itself and, therefore, allowed for further expansions in stylistic experimentation. Scored compositions are usually received through renditions (performances); the interpretation functions as a somewhat free-standing agent which does not necessarily having to aspire to being a 'true likeness' of the notes on paper. Through these subject-sensitive, culturally-focused tactics, Russell was able, more intensively, to probe the relationship between fact and fiction within the contemporary media and the narrative nature of historiography alike. In defence of his work, Russell states, 'I wanted to dress people up in old clothes and do it in a totally *unreal* way, and thus make it more real than ever, and in the process send up this new civil service/academic way of doing films.'[9] The fantastical qualities of historical representation are thus indulged, whilst a 'fact is stranger than fiction' element is keenly integrated into a critique of hierarchies of authority based on economic class.

Crucially, though, the specific juxtapositions of image and music in Russell's programmes rarely seem surreal or implausible because they are so carefully knitted, through style or content, into the historical and often geographical specificity of their subject. It is this exactness of reference that renders Russell's experimentation with biographical delivery a more meaningful commentary on the processes of history. For example, archive footage of Hungary's violent history of colonisation, from the Habsburgs to the Nazis, is threaded through 'Béla Bartók', insinuating that both the brutal storyline of *The Miraculous Mandarin* that is also playing out on screen and the greater portion of Bartók's tumultuous compositions are a direct response to these events. Like the 'actors' researching their characters' contexts in 'The Debussy Film', we must accept the necessity of penetrating history in order to understand culture and vice versa. What is achieved is a powerful argument for a materialist take on history which denies the often idealised ineffability of music and, in so doing, validates portions of popular culture at the same time.

Russell also forwards a related agenda in his frequent swerves from 'past' to 'present', structural experiments that are anything but whimsical or capricious scramblings of these films' diegeses. The transplanting, in 'Béla Bartók', of Bluebeard's Castle into the modernist New Zealand house with its penthouse views of Big Ben, as well as the overlaying of modern-day performers' and their characters' lives in 'The Debussy Film', latches history not just to the contemporary, but also to contemporary cultural produce. In his 1960s work, then, Russell expertly negotiated and expanded what could become meaningful on television, as well as helping to resituate the status of the medium itself.

Culture and society: changes in value

The amendments that were being made not only to the semantic containment of the concept of 'culture', but also to the composition of the rosters of those qualified to arbitrate on such matters were of great consequence at this historical juncture. Many of the elements of Russell's oeuvre that were considered experimental in their day were, notably, busily attempting to redefine these spheres. The socio-historical shift was also partially signalled by the surprising popularity of three non-fiction books: Richard Hoggart's *The Uses of Literacy* (1957), Raymond Williams's *Culture and Society* (1958) and E. P. Thompson's *The Making of the English Working Class* (1963). All these, in their own ways, greatly extended what could be classified as 'culture' (for those persuaded by their arguments) and their expanded readership suggests a revision in the stereotypes of who might be engaging with such scholarly tomes. According to Caughie, these outcomes parallel the conclusions of the Pilkington Committee (of which Hoggart was also a member) and point to a larger social shift:

> the Pilkington Committee Report came to represent an institutionalization of 'Left-Liberal Leavisism': Left in its extension of culture beyond the educated elite; Liberal in its recognition that entertainment could be excellent; but Leavisite in its hierarchy of values which preferred the challenging to the

comfortable; and an awkward mixture of the three in its insistence that culture, even industrial culture, was serious.[10]

All of these factors seem to leave their scent on Russell's experimentation, as well as on much of the programme-making of the decade.[11] Most fundamentally, it is doubtful that a person of Russell's class would have gained a BBC job in previous decades. Russell was, by and large, an autodidact who had not received a university education. The imprints of such class mobility and influx are readily visible in the contemporaneously novel dimensions of Russell's TV output. Firstly, there is an insistence on the artisanal crafting of culture implanted in most of his biographical treatments. We see, for example, artist Peter Blake at work in 'Pop Goes the Easel' (1962) and 'Song of Summer' is greatly absorbed by the mechanics of musical composition, dedicating much of its running time to the arduous labour involved in such processes and, by the same token, formally disrupting the traditional flow of such a narrative. The overlap between physical and creative toil is stressed at a time of change in British modes of productivity and, at the same time, manual production is valorised by its connection to genius.

This allusion is furthered by Russell's insistent focus upon individuals or individualised groups, a digression from the formats of rival arts programmes of the time, *Tempo* and *New Tempo*, which dealt with more abstract, exploratory themes such as 'noise'. An embracing notion of individualism[12] (itself the work of the various 1960s governments' economic and social policies), plays out across Russell's generosity towards 'the artist himself' through, for instance, his editorial wedding of musical swells to biographical dramas and greater historical currents alike. History is rendered personal and vice versa, with this very predilection alerting us to limitations that may have resulted from the governmental regulation and public funding of the BBC during this decade. That said, Russell's protagonists are more often than not impoverished bohemian rebels who struggle against society, remain acutely perceptive, yet are shaped by its fluctuations, and manage to convey its vicissitudes with more clarity than any 'insider'. What might these recurrent themes say to and about the adjustments enacted and also thwarted within contemporary Britain's class system, including Russell's own ascent to a near-*auteurist* position within the BBC? How might all these dilemmas play out through the figure of the oppositional artist, himself also perhaps a cipher for the (cultural) worker on the rise in this new post-war economy?

These questions are asked, even answered, repeatedly and in surprisingly challenging ways by Russell's programmes. Firstly, his (and *Monitor*'s) populist approach to art music brought elite culture into the home through its transmission to the millions who had only recently become affluent enough to buy television sets. Secondly, through a distinctive amalgam of references and connotations, Russell's stylistic experiments draw previously separated classes and their tastes into alignment. 'The Debussy Film', in particular, argues for a less hierarchical discernment of culture: Debussy's composition *Gigues*, for instance, is justifiably positioned by the programme amid a jazz soundtrack and a Soho jazz club milieu (an efficacious commingling of past and present, which has already been discussed). 'The Debussy Film' also regularly hints at a greater affinity between cinema and art music. A sword-fight sequences that parodies slapstick silent film comedy is set to Wagnerian strains, as if to point out how reliant on this tradition soundtracking often is. In addition, its film-within-a-film structure proposes evident overlaps between the dynamics of a movie crew and those of another artistic community. Of note here is the fact that 'the film director' also doubles up as Debussy's patron Louÿs, a move that implies that the requisite benefactor qualities of empathy, financial support and encouragement (as well as some 'Svengali' tendencies, as the programme points out) are also shared by the contemporary film maker. Consequently, the film advocates the idea that a film director is nowadays more an economically influential, like-minded comrade than a lowly and destructive competitor to other art forms, a line Russell doubtless takes himself. During the programme, we are reminded that '90% of his [Debussy's] work derived from a painting or a play' (*Prélude à l'après-midi d'un faune* starting life as a Mallarmé poem and then serving as ballet music, for example), which stresses that the arts have traditionally cross-fertilised each other. In his role as the actor playing Debussy, Oliver Reed is handed a section of Baudelaire's writing on synaesthesia and 'reciprocal analogies' to prepare himself for his role. Intriguingly, similar allusions to mutuality across cultural taxonomies (the sorts of links that can, for example, connect music to cinema) are most commonly underlined by the programme through recourse to precedents within esteemed high art culture.

This tendency to sometimes defer to established bearers of cultural gravitas in order to stress important points, suggests that this new crop of BBC employees not only stretched the acceptable boundaries of culture, but were also, as Asa Briggs argues, mindful of and genuinely convinced by the previous generation's value systems.[13] Adding another twist to this tendency, Russell's reverent return to a particular and privileged form of 'tradition' frequently provoked his most noticeable deviations from the conventions of formal televisual presentation, thus proving the importance of context in the definition of avant-gardism. The radical restructurings of visual arrangement that are waved into his films by dint of their allegiance to the concerns of canonical music are a vital component of Russell's experimentation. Throughout his work, the music is rarely interrupted or fragmented and the visual or narrative track is persuaded to harmoniously adopt the music's more ponderous temporality, a hierarchical arrangement that is rare in the audio-visual media. Crucially, it was the lacquer of prestige with which art music was seen to adorn the less illustrious form of television that perhaps allowed Russell to suggest alternatives to its standard presentation. Until this point in time, music on TV (as a subject rather than as an accompaniment) had typically followed the outside broadcast format of recorded concerts. This presentational convention was evidently a throw-back to radio style, and something which seemed to fear a cross-contamination of musical and narrative forms. In fabricating a correlation between music and image (giving, as it were, priority to the more evidently culturally sacrosanct work) the narrative and visual elements of Russell's biopics become abnormally *musical*. Bearing in mind the structure of the BBC and its relationship to its workers and its public, it is paradoxical, but not out of character, for this repeated deference to a more conservative stance on culture to open up so many experimental opportunities. In many ways, this complicated alignment of proprieties lies at the heart of what distinguishes experimentation on television from its manifestations elsewhere. Once-challenging, now-respected stylistic particularities concocted by the composer under investigation percolate throughout the film and infuse other registers of the audio-visual realm[14] on the levels of both aesthetic and historiographic continuity.

The prevailing themes and structuring principles of Debussy's work open up all manner of loose yet evocative impressionism for the way his biography is imparted and bifurcated. In 'Song of Summer' hand-held cameras engaging in mist-filled close-ups mirror the lyricism of Delius's *Song of the High Hills*, whilst the vibrancy of Percy Grainger's musical persona is captured by swooping cinematography and vivacious editing.[15] Even 'Elgar', which deals with a much less contemporaneously challenging artist, benefits from a number of speedy lateral tracking shots that, in keeping abreast of the horse or bicycle riding that they depict, blur the landscape into broad, dynamic strokes as an equivalent to Elgar's exhilarating and jubilant music.

An arresting, folk-derived modernism radiates from Bartók's music into the visual spectrum of Russell's treatment of the composer. This is manifest in renditions of both the traditional-agrarian (which is often visually conveyed through ethnographic footage that matches the field recordings of folk music that so inspired Bartók) and invocations of contemporary life (such as the harsh, exclusively twentieth-century architecture on show in the *Bluebeard's Castle* and *Miraculous Mandarin* sequences). The two are linked within the film by Bartók's insistence that 'the very new can only come from the very old' (an adage that was surely close to Russell's heart too, especially given the circumstances of working for the BBC). It is, as Bartók might have insisted, the stable and the eternal that contribute the most unfamiliar shapes to this programme about his life, at the same time offering a solution to the restrictions put in place by the traditions of public broadcasting. Whilst it evidently appeared logical and justifiable to incorporate more stylised and abrasive choreography into the figure placement, camera movement and editing of the reworking of the modernist ballet *The Miraculous Mandarin*, even greater visual abstraction is created by the closely shot sections of tightly flocking herds of sheep and horses included to epitomise Bartók's love of the rural. Quick-fire juxtapositions of dextrous hands playing a piano barge into flickering close-ups of insects, birds, deer and bats. This type of brisk montage aptly describes the disjunctive yet symbiotic elements of Bartók's compositions and their reflection upon his divided experience of life as a refugee and his alienation from, yet dependence upon, modernity.

Changes in direction and acting British

Overall, this indulgence of art music – so understandable and yet so rarely formally capitalised upon in cultural programming – endowed Russell's programmes with increasingly extended evocative passages (the entire duration of *Prélude à l'après-midi d'un faune* is respected by 'The Debussy Film', for instance). During these sections, narrative-factual and historical development is no longer shackled to a script-driven documentary norm with ubiquitous sonic explication. In contrast, earlier films like 'Elgar' and 'Béla Bartók', are accompanied by a consistent voice-over provided by Wheldon (although it always provides biographical detail, rather than explanations of the music) and, consequently, no dialogue is apportioned to the actors who play the two composers. However, whilst Wheldon talks over the music in 'Elgar', just two years later, 'Béla Bartók' forbids the two soundtracks from overlapping too often and the music is mixed at a significantly higher level as Russell tries as hard as possible to sideline this type of commentary.[16]

Increasingly, within the development of this body of work, swathes of good quality music which a person of culture would be too polite to interrupt serve to marginalise the documentary voice-over that Russell admitted to disliking intensely. These subversions of Wheldon's documentary ideals also encourage us to question the meaning of the voice-over, the lecturely intonations from on high so common to television and mainstream film documentaries of the era. Voice-overs are much picked over in the study of media form, but, in this instance, there appears to be a historically-specific dimension, one that eschews the authoritative expert interjection of a particular pedagogical heritage and may well signal the absorption into the media industries of candidates from different class and experiential backgrounds.

Although Wheldon seems more respectful of these modes of information delivery (and they were by no means exclusive to university education, of course), this may also be a legacy of his distinguished army career with its acceptance of even more brutally demanding vocal utterances.

In trying to wriggle free from this approach, 'The Debussy Film' institutes the director character who deliberately usurps Wheldon's role as provider of patrician voice-overs. This strategy once more places the techniques of fictional media production at the forefront of how history is delivered. Interestingly, here Russell's objection to the connotations of the voice-over seek *direction* in systems of esteem derived from the popular cultural, rather than formal educational industries, moving beyond the classroom into, perhaps, the prestige of a nascent concept we would now dub auteurism. Whilst Wheldon can often be found broadcasting in the style of a loud hailer user, the stress for Russell in this word is on the prominent director's privilege: *casting*. The voice (and history) are thrown out into realms where they can be imaginatively reconstituted under terms dissimilar to the ones for which Wheldon may have stood, but which are familiar to other types of mass entertainment. Again, formal experimentation was functioning in accordance with the convoluted remodelling of British systems of class, culture, economy and history.

Within this nexus dwelt the replacements for Wheldon's voice-overs, a very particular, historically-reflexive set of acting performances that mingled improbably with certain of Russell's more 'modern' additions to televisual aesthetics. In the earlier productions, there had always been a hint of British amateur dramatics (the 'dressing-up basket' to which Wheldon had rather dismissively referred), and, in the later more sustained biopics, British stage traditions not only prevailed, but flourished. In 'Song of Summer', Maureen Pryor and Max Adrian (who play the Deliuses) barely contain their wry smiles at their perfection of an older variant of British theatre acting. 'R's are rolled, the diction clipped and there is a batty school-marm tinge (so familiar an archetype in this country) to Pryor's performance. These moments are self-aware, camp and, moreover, positioned against, in this instance, Christopher Gable's more sympathetic Fenby, whose unmannered naturalism is, significantly, tethered to a Yorkshire accent. What oozes from these other performances is not only a nostalgia for a particularly British mode of performance (one eroded by the day by kitchen-sink drama and Hollywood movie products) but also a fondness for eccentricity that, in turn, helps to explain and contextualise Russell's experimentations. Both Delius's obstreperousness and Elgar's peculiar habits tangle this attribute into their genius, thus making their creativity and Romantic inclinations palatable for a certain, although perhaps rather wide, type of British audience.

Eccentricity is, arguably, more tolerated than other forms of difference here, maybe because it is recognisable and 'harmless'; it rarely purports to challenge the status quo. Eccentricity merely quarantines itself off in its own designated zone of quirkiness, respecting the values of, most particularly, individualism and rarely tampering with anything else of a political nature. Any of the jarring qualities of Russell's more left-field formal interventions were, conceivably, partially off-set by the peculiar Britishness, the charmingly dotty quality of the acting that wafted through his programmes. Could there have been a more perfect form of experimentation to set within public, national broadcasting and the sanctity of the British home? Russell's comfortable strain of nonconformity stood him in good stead, both in his renditions of artists' lives and even in his own public persona; certainly his departure from this approach marked his rapid downfall.

As rhetoric in favour of experimentation, the homeliness of Russell's subjects was so astutely judged, so familiar, that a smattering of musically-supported avant-gardism was waved through good-naturedly. Here the wider notions of home – nation, history, culture, the political inscription of the family, the TV viewing space, the familiar – are fused so successfully that they appear almost as one and brush off the somewhat exclusive connotations of terms like eccentricity. In *English Eccentrics* (perhaps the most well-known study of this personality type), Edith Sitwell notes that: 'Eccentricity exists particularly in the English, and partly, I think, because of that peculiar and satisfactory knowledge of infallibility that is the hallmark and birthright of the British nation.'[17] Key phrases in her statement imply eccentricity's privilege, protected by the securities of empire, trade superiority (she says 'hallmark') and feudal heritage (it is 'our' 'birthright'). Englishness absorbs Britishness whole in Sitwell's study (note the title) and, although Russell's subjects never seem to strongly or consciously uphold such elitist ideals of nationhood and, indeed, his tributes encompass non-English subjects such as McBryde and Colquhoun in 'Two Scottish Painters' (1959), it is telling that this foundation supports the roots of eccentricity. Contemporary shifts, such as the rise of Welsh and Scottish nationalism and the increasing dedication to British regionalism from the more leftist outposts of the media, find subtle counterparts in Russell's oeuvre.

The fond mockery of the Englishness of a character like Jelka Delius is, moreover, deliberately confused by her actual Scandinavian identity. This, it seems, is just one facet of Russell's greater recasting and division of the *outlandish* (to render eccentricity geographical) within his work. Firstly, there are characters who are so recognisable to us and whose peculiarity seems so utterly excusable that even their upholding of a specifically privileged Anglo-Britishness is indulgently overlooked, most particularly when they liberate such categories for those who were not born into them (and this would also include Russell himself). These figures can be set among us when it is convenient, but easily banished to the fringes when they endanger our political sensibilities (be they bohemian behaviour or stalwart middle-class Englishness).

More disquieting transgression and less tolerable outlandishness is, notably, cast beyond our waters in much of Russell's work. The syphilitic Delius (himself the child of financially successful immigrant parents, and who dismissed the idea of British music) carries out his indiscretions in France, as do Debussy and his associates. 'Béla Bartók' and 'The Debussy Film', the most formally challenging programmes, chart the lives of mainland Europeans. In a climate where Mary Whitehouse's 'Clean Up TV' campaign was gaining momentum, dumping risqué behaviour 'elsewhere' proved an efficacious distancing strategy which perhaps helped entice a curious, but wary middle England towards *Monitor*'s more audacious aesthetic and cultural proposals.

Considering the country's position in world politics at this time, it is revealing that British public TV and its audiences should cherish such complex and multi-functional incarnations of outlandishness. The Suez Crisis of 1956, the transfer of the right to self-governance to a number of now Commonwealth countries throughout the late 1950s and early 1960s (resulting in violent struggles for power in countries like Kenya and what was then Rhodesia) and the loss of control over Cyprus all took their toll. Britain was being forced to rethink its self-image and, of course, its economic and political agendas, in relation to the rest of the world, a shift in perspective that is ever-present in Russell's work, particularly in his suggestions about the role of the cultural industries. Simultaneously, habitual British isolationism was being displayed in the popular resistance to the idea of a European common market and ambivalence towards the USA on a number of levels. Within the country itself, newly arriving immigrant communities were unsettling various sections of the population to the extent that discrimination had to be legally put in check by the Race Relations Act of 1965. At this point, it is useful to consider the sympathetic treatment of the difficult negotiations of migration that the characters of Delius and Bartók underwent. These narratives evidently took place against the unsteadying backdrop of a fluctuating nation, one whose borders (both actual and imagined) were being drastically reworked. It comes as no surprise, then, that the discussions of these new historical trends might render both the content and the form of Russell's programmes simultaneously innovative and backward-looking. These films are consequently searching for a suitably democratic and creative resolution of these multiple alleged 'oppositions'.

In all this, it is fundamental also to acknowledge that the true heroes of this set of films (and the best loved if we are to consider audience ratings and the BFI's decision to release only 'Elgar' and 'Song of Summer' on home viewing formats) are Elgar and Fenby: both squarely and uncomplicatedly British, as well as English. Fenby, in particular, stands out as selfless and decent in a world of destructive debauchery. His Britishness is upright and uncomplicatedly moralistic, yet ultimately non-judgemental: he is a true figurehead for changing times. Both characters, as John Gardiner observes of 'Elgar', are 'local boy makes good',[18] a quality befitting the opportunities available in the contemporary labour market (from which Russell himself had also benefited). Whilst such prospects opened up to the home-grown and genealogically settled, Fenby was also basically an economic migrant (moving to France), as was Bartók in his exile in New York.

Aired for the first time on Remembrance Day, 'Elgar' encapsulated some particularly divergent sentiments about national pride that would have arisen on that occasion in 1962. The film bulges with a confident nostalgia for a somewhat quaint Britain (one that was provincial, but, tellingly, not industrial) as well as a revised and decidedly pacifist sense of nationalism. The character of Elgar is conveniently ambiguous in relation to Britain's fitful and debated awareness of itself as a world power within the 1960s. As John Gardiner points out, '[there is a] playing down of that "other" Elgar, the Edwardian gentleman who revelled in imperialism and Conservative politics, London clubs and the pursuit of social honors'[19] (a somewhat misconstrued interpretation) in favour of a quiet country-loving man who is profoundly troubled by the jingoism his music arouses in its listeners. This latter sensibility is established most poignantly through the famous *Pomp and Circumstance Marches* sequence. Here a deeply dialectical configuration is presented as Elgar's most nationalistically rallying composition is layered over footage from the Western Front during the First World War, the 'Land of Hope and Glory'[20] 'tune' climaxing as we are exposed to a row of blinded mustard-gas victims followed by accumulating shots of graves.

Other more subtle contradictions to the image of Britain that Elgar has more typically been drafted to support are to be found in the film's treatment of the alienating clutter of (Victorian and Edwardian) bourgeois life. Decorative screens, plants, lamps and other furniture needlessly block our access to the characters and Wheldon describes Worcester as both 'stuffy' and 'dull, provincial and frustrating'. Even when Elgar's wealth supposedly elevates him from this encumbered lifestyle, the vastness of his new home is so cold and intimidating as to encourage us to shun the pointless material gains that fame affords. In one extended *Monitor* programme, then, Elgar is simultaneously vindicated for a less colonially-minded and more peace-loving 1960s audience, yet for the more retrograde viewer he is still the man behind the nationalistic fervour associated with 'Land of Hope and Glory'. Bearing in mind the breadth of *Monitor*'s audience and the host of daring stylistic propositions that lie within these films, polysemic characterizations such as this one of Elgar illuminate the unique contributions of experimental television to the greater inter-media avant-garde project. The diversity of expected response demands an artful multiplicity of messages that are far from straightforward and never simple supplications to a one-dimensional industry or social demands.

A different type of punctuation is required in order to escape rebuke or rejection by television's viewers, one that occasionally interchanges rambling, multifarious interjections with more confirming and emphatic statements (such as those about suitable heroism or outlandishness). In order to get to grips with what experimentation could be at this time and in this place, it is vital to scrutinise when, how and why this reassurance is offered. In 'Elgar', for instance, an unequivocal respect for 'Britain' emanates from Russell's handling of his heroes' relationships to geography rather than any given national population, an alliance that sidesteps the persistent reconstitutions of international workforces at that time. Although Russell's TV work was not specifically designed with its export potential in mind (as other, more contemporary 'heritage' products often are), it does share their promotion of certain recognisable geographical spaces. Since 'Elgar', the Malvern Hills have been advertised as 'Elgar country', thanks, in part, to the film's luscious landscape photography and its Blakean transformation of the area into Calgary during the *Dream of Gerontius* sequence. This was, it would appear, a specific projection of Britain for its own inhabitants, television audiences, who, unlike those attending the cinema during this period, were consuming a largely locally-produced product. Television's particular and multifarious domestic connotations at that time, and Russell's careful compliance with everything that such a term could encompass, enabled his success in the 1960s, despite, and as a result of, their ability to advance new modes of artistic expression. At the turn of the decade, however, Russell completed 'Dance of the Seven Veils', a film that was to deliberately violate this intricate and perhaps ultimately insecure self-perception held within Britain.[21]

Russell's fall from grace: 'Dance of the Seven Veils'

Much nudity, some saucy nuns (now a Ken Russell staple), self-flagellating clerics and a burlesque portrayal of Nazism: these were the elements that provoked a Parliamentary motion against 'Dance of the Seven Veils' buoyed along by the criticisms of twenty MPs. The Strauss family were so outraged by the defamation that they banned the use of their ancestor's music in the programme, effectively rendering its transmission impossible until the expiration of their copyright in 2019. All this deterred Russell from television (and vice versa) for a good many years as he embarked on a successful period as a feature film director. Whilst certain surface details and stylistic flourishes seem to have been the sticking points for these censors, the programme's use of them to destabilise the pleasing balance of historical rendition and Britishness to be found in Russell's earlier work may, more truthfully, have been what stopped him so squarely in his televisual tracks. What, then, were the perceived sticking points in Russell's vision and how did their identification expose the socio-historically-determined restrictions that were placed around experimentation at that time?

Firstly, Richard Strauss, the programme's subject, is neither an odd-ball duffer, nor a lovable curmudgeon; he is avaricious, arrogant and prone to statements like, 'One cannot be a superman the whole of the time ... sometimes it's a relief, a relaxation as it were, to be a mere hero.' Significantly, such utterances not only give audiences little choice but to detest or ridicule Strauss, but they are also carried by voice-overs, as if to channel everything Russell mistrusted about this mode of delivery into a damnation of Strauss. The 'British restraint' that makes 'Elgar' so charming is absent and, instead, Christopher Gable's deliberate over-acting easily becomes grating, especially if one is looking to be endeared to one's protagonist. As cantankerous and dislikeable as Delius can be, Russell's respect for his music never wanes. Contrastingly, the pantomimic gestures and bludgeoning intonation in 'Dance of the Seven Veils' are matched by a soundtrack of Strauss's music which is both restlessly fragmented and unrelentingly domineering (perhaps because only the most dramatic sections have been strung together). The closeness between artists and figures from literature that had been so sensitively explored in 'The Debussy Film' is now practically derided. As he conducts *Thus Spake Zarathustra*, Strauss mythologises himself through his relationship with his fictional subject (also, on screen, played by Gable): 'Leave your refuge Zarathustra. Reveal to us the folly of man. I, Richard Strauss, accompany you in music and in spirit.' In all these actions, it seems as if Russell is aiming to edge the various themes that had initially attracted audience loyalty to him into much less comfortable realms.

Similarly, Russell's notion of 'the domestic', which had thus far proved so popular, takes a much more disconcerting turn. In the treatment of Strauss's two symphonies, the *Domestic* and the *Alpine*, 'home' and 'nation' are, as is often the case, presented as bedfellows. However, the film renders the themes of the *Domestic Symphony* almost entirely sexual in nature and the projection of such allusions (which are dealt with in a comically coarse manner) may not have sat well within BBC television's assumed responsibility to the nation, particularly in matters of 'family-oriented' programming. The key joke of the sequence is that Strauss is so conceited as to have written a large-scale and traditionally epic orchestral work about his own private home life.

As he copulates with his wife, he simultaneously conducts his composition, asking the musicians to pace their melodic climaxes accordingly. Here everything for which 'the domestic' had previously stood is belittled by its transference into no more than the physical cravings of this rather loathsome character. Whilst these ideas are communicated through bawdy comedy (itself a stalwart of British entertainment), it is revealing that so many people refused to appreciate this and many of the other gags in 'Dance of the Seven Veils'.

In the interpretation of The Alpine Symphony, the implications of 'the natural' that had proved so harmonious within 'Elgar', 'Béla Bartók' and 'The Debussy Film' are instead swamped by caricatures of 'German-ness' that would have been altogether alienating to British audiences. Clichéd symbols, such as lederhosen, dirndl skirts and edelweiss, would have led many a British viewer to think of Nazi and proto-Nazi mythology. This is a connection that Russell seems keen to make: an accusation about the historically-embedded position of the composer and his fans that is altogether less palatable. Soon after, it is implied that Strauss was an outright Nazi sympathiser; at one point he bears Hitler on his shoulders and, later, he fails to halt a concert, despite the fact that a swastika is being carved on a Jew's chest in the audience. The implication is that Strauss's proclaimed a-politicism is profoundly misplaced and that he did, in fact, welcome Nazi patronage for financial and social gain. Whilst Russell's other subjects embody and creatively rearticulate history, Strauss exploits historical shifts predominantly for selfish reasons. After a series of tributes to inspired single figures, Russell damningly admonishes the extremes of artist self-absorption.

In contrast, six years previously, great pains had been taken with 'Béla Bartók' to establish the composer's forceful opposition to Nazism. The commentary reveals that he had wished his music to be classified as 'degenerate art' and that his painful exile from his beloved rural Hungary was a direct rejection of the Nazi occupation of the area. Both films insist upon the difficulty of projecting nationalism in a century when such ideologies opened up the potential for widespread corruption, ostracism and cruelty. Although absolutely no sympathy for Nazism soils 'Dance of the Seven Veils', the film was, it appears, harder to swallow because it brought fascism much closer to home than 'Béla Bartók' ever does. If experimental television distinguishes itself by inviting uneasy aesthetics and topics into the living room, here, then, is the point at which this traffic becomes unwelcome.

Furthermore, after suggesting an estrangement between the humble British viewer and the über-ego quasi-Nazi, Russell then rams the two into the same moral sphere by revealing that the performance of *Thus Spake Zarathustra* that starts the film is taking place in our very own Albert Hall as close to the end of the war as 1947. Strauss's rapturous reception is accompanied by his exclamation, 'My British friends, always the loyalist!' High art and fascist tendencies bash indelicately into some of the most central tenets of patriotism, and the delicate sympathies Russell has built up throughout his earlier films for the genius-creator are all but shattered. These are not just connections that link British to Nazi history, but also insinuations that our understanding and cultivation of *culture* (so carefully nurtured by both Russell and the *Monitor* and *Omnibus* series) is worthy of suspicion.

These satires and degradations of various core beliefs seemingly extended past the acceptable parameters set for British televisual experimentation at the time. To deride an artist on an arts programme undermined all television had invested in art's status as something far more important than fruit for documentary entertainment. And, at the same time, to connect this huge potential within culture with an unfavourable notion of national identity evidently did much to anger audiences, copyright owners, MPs and television producers alike, all of whom are much more immediately crucial to the actual airing of experimentation than they might be for, say, avant-garde writing or filmmaking.

Tracing Russell's journey from the runaway success of 'Elgar' to the controversy caused by 'Dance of the Seven Veils' provides an extremely telling picture of what was and was not acceptable within the constraints of 1960s and early 1970s BBC television. The understanding of art, the cultural economies, nation and learning held by so much of Russell's audience and under attack in 'The Dance of the Seven Veils' had been key to his, *Monitor*'s, even the BBC's success. Perhaps the way Russell's work had always been positioned in the middle – the middle space between documentary and fictional modes, in the middle of the many intersections of 'Britishness' of the era – was the most effective means of reshaping what the televisual imagination could be in the 1960s. As such, he can often seem, for contemporary viewers, to sit in the middle of how middle-class middle England (swelling as it did throughout the decade) thought of itself as a nation, as an educated and communicative body, as a tradition, a heritage and a series of leisure activities. To move within this rather rambling space and to look out without truly inviting anything untoward inside must have seemed a peculiarly televisual means of experimenting. Yet to tinker with middle-class values, to illuminate their disintegration and infiltration instigated the drawing of a boundary-line that left Russell on the outside for many years. To return to Wheldon's definition of the medium, television, it would appear, 'resided' somewhere altogether more concrete than 'in the imagination'.

Notes

1. Huw Wheldon in Wheldon (ed.), *Monitor: An Anthology* (London: MacDonald, 1962), 13.
2. Russell interviewed in John Baxter, *Appalling Talent: Ken Russell* (London: Michael Joseph, 1973), 113.
3. John Gardiner, 'Variations on a Theme of Elgar: Ken Russell, the Great War, and the television "life" of a composer', *Historical Journal of Film, Radio and Television*, 23: 3 (August, 2003), 197.
4. A similar argument was also levelled by Grace Wyndham at the *Radio Times*'s explanation of *Cathy Come Home* as a semi-documentary. Wyndham contended that '[s]uch a description surely means we are being offered a production which the BBC accepts as a style, and which deliberately blurs the distinction between fact and fiction. Viewers have a right to know whether what they are being offered is real or invented'. (Goldie, 'Stop Mixing TV: Fact and Fiction', in *The Sunday Telegraph* (8 January 1967), 14. Cited in Julian Petley, 'Factual fictions and fictional fallacies: Ken Loach's documentary dramas', in George McKnight (ed.), *Agent of Challenge and Defiance: The Films of Ken Loach* (Trowbridge: Flicks, 1997), 28–59. My thanks go to Helen Wheatley for alerting me to this source.
5. Ken Russell, *A British Picture: An Autobiography* (London: Heinemann, 1989), 22–3.
6. In actual fact, docu-dramas filmed in the studio had been popular during the 1950s (see Elaine Bell 'The Origins of British Television Documentary: The BBC 1946–1955', in John Corner (ed.), *Documentary and the Mass Media* (Arnold, 1986) 65–80), but, unlike Russell's work, these had most readily dealt with contemporary subjects and social deprivation.
7. Examples of this range from television's *Wednesday Plays* and *Z Cars* (a fictional series produced by the BBC's Documentary-Drama Group), to the novels and films of *Room at the Top* and *Saturday Night and Sunday Morning*.
8. Hayden White, 'Historiography and Historiophoty', *American Historical Review*, 93: 5 (December 1988), 1198–9.
9. Russell interviewed in Baxter, *Appalling Talent*, 138.
10. John Caughie, *Television Drama: Realism, Modernism and British Culture* (Oxford: Oxford University Press, 2000), 84.
11. As Caughie (*Television Drama*) and Corner (*Documentary and the Mass Media*) more broadly argue.
12. Interestingly, regardless of the period under examination, Russell consistently returns to the tropes of Romanticism, a period where art was perhaps most obsessed with 'the self'.
13. Asa Briggs, *The BBC: The First Fifty Years* (Oxford: Oxford University Press, 1985), 324.
14. At around this time, the musicologist Hans Keller remarked that television would be advised to render itself musical, rather than to force music into being televisual in such instances.
15. In her chapter in this volume, Helen Wheatley equates such impressionism with

a subjective, point-of-view style and this fits very well with my earlier arguments about individualism.
16 Interestingly, the 2002 reworking of 'Elgar' replaces Wheldon's original voice-over with Russell's own musings. The authorial ego is again repositioned in line with the reasoning that underlies the second version, a homage to Russell as well as Elgar.
17 Edith Sitwell, *English Eccentrics* (Harmondsworth: Penguin Books, 1973), 16.
18 Gardiner, 'Variations on a Theme of Elgar', 196.
19 Ibid., 200.
20 The transformation of this march into the popularly-recognised song took place well after its composition and Elgar is reported to have loathed the sentiments of the lyrics.
21 It is interesting to note that Russell falls foul of the televisual authorities when he is no longer working under the guiding influence of Huw Wheldon.

5

From art to avant-garde? Television, formalism and the arts documentary in 1960s Britain

Jamie Sexton

Arts programming has been a mainstay of British television since its early days, a tradition tied up with the public service ethic contractually enshrined in both public and commercial services. This chapter looks at two series that attempted to experiment with the presentation of art to British television viewers: *New Tempo* (ABC, 1967) and *Who Is?* (BBC2, 1968). These programmes played with, and challenged, the conventions that had hitherto been established within arts programming since the 1950s, and their experimentation must be linked to technological, cultural and institutional developments within the late 1960s. Technologically, the take-up of 16 mm lightweight film cameras and mobile sound recording brought a new, non-studio based, style to television. Culturally, new 'post-modern' trends, including both the merging between 'high' and 'low' art and the increasing permeability between art and other areas of life, such as science and technology, affected the content of the programmes. Institutionally, new opportunities and possibilities for programme making opened up in the late 1960s: for example, the increasing use of independent, freelance television personnel and the increased openness towards 'challenging' programming inaugurated by the growth of television channels (BBC2 becoming the third terrestrial channel in 1964).

Both *New Tempo* and *Who Is?* featured filmmakers from the Canadian, London-based freelance company Allan King Associates (AKA), and attempted to use television in a stylistically progressive manner that reflected a number of social and institutional shifts in Britain at the time. These programmes have been relatively overlooked in histories of British television, even those of arts documentaries.[1] Yet, these two historically and aesthetically interesting series show that there were actually more experimental approaches to television arts programming in the 1960s beyond the more documented elements, for instance: Ken Russell's contribution to *Monitor* (BBC, 1958–65).

Arts programming

Programmes about art were a staple of television from its very beginnings. Between 1936 and 1938 critic and artist John Piper presented discussions of paintings and sculptures. And in the 1950s both *Painter's Progress* (beginning in 1954) and *Sketch Club* (beginning in 1955) showed people 'how to' make art.[2] Whilst the lecture and the 'how to' programme were constructed differently, both were characterised by the style of 'live' broadcasting: studio presentation, relatively static cameras and a general formal sobriety.

In 1951 John Read made a profile on Henry Moore, significant because of its use of film (hardly used in British television at this stage). He continued to make filmed portraits of various artists during the 1950s. Despite the use of film (which allowed cameras to film both interiors and exteriors) camera movement was still relatively scarce and the presentation sober. John Wyver claims that the profile format has been one of the most enduring approaches to arts programming.[3] He adds that the 'profile' format largely adopted a common set of assumptions, which include: an explanatory commentary; a focus on already established artists; and a conception of the artist as a visionary 'genius', who is able to transcend the society that encases her or him.[4]

The profile template greatly influenced *Monitor*, BBC's critically acclaimed arts series. Mostly shot on film and linked in the studio by Huw Wheldon, each programme in the series primarily focused on three subjects or artists. Whilst for the most part *Monitor* tended to adopt a conventional approach both to subject matter and filming methods, John Schlesinger was able to delve into more innovative territory. He used film in *The Class* (tx. 9 April 1961) to record the activities of a drama class at the Central School of Speech and Drama, Swiss Cottage. Shot entirely within the four walls of a classroom, the cameras were fitted onto lightweight 350 mm dollies in order to gain a fluid sense of movement, and Schlesinger coordinated a system of signals with the teacher so that his camera could anticipate the movements of the actors.[5] This programme not only used an innovative filming method, but also covered an event that lay beyond the traditional subject matter of the arts programme. Likewise, Ken Russell made a number of boundary-breaking documentaries for *Monitor*. These include his famous biographical portraits (including *Elgar*, tx. 11 November 1962), which mixed fact and fiction; *Pop Goes the Easel* (tx. 25 March 1962), which included location filming and mixed high and low art, reflecting its controversial subject matter (Pop Art); and *The Dotty World of James Lloyd* (tx. 5 July 1964), which strayed outside of the confines of many arts programmes by documenting an 'outsider artist'.

Such programmes reflected the changing social and technological climate but they were nevertheless exceptional. The profile/biography of an artist presented in a straightforward manner and traditional assumptions about the nature of art continued to remain the norm of arts programming. If film was used, it was usually done so to capture people in more exotic, picturesque locations than the studio.

The adherence to familiar templates was evident in *Tempo*, ITV's main challenger to *Monitor*, which aired between 1961 and 1967. *Tempo*, produced by ABC and in its first year edited by critic Kenneth Tynan, followed the approach of *Monitor* in many ways. It was usually filmed in a straightforward manner, avoiding adventurous formal techniques and presenting film clips with studio links. The programme received negative critical reactions from reviewers who contrasted it unfavourably to *Monitor*, leading to a number of changes, including budget cuts and format modifications. *New Tempo* was to emerge from these modifications.

Tempo and its offshoots

In the face of reviewers' criticisms, in 1965 ABC hired a new producer, Mike Hodges, to take over from Reginald Collins. Hodges had previously worked as a producer for current affairs series *World in Action*, where he had taken a leading role in promoting the use of small crews and lightweight 16 mm film equipment. His arrival heralded a new era for *Tempo* as he used this experience to alter radically the style and format of the programme. Furthermore, *Tempo*'s production context allowed Hodges a great degree of freedom to experiment. ABC were producing *Tempo* out of public service requirements demanded by the Independent Television Association (ITA) so that commercial interests were balanced by an obligation to educate and inform.[6] *Tempo*'s increasing budget cuts reflect the fact that ABC saw it as an obligatory necessity, emphasised by its Sunday afternoon slot, traditionally known as the 'graveyard slot'.

Hodges produced a sequence of thematic *Tempo* programmes, altering the previous template of the series. *Tempo Profile*, *Tempo Entertainers* and *Tempo International* were all produced before the creation of *New Tempo*. While *Tempo Profile* was still quite close to the more traditional 'profile' template, it did insert 16 mm footage within a studio-based format. The next two series, however, were shot on film and were marked by a greater amount of location filmmaking,[7] bringing to arts television the sense of urgency that was usually associated with current affairs. Interviews were shot on the move so that a greater sense of mobility was evident and cameras began to cover a diverse amount of geographical space. Increasingly, Hodges also began to experiment with style and has commented that in *Tempo International* he attempted to find an appropriate filming style that in some way reflected the personality of the interviewee.[8]

To move *Tempo* in a new direction and create a sense of urgency and freshness to arts programming, Hodges hired technical staff from Allan King Associates (AKA). AKA was a London-based, independent production company set up by Canadians Allan King and Richard Leiterman in 1961. King was a documentary filmmaker who had made many programmes for the Canadian Broadcasting Company (CBC) network and went on to direct some important 'direct cinema' films in the mid-1960s, including *Warrendale* (1966). AKA specialised in 16 mm film technology and hired out equipment as well as crews who were skilled at using such equipment (some of whom had, like Hodges, worked on *World in Action*): Dick Fontaine (camera and direction), William Brayne (camera), Christian Wangler (sound), Richard Leiterman (camera) and Ivan Sharrock (sound) were all hired from AKA to work on the *Tempo International* series, importing the significant influence of direct cinema to an arts programme. Whilst narration and interviews were still used, they were covered in a more dynamic manner through a fluid, mobile camera resulting in a continual sense of movement. *Tempo International* marked the moment where the arts programme collided with direct cinema and current affairs.

This type of filming was, however, largely abandoned in the next *Tempo* series *New Tempo*, which consciously moved yet further away from traditional arts programmes. Stylistic elements from direct cinema and current affairs were occasionally used, but the most striking aspects of the series was its rigorously experimental approach, incorporating extremely rapid montage sequences and disjunctive sound/image combinations, and lengthy abstract, time-lapse sequences. Made in 1967 and again employing the services of AKA (as well as research assistance from people in the fields of advertising and journalism), *New Tempo* aimed to reflect the changing notions of art and culture in the 1960s.

New Tempo

New Tempo differed from the conventional template of arts programming to such an extent that it was barely recognisable as such. It did not focus on a specific artist, but for the most part featured a cultural figure (sometimes fictional) discussing philosophical ideas in relation to technology and the social environment. It was not so much an attempt to document an artist or an artistic movement, but to capture and reflect stylistically changes in both contemporary art and society (which in the series are posited as inseparable).

The ideas of Marshall McLuhan, whose book *Understanding Media* was published in 1964, had a direct influence on the series.[9] McLuhan was a truly popular academic analyst. He argued against 'old-fashioned' analyses of media, preoccupied with studying media as content. In contrast, he argued that it was the *forms* of different media that were important. He believed that new media and communications technologies were profoundly altering society, ripping 'man' from 'literate' culture just as the 'Gutenberg revolution' had ripped 'man' from a 'tribal', 'oral' culture. In order to avoid the potential stresses accompanying such a shift, he emphasised the importance of thinking about such technologies in new ways. For McLuhan, new media forms were obliterating sequences and fragmentations derived from a cause/effect relationship (central to mechanistic culture), replacing them with connectivity, instantaneity and wholeness. He wrote that 'automation in industry replaces the divisibility of process with the organic interlacing of all functions in the complex'.[10] He used the artist as a figure for engagement with the new mediascape: 'The mind of the artist is always at the point of maximal sensitivity and resourcefulness in exposing altered realities in the common culture.'[11]

Other trends fed into the style of *New Tempo*. Pop Art was one important influence, as well as the more general climate in which counter-cultural ideas were entering the mainstream. Emerging in the 1950s, Pop Art questioned distinctions between 'high' and 'low' art and moved to integrate art within the world of the 'everyday'. The Royal College of Art had nurtured British Pop Artists, such as Peter Blake, Derek Boshier and David Hockney. *New Tempo* directors Denis Postle (who had previously made an experimental collage film with Pop Artist Eduardo Paolozzi in 1963, entitled *The History of Nothing*), and James Goddard were both former RCA students, and brought an aesthetic of Pop to the programme. Ken Sequin (designer), Mike Myers and Trevor Preston (both researchers) had also studied at the RCA.

At the time of its emergence – when popular culture was often routinely dismissed in a generalised manner – Pop Art was a movement that challenged conventions, confronting as it did traditional 'Britishness', associated with high art and class entrenchment. As Frances Spalding has written: 'Pop Art, seeking, like Dada had done before, to expand the parameters of art, was a deliberate affront to accepted taste. It preferred the lightweight and, in its choice of encoded imagery, helped broaden the audience for art and made the fine arts less exclusive.'[12]

Pop Art would feed into the look and attitude of *New Tempo*, which drew on the iconography of popular culture and approached a variety of disparate cultural subject matter with equal seriousness. Although fascinated by mass culture, the programmes were also concerned with the proliferation of media and of images, especially advertising.

The rise of Pop Art developed at a time when the media and popular culture came under increasing scrutiny. In Britain, McLuhan's ideas were influential but cultural critics tended to avoid his more hyperbolic interpretations of technological mediation. Nevertheless, whilst dismissive attitudes towards popular culture were still prevalent, a number of cultural theorists – such as Raymond Williams and Stuart Hall – were taking such issues seriously. Reflecting such analyses, the definition of culture was expanded from an elitist preserve of great works to a broader notion of a whole way of life (including rituals, popular pastimes and the use of commodities). Dominant cultural life was also being attacked by a number of countercultural voices, whose prominence brought a greater sense of variety and radicalism into the mainstream. The growth of alternative magazines such as *Oz*, of psychedelic and occult movements, and of radical political demonstrations, reflected a dispersion of the cultural consensus that characterised – at least on the surface – the first half of the 1950s.[13] Such radicalism was also feeding through to television: the Pilkington Report of 1962, leading to the addition of a third channel, BBC2, in 1964, and the reign of Hugh Carleton Greene from 1960 to 1969, have generally been seen as contributing to a more daring sense of television in this era.

New Tempo consisted of nine programmes, which were shown on Sundays at 2.15 p.m. between 1 January and 5 March 1967:[14] *Information Explosion, Nostalgia, Noise, Violence, Heroes, Expendability, Leisure* and *Reprise*; a further programme, *Stimulants*, was made but was not allowed to be broadcast due to its controversial subject matter (hallucinogenic drugs).[15] The programmes were conceived of as one interconnected piece, often cross-referencing other programmes and touching on recognisable themes. This style mirrored the aims of the series itself: to show how the rapidly changing world was becoming more and more interconnected (which itself was mirrored in the cross-generic background of those who worked on it), thus constituting a 'social matrix'.

New Tempo attacked a number of the 'traditional' views that characterised many arts programmes. One of these was the idea of the genius artist transcending the social environment that he or she was embedded within and creating 'timeless' pieces of work. *New Tempo* firmly rooted an artistic/cultural figure within a social environment to such an extent that society overwhelmed the individual on many occasions. Lightweight, 16 mm technology enabled the documentation of many hitherto unexplored areas of social life and moved away from a focus on an individual within a studio. The camera explores the environment in these programmes, moving around and getting into some novel spaces (such as inside the central computer base of the NatWest bank and inside a shopping trolley, both in *Information Explosion*). The fast pace of the editing allowed the viewer to experience a broad range of social spaces within the half-hour duration of each programme. This collage also simulated the effects of spatial compression, reflecting McLuhan's ideas of a 'global village', in which everything is somehow interconnected.

The series also experimented with narrative strategies. As in most arts programmes, a speaker 'oriented' the images, but here in an unconventional manner. Commentary was often delivered as rhetorical snippets: enigmatic or didactic pronouncements, rather than explicatory interjections. For example, in *Noise*, John Cage bombards the viewer with ideas about sound and about listening in new ways. Intercut with such pronouncements are clips of Roland Kirk playing rasping music in concert, or of Cage making sounds from everyday objects. The whole programme is a kind of continuum of idea and sound counterpoint, more of a rhythmic 'poem' than a linear 'story'. Narration in other programmes could be quite intermittent, eventually becoming overwhelmed by more radical audio-visual montage sequences. This strategy is used heavily in both *Information Explosion* and *Heroes*, both of which finish with long, speechless, abstract sequences (of time-lapse street scenes and a montage of icons, respectively). The last programme in the series, *Reprise*, features different commentaries from previous episodes pasted together, often over images they did not originally accompany.

Speed and free association are two of the most striking aesthetic aspects of *New Tempo*. Speed, of course, characterises the pace of the editing in some of the montage sequences, but it also characterises other aspects of the film: the swift movement of hand-held cameras, the pace of traffic within the frame, or of the intense motion produced by time-lapse photography. The image collages, meanwhile, are pieced together in a kind of 'free association': disjunctive montage sequences are often used not in a linear manner, but as motifs that obliquely connect to some of the central themes of the series. Speed and free association can be seen as attempts to both mirror contemporary reality and mimic the perceptual effects of technological change. Fast, associative montage reflects the increasing speed and connectivity of everyday life in the late 1960s, suggesting that modern life is both fragmented and integrated, and that connections are sometimes hard to grasp because of the pace of acceleration. Such an aesthetic mode also mirrors strategies in other areas of media, such as advertising. Renée Dickason has written that the 1960s saw a shift in many areas of advertising, from straightforward product placement towards speed, excitement and 'free association'.[16] (It should not be forgotten that advertising researchers worked on *New Tempo*.)

The intense pace of segments in *New Tempo* metaphorically reflect two polarised reactions to technological change. The first is a kind of giddy excitement and the second is anxiety: both of which could lead to a rush of violent, incoherent thoughts. Even McLuhan, often accused of glorifying technology, was disturbed and anxious about this. He believed that people would have to alter their sense ratios in order to avoid the trauma of being overwhelmed or 'numbed' by new technological infrastructures. There is no doubt that *New Tempo* was positive about technological change (hence the underlying order of these associative audio-visual fragments), yet its aesthetic can also be seen as reflecting an underlying sense of anxiety.

New Tempo also brought abstract filmmaking into television. The programme not only reported on new perceptual paradigms needed to cope with the technological environment but also attempted to institute new formal structures that could, drug-like, affect the perceptual apparatus of the viewer. The two concluding montage sequences of *Information Explosion* and *Heroes* were both sensorial representations, but possibly the most vivid example occurs in *Stimulants*. The programme features an interview with radical psychiatrist R. D. Laing about drugs intercut with a man walking downstairs into a room, drinking water and lighting a cigarette. This scene is repeatedly shown at different angles and speeds. Eventually, through lens distortion and manipulation of film speed, the picture slows and swirls as though mimicking drug-like sensations, whilst sitar music on the soundtrack is treated and warped. In this episode, like others, a programme about the use of drugs eventually gives way to an attempt to reproduce the sensory affects of drugs themselves. The constant fluctuation in the series between information on a subject and sensorial impressions of a subject merges abstract and documentary modes in order to show that the 'cultural' and the 'social' are inseparable. In this sense, to quote the narration in *Information Explosion*, 'the whole environment starts to become a living, changing, electric art object'.

In *New Tempo*'s concept of a radical arts programme, and in line with its McLuhanesque ideology, the series continually foregrounded technological mediation. This is evident even in many narrational aspects of the series: in *Leisure*, the narrator speaks into a tape recorder on occasions; in *Information Explosion*, questions are posed to the central character in a voice that has been electronically modulated; in *Nostalgia*, the main orienting links feature a series of questions and answers conducted by telephone. Some representations of technological mediation were more stylistically rendered. For example, in *Expendability*, the narrator's profile is at one stage used as a projection screen, so that as he speaks different stills of urban environments alternate upon his head. The most extensive foregrounding of technological mediation appears in *Heroes*, which surveys the way in which the image-saturated technological landscape is transforming the manner through which celebrity is constructed, and the roles that such celebrities play in peoples' lives. The programme is constantly drawing attention to image and sound technologies, including the Nagra III tape recorder, slide projectors, camera lenses and television sets.

Overall, this mediation of technologies can be read as both a declaration that life was becoming increasingly filtered through communications technologies, and also a turn towards self-consciousness in the arts documentary. This self-reflexive foregrounding of technological construction was accompanied by the overt manner in which the series presented itself as 'new' in opposition to 'old'. Whilst *New Tempo* continually blurred boundaries, such as between 'high' and 'low', 'fact' and 'fiction', between 'art' and 'science', it remained binary in its demarcation between 'new' and 'old'.

Although *New Tempo* employed the lightweight film equipment that was becoming increasingly common within British television production, it did so in a manner that diverged from predominant, 'vérité'-type applications. The adoption of 16 mm film equipment led to a televisual shift in the early 1960s, as the medium's dependence on 'liveness' was weakened and emphasis on 'immediacy' became marked. The former aesthetic reflected television's confinement to the studio and its use of electronic cameras that broadcast live pictures, and its early reliance on theatre and radio. The increasing use of lightweight cameras, on the other hand, meant that television programmes began to be filmed on location, breaking out of the studio, so that mobility and immediacy became more important aesthetic qualities. This was the case particularly within the field of documentary, although this aesthetic also seeped into other areas of programming, such as television drama.[17] This trend was also apparent within the arts documentary, as programmes such as *Tempo International* and selected episodes of *Monitor* demonstrate. Yet whilst the arts programme may have been adapting to this major aesthetic shift, *New Tempo* was moving into alternative pathways. Its form still used the 'filmic' heritage of the vérité paradigm, but incorporated this into a much more self-reflexive and fragmented structure indebted to influences such as advertising, collage, photography, montage-based film-making and cultural theory.

In this sense, *New Tempo* was a manifestation of an increasing 'post-modern' influence within television production, as Lynn Spigel has also noted within the context of US television in the 1960s.[18] Whilst we cannot conflate US and UK television, there was, in both countries, a 'post-modern' blurring between once distinct categories within cultural life, which also encroached upon the televisual landscape. As Spigel points out, television was a medium that merged the scientific, commercial and artistic: it was a technology produced through and used as a tool for science, a form for commerce and commercial culture, as well as a potential forum for the fine arts.[19] *New Tempo* took advantage of this hybridity on the level of both form and content, reflected in its mélange of techniques and by its addressing technological, social, cultural and commercial issues.

Although *New Tempo* attempted to blur distinctions between 'high' and 'low' art, it nevertheless remained bracketed within the 'specialist' category of arts programming. Its low viewing figures highlight that, whilst it attempted to locate 'cutting-edge' experimentation within the popular (especially in the realm of advertising), it never itself entered the realm of the popular.[20] Its status as an arts programme scheduled on a Sunday afternoon may have made popularity unlikely, but the series also failed to achieve critical acclaim.[21] Even Reyner Banham, who helped organise the Pop Art-inspired exhibition *This is Tomorrow* in 1956, was hostile to the series, criticising its excessive privileging of form over content.[22]

The manner by which *New Tempo* attempted to depart from the conventions of arts programming meant that it was extremely difficult to categorise: was it an arts documentary, or was it a more general documentary about the state of culture and society? Such absent markers may have contributed to the general negative reaction to the series. It was no surprise, then, that subsequent arts documentaries tended to eschew such an experimental approach. Nevertheless, many of the figures involved in *New Tempo* also contributed to another experimental arts series the following year: *Who Is?* Perhaps as a result of the reception of *New Tempo*, this series returned, in part, to a more recognisable template of arts television, focusing as it did upon a single individual artist. Yet within this more recognisable format, *Who Is?* also experimented with the format in more subtle ways.

Who Is?

Whereas *New Tempo* was a programme made for a commercial network containing input from freelance contributors, *Who Is?* actually emanated from Allan King Associates. The idea for the series grew out of a documentary made by AKA in 1967, *The Life and Times of John Huston Esq.* (directed by Roger Graef). After this, Roger Graef and Allan King decided to devise a whole series based around portraits of individual artists.

The Life and Times of John Huston Esq. was co-produced by AKA in conjunction with the BBC, National Educational Television of America and the Canadian Broadcasting Corporation. AKA managed to agree a similar deal for a series of thirteen programmes along the same lines: *Who Is?* was co-produced by the same companies, plus the German company Bayerischer Rundfunk. It was the first complete series commissioned by these companies for an independent production unit and was the first international co-production of its kind.[23] The BBC directly commissioned four of the thirteen programmes and purchased the other programmes. All of the material was shot on 16 mm colour film (BBC2 had started showing colour in 1967), produced by Roger Graef and executive produced by Allan King. The programmes had various directors, including Dick Fontaine, William Brayne, Alan King, Roger Graef and Denis Postle. The series was shown on

BBC2 on Monday evenings, between 23 September and 23 December 1968.[24] The only change that the BBC made for British transmission was the design of its own credit logo sequence, which was accompanied by a short burst of electronic music made by Delia Derbyshire (from the BBC Radiophonic Workshop).

Who Is? was composed of thirteen programmes, each based around an artist. These were (in order of British schedule): *Maurice Béjart, Max Frisch, Walter Gropius, Norman Mailer, Rufino Tamayo, Pierre Boulez, Richard Smith, Sonny Rollins, Oscar Niemeyer, Jacques Lipchitz, James Jones, Victor Vasarely* and *Sean Kenny*. Each programme was approximately 28 minutes in length, with the exception of the *Norman Mailer* programme, which was a double-length episode entitled *Will the Real Norman Mailer Please Stand Up*.

While *Who Is?* was more recognisable as an 'arts programme' than *New Tempo*, it did experiment with the more conventional, humanist templates within which it worked. Like *New Tempo*, it was a self-conscious arts programme that situated itself on the side of the 'new' in opposition to the 'old'. This was stated in the publicity release for the programme, which claimed that those involved in making the programmes shared the producers' antipathy to 'old-fashioned formal film-making'.[25]

One of the most striking instances of the old being rejected and the new being promoted is in *Who Is Vasarely?* (directed by Mark Peploe). The programme begins by parodying old-fashioned art programmes: a slow, admiring pan across a picturesque landscape in Provence is accompanied by narration lovingly extolling the landscape. A romantic harp melody plays on the soundtrack, adding to the idealised portrayal. The narrator describes people harmoniously at one with the surrounding environment and mentions that the area is a favourite place of artists. Accompanying a shot of an artist leaving an old building, the narrator says that 'he' can often be seen leaving home with an easel and a brush. A sudden yet prolonged drone on the soundtrack then punctures this filmic mode, as the camera shows a fairly low-angled shot of Vasarely standing alone in the same landscape. As the camera slowly moves in closer to his face, his voice on the soundtrack ridicules attempts to describe art in Renaissance terms. We cut back to the landscape that dominated the opening scene, but now it is overlaid with a succession of abstract shapes that are superimposed over the natural backdrop and accompanied by chopped electronic sounds (composed by Tristram Carey).

Immediately, the 'traditional' arts programme is parodied as idealistic, old-fashioned, and picturesque. The sharp transition from harp music to an electronic drone, and from long-shot to close-shot, emphasises the rupture that this type of documentary is attempting to make. The stylised opening sequence, eventually giving way to 'Vasarely' titles flashing in symmetrical lines, encapsulates what the programme is about. It is at once a portrait of an artist and an attack against the conventional portrait of an artist. A female narrator (Emma Tennant) describes Vasarely in quite a cold and unemotional manner, contrasting with the opening narration (soft, mellow, male tones). The biographical details are sparse and basic, so that a sense of distance and pragmatism is set against the initial warmth and romanticism.

Whilst some elements of the Vasarely programme radically break with conventional arts programmes, others are more conventional. The programme wavers between using conventional techniques and attacking them. This strategy is extended in *Who Is Richard Smith?* (directed by Denis Postle). This was the most experimental programme of the series and the one most similar to *New Tempo*. It mixes audio-visual montage segments with self-reflexive ruminations on how to present a documentary on a single artist. Smith himself places doubt upon 'traditional' approaches to artist documentaries, claiming that shots of him at work and biographical details would not do his work justice. In contrast, this programme (and *Who Is?* as a series) would take new approaches to documenting individual artists. Against the types of artist documentaries questioned within the programme, *Who Is Richard Smith?* mixes mobile interview segments with more abstract, fragmented image permutations, including Smith's own work and images considered influential on his work (particularly imagery associated with popular culture, including advertising). The result is a fast-paced and original programme that at once questions representational conventions and attempts to create a new type of televisual documentary, one that is not only *about* art but which also attempts to *be* art.

Movement between traditional – or at least relatively straightforward – modes of narration, and stylistically experimental sequences, fed into the series of *Who Is?* as a whole. Whereas many of the programmes are experimental, other programmes are more straightforward. The programme on James Jones (directed by Allan King), for example, is a rather uncomplicated portrayal of an artist. It documents the writer's thoughts and biography in mainly interview form, and in much of the earlier portion of the programme we see Jones describing aspects of his childhood and writing from behind his desk at home, the camera rarely moving. The latter part of the film follows Jones walking through Paris, yet the pace of the filming is relatively sober. Likewise, the programme on Norman Mailer (directed by Dick Fontaine) is more reminiscent of a vérité documentary, where the mobile film crew trail Mailer on lecture tours, television appearances and anti-Vietnam demonstrations.

There are two main reasons why the programmes in the series varied in style: firstly, because different creative teams were assigned to specific programmes, and inevitably imprinted their creative marks on the programmes they made; secondly, there was also an attempt within *Who Is?* to mould the style of the programme to the temperament of the artist being documented.[26] To return to the Mailer programme, then, we can link the vérité style of the programme to Dick Fontaine (who produced, directed and wrote the programmes) and his background in making groundbreaking 'televérité' television such as the *World in Action* special *Yeah, Yeah, Yeah: New York Meets the Beatles* (tx. 11 February 1964, made with the Maysles brothers). Also, such a stylistic mode can be seen as suitable not only to Mailer's engagement with journalism but also for covering the demonstration and Mailer's subsequent arrest, events that could not be controlled by Fontaine.

Who Is Max Frisch? (directed by Mark Peploe) also found ways to mirror the preoccupations of the artist under consideration. Frisch was concerned with identity, role-play and the structure of time, issues that inform the aesthetic of the documentary. The emphasis on role-play is highlighted in the style of the film; there is a playful tone to it (emphasised by the bouncy, music-hall type of piano motif at the beginning), in which different people take on different roles. Early in the film a montage of different, 'ordinary' people introduce themselves in short, static shots; these people appear throughout, commenting on Frisch's characteristics and appearance. They are, then, 'playing' roles normally undertaken either by broadcasters or by close associates of Frisch. Later in the film there is a playful approach to the interview format: Frisch often assumes the role of interviewer, and the role of interviewee is played not only by him, but also by other people who have already appeared within the programme.

While the unconventional interview format relates to the theme of identity and role-play, the way in which the programme constantly undergoes spatial and temporal shifts mirrors Frisch's interest in the structure of time. The actual format of the programme, whilst symbolising his concerns, also mixes a more traditional documentary format with experimental sequences. The film investigates the biography and themes of an artist and his work, and it uses extensive location filming so as to position the artist in his social milieu. These sequences, though, are often interrupted by direct address and playfulness with form, a strategy that begins to blur the boundaries between fact and fiction.

On the whole, *Who Is?* was stylistically varied, adopting a range of different approaches that challenged the conventions of documenting individual artists. In addition, those artists covered tended to be less established than was common and also were marked by internationalism: only two of the artists portrayed were British and they were filmed in a number of different locations around the world. Reviews of the series were not as harsh as criticisms of *New Tempo*, yet there was still a general consensus that the series was pretentious and often obscure, a regular critical response to programmes that experiment with form. However, this was not always the case: the films of Frisch and Norman Mailer did both receive good reviews, but these were exceptional.[27] Resistance was also met from within the BBC on occasion, because of the quick, mobile shooting methods sometimes employed. A. Branson (Assistant Film Technical and Training Manager) wrote a letter to C. V. Phipps (Head of Film Operations) complaining about the poor quality of the Gropius programme.[28] Despite such protestations, this programme – the only episode of the series that has a full Audience Research Report – was favourably received by a sample audience. Yet, with viewing figures generally low (varying from 0.5 per cent of the UHF public, approximately 80,000, to 1.7 per cent, approximately 280,000).[29] It is clear, then, that even within the 'specialist' realm of arts television, experimentation often met with resistance, highlighting the tension between the desire to produce new modes, and the adherence to more established aesthetic templates.

Conclusion

Both *New Tempo* and *Who Is?* are historically and aesthetically interesting for a number of reasons. Firstly, they are relatively neglected arts programmes that show there were experiments in the genre beyond the more canonical programmes such as *Monitor*, and which also pre-date some of the more well-known, subsequent experiments in the genre, such as Illuminations' *State of the Art* (Channel 4, 1987). Secondly, they capture and reflect experimental practices, concepts and aesthetics across a range of cultural practices throughout the period, from Pop Art to media theory, from experimental drug use to new approaches to sound. Thirdly, they not only document cultural and artistic activities, but they do so through an appropriate form of televisual presentation, in which form mirrors content. Deviating from the traditional format in which pre-existing artworks were presented to an audience, the series used art as a stimulus through which a new kind of televisual aesthetic was produced. Out of this, an avant-garde television practice tentatively emerged, in which the documentary style, associated with current affairs, both clashed with and enhanced the more conceptual and abstract style of filmmaking in this attempt to not only document art, but also to portray its aesthetic dimensions.

Who Is? and *New Tempo* undoubtedly made innovative interventions within the medium, and reflect both the opportunities as well as the constraints operating within British television at that time. The fact that they were commissioned and broadcast was undoubtedly connected to the opportunities afforded by the increased need for programmes with the advent of three terrestrial channels, as well as a public service stipulation to cater to cultural edification. Furthermore, given the surrounding cultural climate of the late 1960s, television as a medium was undergoing change. The influence of Pop Art, for example, can be found in drama series such as *The Avengers* (ABC, 1961–69) and *The Prisoner* (ATV, 1967–68). Yet when these elements were incorporated into more radical, experimental structures of *New Tempo* and, to a lesser extent, *Who Is?*, they met with far more hostility. As a 'specialist' genre, arts programming would not expect to gain huge audiences. As a 'prestige' form of programming, though, critical reception was crucial to its status, and the reception of these programmes was not positive.

It would appear that the resistance towards such programmes hinged on their combination of modernist experimentation with what has become identified as more 'post-modernist' features (such as the conflation between the popular and 'high art'). The adherence to a notion of arts television as relaying information about art, as opposed to portraying experiential dimensions of art, was a persistent trend. Well-received programmes that diverged from such a template tended to be those that portrayed a single, established artistic figure (an example being Russell's *Elgar*, BBC, 1962). Those that diverged from such a template and which also interrogated traditional conceptions of what constituted art, were less likely to meet with critical approval.[30] Antipathy towards television that is not just about art but which also attempts to be art has largely remained. In 2005 Michael Morris, co-director of the arts commissioning body Artangel, complained that 'There's a lot of TV about the arts, and not enough that is art.'[31] In the light of renewed discussion about the need to create new types of arts programmes, it is time that more people were alerted to *New Tempo* and *Who Is?*: they may be almost forty years old, but perhaps point to the future of arts programming.

Notes

1. An exception is an MA dissertation written by Emma Tutty, '*New Tempo*: the Search for an Alternative Arts Programming Aesthetic' (Birkbeck/BFI, 1997).
2. John Walker, *Arts TV: A History of Arts Television in Britain* (London: John Libbey/Arts Council of Great Britain, 1993), 20–5.
3. John Wyver, 'Representing Art or Reproducing Culture? Tradition and Innovation in British Television's Coverage of the Arts (1950–87)', in Philip Hayward (ed.), *Picture This: Media Representations of Visual Art and Artists* (London: John Libbey, 1988), 28–9.
4. Ibid., 35.
5. BBC WAC T32/996, *Monitor, The Class* (held at BBC Written Archive Centre, Caversham).

6 Bernard Sendall, *Independent Television in Britain, Volume Two: Expansion and Change, 1958–1968* (London and Basingstoke: Macmillan, 1982), 23–4.
7 Tutty, 'New Tempo', 33–4.
8 Mike Hodges interviewed by Rodney Giesler, 3 March 1998 (BECTU History Project interview tape).
9 An influence that Hodges openly admits in the interview with Giesler.
10 Marshall McLuhan, *Understanding Media: The Extensions of Man* (London: Sphere, 1967), 46.
11 Quoted in Arthur Kroker, 'Digital Humanism: The Processed World of Marshall McLuhan', *CTheory.net* (May 1995), www.ctheory.net/text_file.asp?pick=70 accessed April 2006.
12 Frances Spalding, *British Art Since 1900* (London: Thames & Hudson, 1986), 194.
13 Robert Hewison, *Culture and Consensus: England, Art and Politics Since 1940* (London: Methuen, 1997), 50–87.
14 Bar the first programme, which was shown at 2.30 p.m.
15 It was replaced by a repeat of the first programme in the series, *Information Explosion*. See Reyner Banham, 'The Message is a Monkee' [sic], *New Society* (23 February, 1967), 284.
16 Renée Dickason, *British Television Advertising: Cultural Identity and Communication* (Luton: University of Luton Press, 2000), 49.
17 See Jamie Sexton, '"Televérité" hits Britain: Documentary, Drama and the growth of 16 mm Filmmaking in British Television', *Screen*, 24: 4 (Winter 2003).
18 See Lynn Spigel, 'High Culture in Low Places: Television and Modern Art, 1950–1970', in Spigel, *Welcome to the Dreamhouse: Popular Media and Postwar Suburbs* (Durham and London: Duke University Press, 2001).
19 Ibid., 285.
20 Banham noted the low viewing figures for *New Tempo* in 'The Message is a Monkee'.
21 Review clippings of *New Tempo* are collected in the BFI Library on microfilm.
22 Banham, 'The Message is a Monkee', 284.
23 Details from the publicity release for the series, in *Roger Graef Special Collection, Box 5: Who Is?* (BFI Special Collections, BFI Library, London).
24 Programmes were usually shown between 9.55 p.m. and 10.25 p.m., but were sometimes shown at slightly different times.
25 Publicity release, *Roger Graef Special Collection, Box 5: Who Is?* Also see Graef's introduction to the series in the *Radio Times* (19 September 1968), 46.
26 This was openly declared in the Publicity Release for the series. In the *Roger Graef Special Collection, Box 5: Who Is?*
27 P. Porter reviewed both the Frisch programme and the Mailer programme favourably in the *New Statesman* (18 October 1968), whilst George Melly reviewed the Mailer programme positively in the *Observer* (20 October 1968).
28 Letter from Branson to Phipps, 12 November 1968. From *BBC* WAC File: *T51/150: Who Is Walter Gropius?* Branson expressed concern that the reputation of the BBC would suffer. It has to be said that the Gropius film does appear to be strikingly monotone, dominated by a light, brownish tone.

29 *Roger Graef Special Collection, Box 5: Who Is?*
30 In contrast to his biopics, Ken Russell's *Pop Goes the Easel*, perhaps the first arts documentary to experiment with this slot in order to present the new merging between commercialism and high art, was negatively received. It had the lowest reaction index rating for a *Monitor* programme at the time of its showing. BBC WAC, T32/1, 021: *Monitor, Pop Goes the Easel*.
31 Charlotte Higgins, '"Give Camera to Artists" Plea as TV Arts Lambasted', *The Guardian* (8 April 2005), 9.

6

An experiment in television drama: John McGrath's *The Adventures of Frank*

Lez Cooke

In Chapter 3, on *Diary of a Young Man* (BBC1, 1964), John Hill explores the relationship between the series and Troy Kennedy Martin's 'Nats Go Home' manifesto,[1] a polemic against naturalism in television drama which provided a theoretical rationale for the experimentalism of *Diary of a Young Man*. As Hill notes, *Diary* was a collaboration between Kennedy Martin and John McGrath, who had previously worked together on the groundbreaking police series *Z Cars* in 1962. According to McGrath, *Diary of a Young Man* had its origins in an unperformed stage play, *Jack*, which he wrote for the Royal Court Theatre in 1960.[2] In the late 1970s McGrath returned to the theme of *Diary* in a theatre play, *Joe of England* (1977), produced the year after he revived Kennedy Martin's attack on television naturalism at the 1976 Edinburgh Festival, when he delivered the inaugural MacTaggart Lecture.[3] McGrath's 'case against naturalism' argued that television drama was as much immersed in naturalism in the mid-1970s as it had been in the early 1960s and he challenged television executives, writers and directors to be as bold in challenging naturalism as those involved in the making of *Diary of a Young Man* had been in 1964.

Four years later, following the production of *Joe of England*, McGrath took up the challenge himself, returning to television after an absence of several years to make *The Adventures of Frank* (BBC1, 1980), a non-naturalistic drama combining the agit-prop music-theatre of *Joe of England* with new video effects. The result was an experiment in television drama that attempted to update *Diary of a Young Man* for a new conjuncture, utilising the non-naturalistic potential of new video technology while giving the subject an overtly political dimension lacking in *Diary of a Young Man* (see the conclusion in Chapter 3). This chapter examines the product of that experiment, placing it in the context of McGrath's other work and his own 1979 'manifesto' for progressive television,[4] while also considering the production in relation to other radical and experimental television drama produced in the 1970s and early 1980s.

While McGrath later admitted that *The Adventures of Frank* was 'a bold attempt that didn't come off',[5] the production is a rare example in British television of a drama that attempts to combine Brechtian ideas with experimental television techniques in order to explore socio-political developments in Britain at the beginning of the 1980s. For this reason *The Adventures of Frank* is worthy of examination, especially in relation to *Diary of a Young Man* and the television version of McGrath's theatre play, *The Cheviot, The Stag and the Black, Black Oil* (BBC1, 1974), but also with regard to the experimental potential of new video technology which, in the 1970s and 1980s, was primarily used for aesthetic effect, rather than as a tool for exploring political ideas.

John McGrath and the background to *The Adventures of Frank*

John McGrath entered television when he joined the BBC Script Department as a scriptwriter-adapter in 1960, working alongside other young writers such as John Hopkins, Troy Kennedy Martin and Roger Smith. Although McGrath wrote one episode of *Z Cars*, he mainly worked as a director on the series, developing a new fast-paced style for the drama in an attempt to get away from the theatrical naturalism which defined much studio drama at the time. The achievement of *Z Cars* in its early days was considerable but, frustrated with the limitations of series drama, McGrath and Kennedy Martin left before the end of the first series, collaborating subsequently on *Diary of a Young Man* before going their separate ways, reuniting once more in 1978 for the final episode of *Z Cars*. After *Diary of a Young Man* McGrath produced two series of 'experimental' films for BBC2 in 1964–66, made by directors including Ken Russell, Philip Saville and McGrath himself.[6] In 1966 McGrath's *Events While Guarding the Bofors Gun* was produced at the Hampstead Theatre and subsequently made into a feature film, *Bofors Gun* (1968), directed by Jack Gold. By this time McGrath had left television to concentrate on writing screenplays for films such as Ken Russell's *Billion Dollar Brain* (1967), John Dexter's *The Virgin Soldiers* (1969) and Jack Gold's *The Reckoning* (1970).

McGrath spent most of the 1970s working in alternative theatre, founding the socialist 7:84 Theatre Company in 1971 (the name derives from a statistic published in *The Economist* that 7 per cent of the population in Britain owns 84 per cent of the wealth). In 1973 the company was split into Scottish and English branches with McGrath acting as artistic director for both companies, writing most of the plays they performed. It was the Scottish company that produced *The Cheviot, The Stag and the Black, Black Oil*, an agit-prop drama based on the traditional Highland ceilidh, as its first production in 1973. The show toured extensively in Scotland and was reworked as a BBC *Play for Today* in 1974, directed by John Mackenzie, who had worked on *Diary of a Young Man* as a floor manager and assistant to director Ken Loach. The television version of *The Cheviot* combined material from the theatre production with new scenes, shot on film, dramatising the Highland clearances of the nineteenth century and documentary footage about the oil boom of the 1970s, to produce a radical, 'Brechtian' television drama.[7]

It is in the juxtaposition of different forms that *The Cheviot* most clearly departs from the aesthetic of naturalism in television drama. Mackenzie had seen the touring show and asked McGrath if he would write a screenplay based on the stage production. In doing so McGrath was concerned that a television version should retain the interactive agit-prop spirit of the theatre play. He proposed using the stage play as a Brechtian alienation device, cutting between the stage play and the documentary and drama footage that was filmed for the television version. The approach was a self-consciously Brechtian one, as McGrath later admitted, designed not only to politicise the audience but to involve them as active participants in the production of meaning, rather than positioning them as passive consumers of a predetermined, closed narrative: 'Oh yes, that was consciously Brechtian that was. Brechtianised television – it wasn't a Brechtian stage play but it was a Brechtian way of approaching television, fairly consciously.'[8]

The approach was qualitatively different to the non-naturalism of *Diary of a Young Man*, where the juxtaposition of different forms – studio scenes, vérité and montage sequences, stills sequences, diegetic conversation and voice-over narration – was informed by the theories elaborated in Kennedy Martin's 'Nats Go Home' manifesto, which owed as much to Eisenstein's theories of montage as they did to Brechtian theories of alienation. While Brechtian ideas were certainly evident in 'Nats Go Home' Kennedy Martin principally invoked Brecht's theory of distanciation in support of his argument about the 'objectifying' quality of the television image,[9] although John Hill argues that Kennedy Martin's distinction between 'story' and 'plot' is similar to Brecht's distinction between 'dramatic' and 'epic' theatre.[10]

With the television version of *The Cheviot, The Stag and the Black, Black Oil* McGrath wanted to use montage in a more 'consciously Brechtian' way. In *Diary of a Young Man* montage was used within a repertoire of non-naturalistic techniques in order to create an innovative modernist drama, rather than a political drama. In *The Cheviot* montage was used not for aesthetic effect but to reinforce the political message of the drama. The difference owes much to the different political and institutional contexts within which *Diary of a Young Man* and *The Cheviot* were produced, but the more 'consciously Brechtian' strategy of *The Cheviot* also results from McGrath's increased involvement with socialist politics in the 1970s. His decision to go to Paris in May 1968, when students and workers clashed with French police on the streets, was indicative of his growing political involvement and there is no doubt this was a formative influence prior to the setting-up of 7:84 as a radical theatre company. The political nature of 7:84's theatre work is clearly evident in *Joe of England*, where McGrath returns to the basic story of *Diary of a Young Man* – a young man coming down to London from the North seeking adventure, romance and his fortune – but updates it for the late 1970s, in the process making it more overtly political. McGrath describes the political context in which the play was produced in his book, *Naked Thoughts That Roam About*:

> It was the year when Callaghanism and the heavy tread of the police federation running the government became apparent. *Joe of England* was a response to the nihilistic feeling one got at that time that politics was becoming pointless on a parliamentary level. They were beginning to sort out inflation but everyone was very fly; all socialist principles had been abandoned and the ability of Callaghan and his cabinet to absorb opposition and the militancy of the working class, cast people with any principles into a certain gloom and cynicism about the way people in the country were going. So to have this boy coming to the heart of the nation he is proud of, to see it in need of a transplant, was what the play was about.[11]

The 7:84 (England) company toured *Joe of England* from November 1977 to June 1978, but McGrath was not happy with it, describing the play as 'disappointing'.[12] Nevertheless, he thought there was enough merit in the idea to rework it again for television in 1980, by which time Margaret Thatcher's Conservative government was in power and the political pessimism expressed in *Joe of England* had become a reality.

In the first three months of 1979, prior to the election of Thatcher, McGrath gave a series of six talks, mainly about theatre, to students at Cambridge University, demonstrating his concern to provide a theoretical basis for his theatrical practice. In the final talk he discussed 'The Challenge of Film and Television' for those writers and directors wanting to make a progressive intervention within these media. Together with his 1976 MacTaggart Lecture, 'TV Drama: The Case Against Naturalism', this talk represents the nearest McGrath came to providing a manifesto on television drama. Delivered little more than a year before *The Adventures of Frank*, McGrath provided a list of recommendations for 'the serious writer in television' which summarise his ideological approach to the medium. The recommendations included the need to:

> analyse the real nature of television communication, and the process of material and ideological production; intervene in the situation in order to challenge

the stifling 'TV naturalist' form that reduces the world either to a small bowl of emotional stew, handed out in weekly dollops, or to a series of criminal acts performed by deviants ... re-assert the possibility of forms in television which do allow a small degree of theoretical thinking into the act of creation and communication ... create vigorously and well, with an awareness of the limitations of the medium, in such a way as to command a deeper response from a popular audience; use words, images, ideas with a historical awareness as well as an awareness of the audience.[13]

While not as extensive as Troy Kennedy Martin's 'Nats Go Home' polemic, McGrath's recommendations provided a theoretical manifesto for the production of progressive television drama which he attempted to put into practice the following year with *The Adventures of Frank*.

The Adventures of Frank as a *Play for Today*

Having had little involvement with television since the early 1970s McGrath saw an opportunity in 1980 to make an intervention within the *Play for Today* series on the subject of Thatcherite politics. This was facilitated by the fact that Richard Eyre, a friend of McGrath's who had directed some of his theatre plays in the 1970s, was the producer in charge of *Play for Today* at the time. Changing the name of his central character to Frank, McGrath retained the basic idea of a Northern working-class lad who travels to London seeking his fortune, only to find that in order to succeed he must adopt capitalist values of ruthlessness and greed, and forsake the values of his working-class upbringing in Sheffield.

The Adventures of Frank was shown on BBC1 in two parts on 4 and 11 November 1980. Originally envisaged as a single play, *Frank* was a departure from the social realist dramas for which *Play for Today* was well known. By 1980 *Play for Today* had a reputation for progressive drama engaging with contemporary social issues in a predominantly realist style. This tradition is represented by plays such as Jim Allen's *The Rank and File* (1971), *The Spongers* (1978) and *United Kingdom* (1981), Jeremy Sandford's *Edna, the Inebriate Woman* (1971), Mike Leigh's *Hard Labour* (1973), Tony Perrin's *Shutdown* (1973), Colin Welland's *Leeds – United!* (1974), David Edgar's *Destiny* (1978) and Alan Bleasdale's *The Muscle Market* (1981). With the exception of *Destiny* these were all filmed dramas, a number of them concerned with aspects of working-class labour, representing classic examples of the 'gritty social realism' that has a long-standing tradition in British film and television. While by no means the only type of drama to be produced within *Play for Today*, these social realist dramas are among those most associated with the series, to the extent that it is sometimes seen as synonymous with this type of drama.

The Adventures of Frank, however, marks a distinct departure from this tradition. Firstly, the play drew upon aspects of pantomime and agit-prop theatre practised by the 7:84 Theatre Company. In fact, many of the scenes in *The Adventures of Frank* were studio reconstructions of scenes from *Joe of England* and the play used songs from the stage play throughout, with members of 7:84 performing them in the studio. Secondly, *The Adventures of Frank* made use of video effects technology in a conscious departure from the naturalistic aesthetic of social realism.

McGrath wanted to use the relatively new and expensive Quantel digital video editing machines in an exploratory way, in order to achieve some patently non-naturalistic effects. However, the decision to experiment with new video technology raised the cost of production beyond that available for a single play. Consequently, the play was divided into two, in order to spread the cost across two budgets. While Quantel had been used for other television programmes, such as *Top of the Pops*, the technology had been little-used in drama. It was McGrath's interest in exploring its potential for creating non-naturalistic drama that primarily locates *The Adventures of Frank* as an 'experimental' drama, although the use of video effects technology was only one of a number of ways in which *The Adventures of Frank* departs from television naturalism.

Other television drama directors were experimenting with new video technology in the 1970s and early 1980s. James MacTaggart was one of the first to do so with his 1973 dramatisation of *Candide*, in which he used the process of colour separation overlay (CSO) to place his characters in an entirely artificial, electronically-generated world. In the same year, Howard Schuman's untransmitted *Censored Scenes from King Kong* also used CSO, and other video effects, for a non-naturalistic purpose, while in the mid- to late 1970s Schuman's two *Rock Follies* series used video effects technology in many of the musical sequences. In 1980, while McGrath was working on *The Adventures of Frank*, the director Philip Saville, renowned for pioneering new techniques in television drama since the early 1960s, was also experimenting with video technology in *The Journal of Bridget Hitler* (BBC2, 1981). This BBC *Playhouse* production was about a trip that Adolf Hitler supposedly made to Liverpool in 1912 to visit his half-brother Alois, who was living there with his wife, Bridget. Rather than present it as a conventional historical drama, however, Saville staged it as a documentary investigation taking place in a television studio, making extensive use of CSO in order to superimpose archive film and other images onto a screen in the studio, as part of the inquiry that was being enacted. In Saville's hands the 'investigation' in *The Journal of Bridget Hitler* was as much an investigation into the creative potential of video effects technology as it was an inquiry into the claims made by Bridget Hitler in her journal.

The Adventures of Frank, however, was the first television drama to use the image manipulation possibilities of Quantel in a self-consciously Brechtian manner, as distanciation devices to interrupt the narrative flow and encourage the viewer to see the drama not as a 'window on the world', but as a constructed piece of television with a particular ideological viewpoint. As McGrath explained in the *Radio Times* in November 1980:

> In terms of drama, it says to the audience 'this is just a succession of images'. So, as the audience, you become aware that what you're watching is not a slice of life or a chunk of reality and therefore that somebody is creating it and there is a purpose to that creation. What it's capable of doing is to produce alienated television in the way that Brecht was aiming at alienated theatre. Not alienation in the sense that people stay away but that you step back a little bit from the picture and examine it more closely.[14]

Throughout *The Adventures of Frank* different forms are played off against each other in a dialectical strategy intended to produce a politically active viewer. At the beginning of Part One, 'Everybody's Fiddling Something', a montage of colour stills introduces Frank as he sets off from his home in Sheffield to seek his fortune in London. Narration is provided in the form of a song as Frank hitches a lift on a lorry, indicating from the outset that this is not going to be a naturalistic drama but a musical in the style of McGrath's work with the 7:84 Theatre Company. Quantel is used for the first time when three smaller images are superimposed onto a shot of the motorway as the lorry travels down to London. In the superimposed images we see Frank, the lorry driver, and an aerial shot of the lorry, the three images breaking up the naturalistic perspective of the single frame. Frank falls asleep and, in a dream sequence illustrated with stills of the rich and famous, imagines meeting the Queen, Margaret Thatcher and other VIPs when he arrives in London.

On arrival, in the first of many such sequences, Frank addresses the camera against a superimposed backdrop of busy street scenes. This is not filmed on location but achieved through colour separation overlay: recording the actor in the studio against the backdrop of a blue screen onto which images are superimposed electronically to achieve a composite image. This technique is used throughout the drama and is one of the ways in which *The Adventures of Frank* most obviously departs from a naturalistic mode of representation. Frank sets off to find accommodation in a private hotel, from which he is chased away by a fierce, but all-too-obviously dummy, dog. If it were not already evident, the dummy dog makes it clear that the drama is not going to conform to the conventions of realism that the viewer might normally expect from television drama. Instead, the mode of representation is more akin to that of pantomime than to the naturalism more usually associated with *Play for Today*.

Taking refuge from the dog up a lamp-post, high above the traffic passing in front of King's Cross railway station, Frank continues his narration to camera. At this point there is a Brechtian interruption as he explains: 'This here is a play' (cue for the *Play for Today* title to appear on the screen behind Frank, accompanied by its signature drum roll) 'about me coming to London. Ay, I'm Frank of England. Frank of Sheffield in actual point of fact ...' He explains his reason for coming to London, to get work because the steel industry in Sheffield has been shut down. The play (and the term 'play' seems more appropriate here than in many of the filmed dramas being shown in the *Play for Today* series at the time) continues with another montage of still images as Frank resumes his quest to find accommodation. This sequence echoes a similar sequence in *Diary of a Young Man*, down to the use of an upbeat music track and a repeat of a scene in which Frank is kicked out of the London Hilton, following which – and this is where *The Adventures of Frank* introduces new elements made possible by the use of video technology – Frank uses his willpower to make the Hilton wobble and disappear, realised through the image manipulation effects of Quantel.

Frank makes his first journey on the London underground, presented as a journey into a surreal subterranean underworld through the use of solarised images, travelling to Oxford Circus, 'the circus at the heart of the city', which is represented literally as a circus through a series of images that scroll on the screen, to the accompaniment of circus music. Leaving the station and emerging on to the streets, however, Frank is disappointed to find the reality is 'more like Leeds on a Saturday morning', but then he discovers the wealth of Bond Street.

The use of still image sequences to progress the story in a lively and elliptical manner, accompanied by music and/or Frank's narrational voice-over, replicates the formal strategy of *Diary of a Young Man*. However, in *The Adventures of Frank*, in addition to the use of colour, the development of video technology such as Quantel allows the non-naturalistic strategy of *Diary* to be taken much further. As McGrath explained to Stephen Gilbert in the *Radio Times*:

> Because it's an adventure story with lots of movement through it, there were possibilities for using still sequences, as we'd done in the 60s, but for using them in a totally different way with the new electronic devices. We were breaking completely new ground with some of these microchip and floppy disc devices, ways of storing computer information electronically. You can take the picture and reduce it in size or motor it out so that it blows out of the frame. You can take the picture and turn it round and put it into any shape by making the picture into computer information, feeding it into a microchip and then playing instructions on to a floppy disc. They use it on *Top of the Pops* all the time.[15]

The utilisation of these techniques within what is essentially a musical, or a play with songs, together with a more exaggerated, 'theatrical' acting style replacing the naturalistic acting usually found in television drama, makes *The Adventures of Frank* 'experimental' in more ways than one. Like many experiments, it does not entirely succeed, as McGrath was himself prepared to admit: 'It just didn't work. It was a bold attempt that didn't come off, partly for casting problems, partly I was trying to do far too much, to get too far ahead of the technology.'[16]

Certainly Mick Ford, coming from a background of realist film and television drama (he had recently appeared in the feature film version of Alan Clarke's *Scum*, released in 1979), often seems uncomfortable in the central role, and the clash of styles between him and some of the other actors, who were from a background of alternative theatre, made for some awkward exchanges. Jim Broadbent, as the city capitalist Brutus Champing, gets into the spirit of things with an extrovert performance, but the acting too often seems laboured when a greater urgency is needed. Also, splitting the drama into two parts, while necessary to get sufficient money for the effects work, undoubtedly weakened it, extending it to nearly two and a half hours when greater economy was needed. 'That broke its back really', McGrath later acknowledged.[17]

There is also an awkward contrast between some of the studio scenes, especially when they are electronically generated using CSO, and the stills sequences, with the latter generally achieving a faster narrative tempo while the studio scenes slow things down. The musical numbers also contrive to slow the pace, although some of these Brechtian interludes, especially when video effects are employed, are among the most successful sequences in the drama, communicating the political message in a pleasurable and entertaining way.

One of the more successful scenes combines music and video effects in an innovative manner. Frank, having just visited a job centre, is sitting on a bench reading the job ads in the *Evening Standard*. He is, of course, in a studio and behind him a classical-style building is shown by means of colour separation overlay. Superimposed onto the portico, using Quantel, six faces 'sing' the ads Frank is reading, while he comments on them. Another sequence that successfully marries music and video effects comes during Part Two, 'Seeds of Ice', in a reprise of the 'Going Up' number that closed Part One. This time, as Frank is superimposed onto the screen, a sequence of stills scrolls down, creating the illusion that Frank is 'going up in the golden elevator'. While doing so, CSO is used to have him transform from his old clothes into a suited city gent, complete with umbrella and bowler hat. The superimposition of cardboard cut-out representations of a hot-air balloon and an aeroplane indicate he has 'taken off'. At the end of the sequence he is in outer space, represented by a cartoon spaceship and a backdrop of stars. Such fantasy sequences illustrate what could be achieved, through an innovative use of video technology, in the pursuit of a non-naturalistic television drama.

Form and politics

While some critics may have appreciated the use of 'electronic trickery' in *The Adventures of Frank* it was the socialist politics that, predictably, brought forth some scathing reviews from the right-wing press: 'In effect this play is drama by slogan, which means by definition that the design of the banners is more interesting than what they shout' wrote Sean Day-Lewis in the *Daily Telegraph*,[18] while in the Daily Mail Herbert Kretzmer concluded: 'McGrath employs all manner of electronic effects to enliven the screen, but what lingers is the taste of sour grapes, class hatred and humourless earnestness. Dire stuff'.[19] Other reviewers, who might have supported the political sentiments expressed in the play, such as Stewart Lane in the *Morning Star*, nevertheless felt the experiment did not work: 'I'm an admirer of John McGrath's talents, his past accomplishments, and agree with his socio-dramatic objectives. But, for me, this particular exercise failed – on television anyway.'[20]

Whether *The Adventures of Frank* works as a play for television is perhaps the key issue. The experiments with video technology were adventurous but crude, needing more time to perfect than was available, and the attempt to combine them with the musical theatre and non-naturalistic performance style of 7:84 made for an uneasy mix that was only intermittently successful. The problem was partly that the attempt to recreate the live 7:84 performance in the television studio did not really work, although for McGrath the main problem was that there had been insufficient post-production time in which to successfully combine the video effects and the studio scenes:

> The main problem – apart from a casting problem, because the boy who I was made to take for the lead was just not right – was that the Quantel wasn't in an editing room, it was only available in the gallery of *Midweek*, that current affairs programme. So you could only use it when the studio was under maintenance and the gallery wasn't and *Midweek* didn't want it. So I got two days to make major experiments and to use it for two films, and basically what happened was that I made the things roughly in the way I wanted to but when I put them back into the programme they didn't work and I wanted to go back and make them work. I used stills as well, messing about with stills, but the stills were all too slow, they moved too slowly. I wasn't happy with it. Some things I was, but on the whole not. There's some wonderful sequences, however ... the nearer it got to 7:84's show the better it was.[21]

As McGrath acknowledges, given the time available he was 'trying to do far too much'. In an interview published in *Time Out* just before *The Adventures of Frank* was screened, McGrath indicated how much further he was trying to go with the play than the earlier *Diary of a Young Man* had done, by including an element of critical self-analysis in an attempt to deconstruct the motives of the central character:

> The difference between 'Frank' and 'Diary' is that, in a simple way, 'Diary' admired the brashness and aggression of the central character, whereas now, 16 years later, 'Frank' is analysing its central character much more, taking that character apart. In 'Diary' we tended to see Joe as the great immutable image of the lad from the north. But 'Frank' questions that image and examines the vulnerability of that image to the impressions and values he receives as he encounters London. He goes through a sort of learning process – but not one that's uncritically accepted.[22]

The aim to deconstruct and analyse the central character, together with the intention to present a 'state of the nation' play about the politics and morality of Thatcherism in the early 1980s, within an experimental format in which the distancing potential of Quantel and video technology is married to an agit-prop music-theatre style, provides ample testimony to the creative ambition of *The Adventures of Frank*.

The content of the play, focusing on the wheeling and dealing of city stockbrokers and the ruthlessness and greed at the heart of Thatcher's free-enterprise economy, was certainly not the stuff of most popular television drama, as BBC Audience Research Reaction Profiles seemed to confirm, with 68 per cent of viewers seeing it as a 'poor idea' for a play. On the other hand, 74 per cent recognised it as 'original'.[23] Yet, coming barely a year after the election of the first Thatcher government, when the full impact of Tory policies had not yet been felt, *The Adventures of Frank* now seems remarkably prescient in its analysis of the politics of Thatcherism, in addition to being pioneering in its innovative use of digital video effects within a live action drama, anticipating the increased use of digital graphics in television in the 1990s.

In retrospect, however, *The Adventures of Frank* seems more like the end of an era than the beginning of a new one, almost a 'last hurrah' for the kind of experimentation in British television drama that McGrath, Kennedy Martin and others had initiated in the early 1960s. McGrath's experimentation with Quantel and video effects, in order to achieve forms of Brechtian distanciation in the drama, now seems like an attempt to revive a Brechtian tradition that had previously had less impact in television than it had in alternative theatre and in low-budget independent cinema. Had it not been for Richard Eyre, who was clearly sympathetic to this kind of work, it is unlikely that *The Adventures of Frank* would have been made at all, let alone shown on BBC1 in primetime. The fact that it was shows that the possibilities for producing innovative, non-naturalistic drama still existed at the beginning of the 1980s. Three months later, Philip Saville's equally experimental *The Journal of Bridget Hitler* was screened on BBC2 for a 'minority' audience, and in 1986 Dennis Potter's formally ambitious and critically acclaimed *The Singing Detective* was also relegated to BBC2. In the new 'era of cost-effectiveness', as the contemporary situation was described at the Edinburgh Television Festival in August 1980,[24] radical and experimental dramas were likely to be marginalised, if they were made at all.

Given this context, *The Adventures of Frank* represents one of the last examples of an enlightened tradition in British television drama, a tradition where experiment, innovation and the exploration of political ideas were encouraged but which, by the end of the 1980s, had been eroded by the cost-cutting and censorious ideology of Thatcherism. While some producers at the BBC, such as Jonathan Powell and Michael Wearing, continued to commission progressive television drama, such as Alan Bleasdale's *Boys from the Blackstuff* (1982) and Troy Kennedy Martin's *Edge of Darkness* (1985), these were screened, initially at least, on BBC2 rather than BBC1 and adopted more 'popular' forms of social realism and the political thriller, even if they did use those forms in stylistically adventurous ways, eschewing the more overtly Brechtian experimentation of *The Adventures of Frank*.

With the subsequent advent of multi-channel television in Britain the competition for audiences has increased and television companies have generally been disinclined to take risks, opting for more tried and tested formats, such as generic drama and soap opera. McGrath himself recognised that conditions were not favourable to non-naturalistic drama in the 1990s. When he made *The Long Roads* (BBC2, 1993), a BBC *Screen Two* film about an elderly couple from the Scottish Highlands travelling to visit their grown-up children in different parts of the British Isles, he made it as a naturalistic drama, 'because I sussed that the '90s was no time for experiment, so I just went for content'.[25]

While innovative television dramas such as *This Life* (BBC2, 1996–97), *Holding On* (BBC2, 1997), *The Second Coming* (ITV, 2003) and *Blackpool* (BBC1, 2004) have been screened in recent years, 'political' dramas, such as *A Very British Coup* (Channel 4, 1988) and *Our Friends in the North* (BBC2, 1996), have virtually disappeared from the schedules. Meanwhile, there seems to be no space for dramas, like *The Adventures of Frank*, that are both formally innovative and politically radical. In this respect *The Adventures of Frank*, for all of its imperfections, represents the final fling of a radical/experimental/political tradition in British television drama, prior to the onset of the ratings-driven commissioning ethos of the 1990s which eroded the opportunities for such experimentation.

This chapter was originally written as a paper for *Plugged Into History: A Conference to Celebrate John McGrath's Work*, held at Royal Holloway, University of London, 19–20 April 2002.

Notes

1. Troy Kennedy Martin, 'Nats Go Home: First Statement of a New Drama for Television', *Encore*, 48 (March–April 1964), 21–33.
2. John McGrath, *Naked Thoughts That Roam About* (London: Nick Hern Books, 2002), 18–19. Troy Kennedy Martin refutes McGrath's claim that *Jack* was the basis for *Diary of a Young Man*, asserting that *Diary* was primarily written by him and that McGrath contributed little to the writing of the series. The dispute between Kennedy Martin and McGrath over the authorship of *Diary of a Young Man* delayed the production of the series by several months and Kennedy Martin contends that he only agreed to a co-writing credit in order to get the series made. See Lez Cooke, *Troy Kennedy Martin* (Manchester: Manchester University Press, 2007).
3. John McGrath, 'TV Drama: The Case Against Naturalism', *Sight & Sound*, 46:2 (Spring 1977).
4. John McGrath, *A Good Night Out* (London: Nick Hern Books, 1996 [1981]), 114.
5. John McGrath, interviewed by the author, 27 April 2000.
6. The first series was transmitted under the series title *Six* (BBC2, December 1964–January 1965), while the second series, provisionally titled *Five More*, was transmitted, without a series title, on BBC2 in July–August 1966. One of the films in the second series, a *cinema vérité*-style documentary called *Mo* (BBC2, tx. 25 July 1966), featured Troy Kennedy Martin's sister, Maureen, and included an appearance by Troy.
7. Lez Cooke, *British Television Drama: A History* (London: British Film Institute, 2003), 103–10.
8. John McGrath, interviewed by the author, 27 April 2000.
9. Kennedy Martin, 'Nats Go Home', 29–31.
10. See John Hill, 'A "New Drama for Television"?: *Diary of a Young Man*', Chapter 3 in this volume.
11. McGrath, *Naked Thoughts That Roam About*, 107.
12. Ibid., 106.
13. McGrath, *A Good Night Out*, 114.
14. Stephen Gilbert, 'Comedy, with chips', *Radio Times* (1–7 November 1980), 11.
15. Ibid.
16. McGrath, interviewed by the author, 27 April 2000.
17. Ibid.
18. Sean Day-Lewis, 'Drama by slogan – not frankness', *Daily Telegraph* (5 November 1980).
19. Harry Kretzmer, 'The taste of sour red', *Daily Mail* (5 November 1980).
20. Stewart Lane, review, *Morning Star* (5 November 1980).

21 McGrath, interviewed by the author, 27 April 2000.
22 Sandy Craig, 'Have Story, Need ... QUANTEL!', *Time Out* (31 October–6 November 1980), 19.
23 BBC Audience Research – Selected Television Programmes: Reaction Profiles – Week 45: Saturday to Friday, 1–7 November 1980. Part One of *The Adventures of Frank* received a rating of 30, which was very low, while Part Two had a better rating of 51, but still below average.
24 Carl Gardner and John Wyver, 'The single play: from Reithian reverence to cost-accounting and censorship', *Edinburgh International Television Festival 1980*, Official Programme published by *Broadcast*, reprinted in *Screen*, 24: 4–5 (July–October 1983), 47.
25 McGrath, interviewed by the author, 27 April 2000.

7

Don't fence me in: *The Singing Detective* and the synchronicity of indeterminacy

Catrin Prys

> Television's very use of narrative forms pushes them towards an openness that in many other media would seem intolerable, or at least inept.[1]

First broadcast on BBC1 between 17 November and 21 December 1986, *The Singing Detective* is most regularly identified with its writer, Dennis Potter. This does little justice to the important and crucial input of figures such as John Amiel (director) and Kenith Trodd and John Harris (co-producers), not to mention a whole array of choreographers, actors, musicians, and so on, that clearly played a huge role in how it was finally produced from Potter's original script.[2] However, I do not intend to question the way that the drama has usually been understood and analysed through the idea of 'authorship'.[3] My interest lies in *The Singing Detective*'s address to the viewer, particularly its stylistic creation of various and complex levels of meaning that demand to be deciphered but never closed down to understanding. It is these places, where meaning shifts and resists closure, that make the serial so inherently experimental. *The Singing Detective*, because it succeeds in generating different meanings for many different and varied audiences is, in this sense, polysemic. Rather than attempting to 'tie' meaning down, this chapter explores the ambiguities and textual indeterminacies that lie at the heart of Potter's experimental television drama, elements that helped to make it such a rich, dense and complex landscape for its viewers.

Potter and polysemy

John Thornton Caldwell argues that video practitioners today tend to challenge the apparent 'depthlessness' of electronic pixels or scan lines by 'creating images that seem to be layered in depth below the glass surface of the screen'.[4] As such, he suggests that the surface images of the small screen can be used in such a way that it helps to create:

[a] visual complexity, to suggest psychological depth or subjectivity. In fact, many title sequences and program openings that now use layering do so in a way that invokes their characters' personalities, feelings and subjective states. In this way, transparency works to counter two clichés about television. One is the perceived coarseness of its imagery, and the other is the assumed shallowness of its characters and fictions.[5]

The Singing Detective is a quintessential example of 'layered' televisual images merging together to create the illusion of psychological depth or subjectivity, suggesting a visual profundity that is often more than the sum of its parts. 'Depth' is created out of a number of multi-layered and interconnecting 'surfaces', so that the complexity of the televisual image contributes to the complexity of its meaning. These 'layers', in their turn, make it difficult for the viewer to pin down one fixed source or interpretation of meaning.

Such notions of textual indeterminacy have inevitably been applied to the production of meaning found in television, its visual and its aural elements. According to John Fiske, if television is to be popular and reach a diverse of audience it needs to construct 'open' or 'polysemic' texts that avoid pinning meaning down too rigidly. If viewers from different social classes or positions were bombarded only with an unrelenting 'dominant ideology' they would soon switch off their sets. Thus, the 'openness' of the televisual text is vital. As Fiske puts it:

> Meaning is as much a site of struggle as is economics or party politics, and television attempts (but fails) to control its meaning in the same way that social authority attempts (but fails) to stifle voices and strategies of opposition. It is the polysemy of television that makes the struggle for meaning possible, and its popularity in class structured societies that makes it necessary.[6]

This chapter argues that Dennis Potter's drama, and particularly *The Singing Detective*, contributes to experimental television through systematic comment on, and elaboration of, the medium's inherent polysemic nature. This mode of address allows and encourages an active viewer to distil a plethora of meanings that implicitly celebrate the 'bliss' of textual indeterminism. Potter deploys this mode of address, in combination with his 'non-naturalistic' techniques (characters directly addressing the camera, child characters played by adults, characters suddenly bursting into song and the drama's intricate use of flashback, flash forward and montage) to convey a form of 'interior characterisation' that creates, as Caldwell puts it, 'psychological depth or subjectivity'. These devices force the viewers to question the world they are shown and encourage them to grapple with its strongly psychologised landscape.

Potter's television drama (such as *Vote, Vote, Vote for Nigel Barton* (BBC1,

1965), *Moonlight on the Highway* (LWT, 1969), *Casanova* (BBC2, 1971), *Pennies From Heaven* (BBC1, 1978), *Blue Remembered Hills* (BBC1, 1979), *The Singing Detective* and *Blackeyes* (BBC1, 1989) can be defined by this fascination with portraying and conveying 'the inner flux of the mind'. It is the intensely subjective dimensions of human consciousness that fascinate Potter, reflected in an array of experimental techniques that critics have identified as his particular form of 'psychological realism', described by John Cook (borrowing from Raymond Williams) as a form of 'psychological expressionism'.[7] It was certainly a version of reality that revealed a solipsistic mental landscape, filled with unreliable narrators, a breakdown in the generic boundaries between 'fact' and 'fiction' and defined by a constant narrative questioning of the 'real'.

Unlike more explicitly 'post-modern' television drama such as *Twin Peaks* (ABC, 1992), in which meaning is continually allusive and closure seems endlessly postponed, Potter's work appears to search for a central and an underlining core of 'meaning'. As John Caughie points out, *The Singing Detective* employs an essentially 'modernist structure', particularly in its 'concern with the means of representation, symptomatic of a loss of faith in the capacity of the conventions of narrative realism, whether critical or naturalistic, to express complex realities'.[8] However, within this cohesive modernist 'centre' lie a fluidity of meaning and a level of polysemy that has sometimes been ignored by critics who seem intent on tying all meaning down to an exact and identifiable source. Although *The Singing Detective* searches for and (to an extent) reveals a central thread or a core of meaning, it also 'opens up' a whole array of narrative spaces and textual indeterminacies.

Rhythm and blues

Made in association with the Australian Broadcasting Corporation, *The Singing Detective* is an extremely sophisticated, multi-layered example of an experimental television drama, which originally unravelled before its viewers' eyes for six weeks in a process of intense narrative complexity. Suffering from an acute from of psoriatic arthropathy (a dreadful combination of psoriasis and arthritis from which the writer himself suffered), Philip Marlow (Michael Gambon) is literally a prisoner inside his own skin and bones, forced to spend his days and nights (hardly able to move) in a National Health Service hospital.[9] Through sporadic flashbacks we learn a great deal about Marlow's past, particularly of his childhood and his mother's infidelity (he witnesses her having sex with a stranger in his childhood forest), and of his feelings of isolation and guilt when she finally commits suicide (he appears to blame himself for her death, having told her that he actually watched the forest affair). Whilst confined to his bed in the present, he also continually rewrites a pulp detective story in his head (also called *The Singing Detective*), and incorrectly imagines that his wife, Nicola (Janet Suzman), is conspiring to steal the rights to his screenplay. Furthermore, Philip suffers from severe hallucinations; as his body temperature soars out of control, so too does his mind.

As this brief outline suggests, *The Singing Detective* centres on the internal workings of its protagonist's psychological interior. The dramatic techniques employed in the drama all contribute to deflect the viewer's attention away from the external trappings of naturalism, towards the inner 'realities' of this character's psyche. Indeed, Philip Marlow constantly struggles with his memories, desires and deep-rooted feelings of guilt and betrayal, and it is these psychological factors that demand continual acknowledgement and exploration of past events and future consequences. Thus, rather than simply portraying the external and chronological realities of his present life, the serial fully reveals Marlow's *inner* psychology by plunging the viewer into an expressionistic, non-naturalistic, multi-layered narrative milieu. This is particularly produced through a mixing and merging of different narrative worlds so that the viewer is sometimes left unsure exactly which narrative space they occupy or where each narrative space ends and the next begins.

In an interview with Graham Fuller, Potter describes the different narrative strands at work within the serial as 'routes' that the viewer must follow: 'if you go down one you will meet the other. They're not alternative routes; they're more like a maze, except that each step you take inevitably bumps you against the step you would have taken had you gone somewhere else.'[10] This remark gives some insight into how each narrative layer may be understood. In particular, it is generally agreed by critics that the main narrative levels of the drama can be divided into four distinct 'layers'. Yet I would go further to suggest five important narrative 'layers', the last one being the realm in which all four narrative worlds constantly clash and collide:

- *The hospital scenes:* these make up Philip's present and external 'reality'. They have all the makings of a British hospital situation comedy that sometimes borders on farce, situation comedy, comparable, at times, to the British *Carry On* films (particularly those set in a hospital like *Carry on Nurse* [1959]).
- *Flashbacks:* most of the flashbacks refer back to Philip's childhood in the Forest of Dean and his brief time in London, Hammersmith. These are all set in the 1940s, with the Second World War being a prominent backdrop and an ever-present ingredient in the young Philip's life. This is also reflected in his schooldays, under the ever-watchful eye of a tyrannical schoolmistress. Much less often are flashbacks to his later life. However,

these do occur, such as a Marlow's encounter with a prostitute during the 1960s.
- *The pulp detective novel* (also called *The Singing Detective*): that Marlow has written and is trying to rewrite in his own mind. The style of these scenes is a striking pastiche of typical 1940s film noir in the tradition of a film such as *The Maltese Falcon* (1941), and within them we encounter a typical 'Bogart-like' character which appears to act as the sick Marlow's macho alter-ego (hence the irony of his name, Philip Marlowe being the name of Raymond Chandler's hard-boiled detective).
- *Bizarre hallucinations:* due to Marlow's rising temperature we witness many of the characters in the hospital ward dancing and lip-synching to songs from the 1930s and 1940s, such as 'Dem Bones', 'You Always Hurt the One You Love' and 'Don't Fence me In'. Also within this narrative 'level' perhaps is a paranoia narrative in which Marlow imagines that his wife Nicola is conspiring against him to steal his screenplay with her secret lover.
- *Narrative convergence:* these narrative worlds are never clearly separated but often merge and collide with one another. For example, actors playing characters in the detective novel may also appear as different characters in the childhood flashbacks, or songs and performances of songs may momentarily transcend all four narrative worlds.

The job of the critic is to clarify these narrative levels and to outline each 'layer' clearly and separately. But this type of analysis (as crucial as it is in our understanding of this complex and multi-layered drama) fails to acknowledge that the narrative is perhaps not meant to be watched and understood in such a clear and organised manner. On the contrary, narrative *confusion* characterises much of the *mise-en-scène* of *The Singing Detective*. It is this narrative confusion that the serial is at pains to create and through which the polysemic nature of the text (and by implication, the polysemic nature of the human mind) is able to shine through. From this perspective, it is not actually important that the viewer understands where each narrative level begins and ends (as is it not always clear even to Marlow). However, it is important that the viewers feel and experience Philip's psychological journey alongside him and that they witness (and perhaps even empathise with) the slow meandering of his unconscious mind. In order for the viewer to do this, and before any metaphorical connections can take place, the sense of time passing and a feeling of deep inner reflection needs to be expressed and dramatised on screen. Thus, this sense of movement through layers of narrative time and narrative space is significant not only in terms of the serial's density and complexity but also as the means of constructing a time and space for the viewer's engagement with it.

It is the semiotic confusion produced by the text that allows the viewer (one who is not completely overwhelmed by its narrative complexity) real insight into how Marlow's fevered mind is gradually beginning to piece together the painful, and apparently random, fragments of his life. Indeed, it is precisely the point where all is *not* explained that *The Singing Detective* is at its most polysemic. On one hand, the viewer identifies with Marlow's tortured mind, but is, on the other, driven to try to decipher his story and to fill in gaps and spaces. This is crucial to the serial. If all the narrative strands and visual and aural motifs were clearly and immediately outlined and explained, the viewer would neither be able to experience the difficulty of Marlow's own journey nor, possibly, identify his journey with their own.

To summarise: if *The Singing Detective* is to succeed (if all the narrative strands are eventually to come together), the serial has to take the viewer into, both through identification and decipherment, the slow and gradual process of therapeutic investigation that the protagonist himself is undertaking. This is partly achieved through the serial form, which lends itself well to this type of psychological process (that is, we return to Marlow week after week, the passage between episodes – rather than watching it in one showing on DVD – giving us a sense that the narrative is continually unfolding even when we are not watching). As Glen Creeber points out, this slow serialised passage of time is missing from the recent film version of *The Singing Detective* (starring Robert Downey Jnr and directed by Keith Gordon in 2003) as the original script had to be condensed and contained within the more limited parameters of a Hollywood movie.[11] However, I would argue that this sense of time passing is also achieved through a visual and aural rhythm which is a constant reminder of Marlow's temporal world, creating a 'beat' that underscores the whole serial. As Potter suggested to Graham Fuller, when writing the original script, this 'rhythm' of the narrative came before almost every other narrative priority:

> Some of the scenes of *The Singing Detective* were thirty or forty pages long. Normally in a movie a scene is two pages to two-and-a-half pages, or at the most three or four. But you can get three or four scenes on a page. Sometimes that's necessary; it happens in *The Singing Detective*, for example, and it certainly happens in the screenplays that I've done. But what I want to attend to is the natural shape and rhythm of a particular scene. If it takes twenty pages, it takes twenty pages, and that's something I will not compromise on.[12]

This can be explained by looking in detail at the opening of episode three ('Lovely Days'). While important elements of the story (and Marlow's troubled childhood) are clearly presented for the first time in this short sequence (young Marlow leaving his childhood home and travelling to London with his mother by train, leaving his father behind), the mood and the atmosphere of the sequence is also crucial in creating a sense of time and increasing inner reflection. Throughout, the adult Marlow's thoughts are gently 'swaying' and 'melting' between past, present and fantasy. An analysis of the images and the sounds that create these effects reveals the 'spaces' in the narrative through which meaning is suggested and hinted at rather than didactically contained.

Trains of thought

The use of sound in this sequence illustrates how this sense of Marlow's interior perspective is possibly generated. From the very start of the episode we hear the sound of the train taking the young Philip and his mother to London. This steam train ('chug-chugging' its way along the tracks) not only immediately brings an aural 'rhythm' to the sequence, but also suggests a 'journey'. The connotations of the sound are confirmed visually with the image showing the father waving goodbye to his young son from the station platform.[13] While the movement of the train almost certainly mirrors the viewer's 'movement' into the episode, the train (particularly the use of its sound) will also become the 'vehicle' that effects an easy movement from one narrative level to another. Although the sound of the train subsides in the next narrative space (the song 'Paper Doll' begins as the viewer sees Philip sitting pensively in his hospital bed in the present), the whistle of the train is frequently heard throughout this sequence, often announcing a cut to a different fictional space and sometimes accompanying a particular (seemingly significant) moment or memory. Moreover, when the train's 'chugging' does fade or cease, another sound begins, whether it be a song or another noise, continuing the rhythm of the train and the slow progress of the narrative in its absence.

For example, after the slow dissolve from the young Philip in the train to the nurse asleep on Marlow's hospital ward (in the present), the sound of the train and the song slowly (almost seamlessly) bleed into the sound of a heart monitor. Although the heart monitor creates a gentler mood of calmness, it still continues a similar 'rhythm' originally set in motion by the train. The steady 'blip' of the heart monitor also appears to reflect the steady breathing of the patients (their chests slowly rise and fall in their sleep), and helps to create a dream-like quality (perhaps also a sensation of deep thought) that corresponds to Marlow's own state of mind. This aural and visual rhythm adds to the seamless progress of the different narrative layers, but it also evokes a feeling of deep introspection and thoughtful meditation, emphasised by an awake (and clearly troubled) Philip musing over painful memories.

In this way, the calmness of these hospital scenes help to mirror Marlow's own reflective thought process, the 'ticking' of the heart monitor perhaps subtly suggesting the subtle 'ticking over' of his mind. Nevertheless, as he begins to hear his mother's questioning voice something else 'clicks' inside his head that prompts the cut to the next, slightly faster, edited sequence. Even quicker than the previous scene that featured the young Philip, these shots suggest a kind of frenzied state of panic. Clearly, a *realisation* has occurred which connects these quick cuts of the train in the tunnel with his thoughts about his mother.

As this suggests, the very pace and rhythm of the narrative is crucial to, and underpins, its overall structure and meaning. Firstly, the duration of scenes, and the juxtaposition and pace of the shots within them, create a particular sense of mood and atmosphere. In this extract, the scenes vary enormously in terms of time and pace, conveying the speed at which Marlow is slowly beginning to unravel the psychological 'puzzle' before him. Secondly, when Marlow reaches a key point of realisation or personal pain, the pace of the shots mirror or reinforce his moment of epiphany.

In addition to the 'beat' of the train and the heart monitor, 'Paper Doll', one of the popular songs from the 1930s and 1940s that recurs throughout the serial, appears on the soundtrack. Again, the sound creates connections between and across numerous narrative segments. The songs are all from the 1940s, the time of Marlow's childhood and the period of his own novel, adding a convenient connection between these two disparate narrative levels; but they also, like the other sounds, reveal insights into Marlow's innermost thoughts and desires. As in many other parts of the narrative, here 'Paper Doll' works to bind his memories and fantasies together. In keeping with most of the songs in the serial, the lyrics revolve around women, betrayal and sexuality. It is the father who first 'lip-synchs' to the song, then we see the Bogart-like singing detective crooning its lyrics, but it is also possibly a reminder of the mother's sexual betrayal in the forest. The song's lyrics emphasise the idea of one woman belonging to one man, almost like a possession ('I'm going to buy a paper doll that I can call my own, a doll that other fellows cannot steal ...').

Indeed, the young Philip and his mother are actually leaving for London as a direct consequence of her adultery. Thus, when the father is seen lip-synching the song, the lyrics are tinged with intense sadness and regret. However, when the lyrics are associated with the mother (when, for example, the soldiers lip-synch in the carriage in which she and Philip sit), they become more sinister. The song therefore serves a double function: while binding narrative strands together and making the movement in and out of diverse fictional spaces seamless and fluid, it also hints at aspects of Marlow's psychosexual neurosis. Certainly, Potter made no secret of the fact that the songs were used in a very deliberate and calculated manner to reveal deep anxieties. As he told Fuller:

> In *The Singing Detective*, Marlow, sick, trying to reassemble himself, was resisting them, didn't believe in them, or only believed in them in the way he believed in his cheap thrillers. The songs played the same kind of function as his story, his cheap detective novel, which sneaked up on him and revealed to him how much of his own life was in them; how much of his own misogyny and self-pity and his own inner myth was bound up with this cheap writing. In *Pennies [From Heaven]* the songs were believed in by the character. In *The Singing Detective* they were hard little stones being thrown at Marlow... In *The Singing Detective*, the cheap fiction, the illness and the cheap songs – well, not so cheap – were together conspiring to force him to recognize what he was: stark, stripped down, with nothing but a ferocious rhetoric, plus self-pity.[14]

Yet, how this insight into Marlow's mind is achieved through the use of popular music is surprisingly subtle and complex. Seen from a contemporary view the song seems shockingly sexist: the desired 'paper doll' would replace a real woman to control her and stop her from straying, thus transforming her into something lifeless, objectified, a subject of man's will. The Singing Detective's version (set in the past) is perhaps simply anachronistic (his Bogart persona would clearly not understand its pre-feminist nuances), but sung by Marlow's sad and mournful father it becomes imbued with the care and longing of a man deep in pain. Furthermore, Marlow's memory of the song may be a symptom of his own personal problems, an old-school misogynist whose difficulties with women and sex are probably at the root of his painful illness and psychological unease.[15] So to give this song one meaning or to attempt to tie meaning down would clearly be reductive. Indeed, it is the polysemic nature of this and the other songs in the serial (particularly as they have 'travelled' from the 1940s to the present) that gives them potency and brings so many meanings to their deceptively 'banal' and 'sugary' melodies. As K. J. Donnelly puts it, film and television music (and sound) is rarely about producing conclusive or didactic meaning, it is often indicative of more subtle inflections of mood, atmosphere and occasional 'elsewheres':

> the soundscape itself might be conceived as an analogue to the virtual space of mental processes, as a repository of half-memories, primal emotion and the seemingly illogical. 'Ghosts' inhabiting a film are often little more than shapes, momentary musical configurations or half-remembered sounds. Music can suggest, or even lead directly to, an elsewhere, like a footnote.[16]

Throughout the whole of this excerpt there is never a moment of complete silence: the sounds and the music, whether they are at the forefront or tugging away in the background, are always there. The concept of the serial as a whole revolves around the erosion of time, which is then underscored and reflected in its rhythm or 'beat'. The chugging of the train, the beeping of the heart monitor, even the languid rhythm of the song, all create a sense of the inexorable and inevitable feeling of the passing of time. Whether it is the psychological 'time' of Marlow's mind or the linear, chronological 'time' of the hospital ward, the beat of life is constantly heard, thus creating a sense of temporal flow regarding Philip's present condition and the slow process of his recovery. The sense of 'intimacy' and 'immediacy' associated with the process of watching television, combined with this sense of urgency, heightens the serial's emotional trajectory.[17] Thus, these aural elements work independently from the visual imagery and draw the viewer emotionally into the serial, the allure of its rhythm continually unravelling more 'clues' along Marlow's psychological journey.

Signs and synchronicity

This sequence is no less complex in its use of visual motifs and imagery. A key recurring image is the father's wave from the platform of the station to his son (fig. 1). The young Marlow leans out of the window to wave back while his mother sits, seemingly unconcerned, in the carriage. The father's sad wave later returns in two separate contexts: first, copied exactly by a scarecrow standing in the field that the young Marlow spies from his train carriage (fig. 2) and then by the 'Singing Detective' in a fantasy sequence, as he 'sings' 'Paper Doll' (fig. 3). When the scarecrow assumes the father's pose, the eerie music of the detective story is heard (often connected to Philip stumbling across a psychological 'clue'). In the following shot we see and hear the speed of the train quicken, perhaps reflecting his increasing panic, before the cut into the next scene. Something has now 'clicked' in Marlow's mind, even though neither he nor the viewer may yet understand its significance. The scarecrow, then, perhaps acts as a symbol of interchange between the unconscious and conscious mind, an image of deep psychological unease.

Yet, to make matters more confusing, during this sequence the scarecrow morphs into a frightening caricature of Hitler (fig. 4), whose distorted face is suspiciously like that of Marlow's frightening schoolmistress (played by Janet Henfrey). Further connotations suggest themselves: there could certainly be a clear connection between Hitler and this domineering teacher. The young Philip lives in fear of both, and the iconography of the scarecrow is often traditionally connected with witchcraft and the occult, perhaps also reflecting a wider social paranoia related to the war. As it mimics Mr Marlow's wave, connections can also be drawn between this inhuman figure and his own repressed father. Marlow's father is, however, unlike the frightening figures of Hitler or the schoolmistress, so the association never seems to be made clear. Indeed, if such literal connections were made they could appear dangerously simplistic and perhaps suggest little about the complex means by which an image like the scarecrow may actually work.

Figures 1–4 *The Singing Detective*

The scarecrow is clearly a densely complicated image invested with more meaning than any viewer could immediately decode. Even for the bed-ridden Marlow, the image of the scarecrow and his symbolic significance does not seem entirely transparent. Just as the sound of the train that 'bleeds' between scenes becomes connected with other sounds, the formal devices that displace the wave create a shift between narrative levels. These displacements work as 'floating signifiers', producing a form of dramatic 'free association' within the narrative itself. As a 'floating signifier' the scarecrow means many things to Marlow, some of which can be explicitly understood, others which hint at deeper, unconscious connections that are left hanging.

Perhaps what is most important here is that the images of the father, the singing detective, the schoolmistress and Hitler, do not cohere into a logical sequence. They are signifiers of Marlow's deeply troubled state and lead back to his journey away from his childhood home, signified ultimately by the sight of his forlorn father waving him goodbye. As this sequence flickers quickly across the screen (much like the images we might watch from the window of a train), the viewer perhaps is meant to share the sense of deep reflection that Marlow is now experiencing. 'All clues, no solutions. That's the way things are', Marlow says later on in the serial.[18] Of course, he does find *some* solutions to these 'clues' (and does finally begin to recover from his illness), but not even he expects to untie and understand everything. The song at the end of the serial, Vera Lynn's 'We'll Meet Again', signifies that Philip's understanding of his psychological problems will never truly be 'complete' and that the 'semiotic excess' that confronts him around every corner is filled with as many 'red herrings' as 'clues'.

As many critics point out, *The Singing Detective* is a loosely 'Freudian' piece of work, dramatising one man's therapeutic search for psychological recovery by exploring and re-examining his own past life.[19] In particular, it dramatises the way that unconscious repression will eventually damage the human psyche (even, as in this case, creating symptoms on the human body itself), unless its source is gradually and carefully exposed and acknowledged by the subject. Freud used free association in therapy to freely allow the patient's mind to associate ideas in order to uncover 'clues' to traumatic memories. This process is reflected in *The Singing Detective* (its structure, content and style), as it is in many modernist novels.[20] Everything on screen is potentially relevant, although not always decipherable, as symptoms of Marlow's cathartic and profoundly psychological journey. However, perhaps the clear significance of Freud has overshadowed the relevance of Jung to an examination of Potter's narrative universe and the distinctively experimental style of its *mise-en-scène*. In particular, Jung's notion of *synchronicity* suggests a possible way of interpreting the more 'polysemic' elements in *The Singing Detective*.

Jung uses the term synchronicity to convey the idea of 'meaningful coincidence': how chance events are connected in such a way that their occurrence seems to defy the calculations of probability. In other words, these 'coincidences' are not merely accidental but suggest a deeper and underlining meaning at work. Synchronicity can be likened to déjà-vu: the sense that something has happened before or the feeling that an event was somehow 'predestined'. For Jung, little is coincidental: chance reflects and hints at deeper connections taking place within a wider alignment of 'universal forces'.[21] In particular, he connected synchronicity to his notion of the 'collective unconscious': the belief that we all share a collection of 'myths' or 'archetypes' that inform our understanding of the world. It is at moments of synchronicity that we are briefly allowed a glimpse into the overall, inherently meaningful, structure of the human universe. As Peter A. Jordan explains:

> Because Jung believed the phenomenon of synchronicity was primarily connected with psychic conditions, he felt that such couplings of inner (subjective) and outer (objective) reality evolved through the influence of the archetypes, patterns inherent in the human psyche and shared by all of mankind. These patterns, or 'primordial images', as Jung sometimes refers to them, comprise man's collective unconscious, representing the dynamic source of all human confrontation with death, conflict, love, sex, rebirth and mystical experience. When an archetype is activated by an emotionally charged event (such as a tragedy), says Jung, other related events tend to draw near. In this way the archetypes become a doorway that provide us access to the experience of meaningful (and often insightful) coincidence.[22]

John Izod is one of the few critics to have explicitly used Jungian psychoanalysis to interpret Potter's work, particularly in relation to his last two posthumous serials, *Karaoke* (BBC/Channel 4, 1996) and *Cold Lazarus* (Channel 4/BBC, 1996). For Izod, Daniel Feeld's (Albert Finney) belief in *Karaoke* that the people around him are reciting words from his own script is a clue to synchronicity at work within the drama as a whole. He argues that Feeld's 'anxiety produces a nightmare vision in which the archetypes have complete power to determine the tenor of the individual's life and consciousness and experience count for almost nothing'.[23] Certainly, Marlow does seem to share a similar feeling of déjà-vu; the aural and visual motifs and repetitions that are so carefully woven into the *mise-en-scène* suggesting that everything he witnesses is part of some wider psychic experience that he can never fully comprehend.

The frequent repetition of the drama's narrative and visual motifs further suggests synchronicity. Both visual and aural repetition could be seen as adding a crucial sense of déjà vu to the viewing experience that has often been ignored by more 'prescriptive' Freudian interpretations. The recurring noise of the train or the mirroring of the wave by different characters and figures suggest that all elements in the drama are interconnected and that Marlow is sifting through old memories, so that the images and their role in the story are randomly but intimately connected, as though in a maze. It is not necessary that the full significance of all the images on view should be comprehensible, but how they shift and slide together (similar to the processes of displacement and condensation) is important. Ultimately, they build up into a rich and dense insight into the very process of self-knowledge. The appearance of different characters played by the same actor produces a similar effect. The significance of this type of 'doubling' may not be apparent nor is it always meant to be. But the viewer is made aware of the complexity and interconnectedness of Marlow's thought processes, and the way that they all are part of some wider and deeper network of 'universal forces'.

In this way, the process of decipherment is essential to the mode of address built into *The Singing Detective*. This process constructs a particular kind of viewer who is forced to struggle to make sense of all the images and the seemingly disparate narrative strands (and visual/aural motifs). Through this struggle to decipher, the viewer is 'bonded' with Marlow's own dilemma, and thus effectively 'journeys' with him through a maze of 'clues' that gradually begin to form a 'whole' out of all the serial's colliding fragments. This is not because the meaning is coherent, but because it is always threatening to shift and transform itself.

The scarecrow remains an indecipherable image. It is probably a shadow of something that haunts Marlow, a 'ghost' or 'primal emotion' that can never be entirely deduced or explained. As such, it also suggests a symbolic moment of déjà vu or synchronicity with the realisation that his father's sad wave no longer belongs to a single moment of time. Seen in this light, *The Singing Detective* should not be comprehended as a serial with a straightforward teleological structure; rather, its intricate narrative maze reveals the complexity and indeterminacy of a world that none of us will ever completely understand.

Conclusion

The Singing Detective is not so much about universal truths as the personal truths that litter and inform all human life. It is about building and understanding the ambiguities of identity in the most desperate of situations. It asks of its audience an active collaboration in the production of meaning, a relationship that encourages meaning to be sought after and decoded rather than simply perceived. It is the density of its narrative readings that is the greatest legacy of the serial as it intuitively recognises and appreciates the democratic potential of television's textuality. As John Fiske explains with reference to the 'producerly text':

> The producerly text ... draws attention to its own textuality, it does not produce a singular reading subject but one that is involved in the process of representation rather than a victim of it, it plays with the difference between the representation and the real as a producerly equivalent of the writerly mixing of documentary and fictional modes, and it replaces the pleasures of identification and familiarity with more cognitive pleasures of participation and production ... it treats its readers as members of a semiotic democracy, already equipped with the discursive competencies to make meanings and motivated by pleasure to want to participate in the process.[24]

It is the richness of *The Singing Detective* that makes the varied readings, Fiske's 'semiotic democracy', so possible, even desirable. While Marlow's personal search is unmistakable, each viewer will inevitably perceive that journey in their own way and bring their own experiences to bear on that voyage of discovery. Polysemy does not imply that *any* reading is possible, or that the text itself is not 'connected' in some way to multiple readings; it suggests that it is within a text's 'spaces' and 'gaps' that its meaning is generated. Perhaps one of the most important characteristics of experimental drama is this ability to suggest where meaning might reside but never to insist that this is the only meaning that there is. Above all, *The Singing Detective* is a serial about the events that define the human mind, things that can only rarely be grasped except, perhaps, on those unusual occasions of psychic insight or 'synchronicity'. Indeed, to reduce the serial to a unifying, homogenous whole would ultimately undermine the very means by which it ceaselessly attempts to suggest the endless possibility and potential of human memory, creativity and interpretation.

Notes

1 John Ellis, *Seeing Things: Television in the Age of Uncertainty* (London: I. B. Tauris, 2000), 82.
2 See Joost Hunniger, '*The Singing Detective*: Who Done It?', in George W. Brandt

(ed.), *British Television Drama in the 1980s* (Cambridge University Press, 1993), 234–57.
3   See Glen Creeber, *Dennis Potter, Between Two Worlds: A Critical Reappraisal* (Basingstoke: Macmillan, 1998), 11–19.
4   John Thornton Caldwell, *Televisuality: Style, Crisis and Authority in American Television* (New Brunswick, New Jersey: Rutgers University Press, 1995), 149.
5   Ibid.
6   John Fiske, 'Television: Polysemy and Popularity', in Roger Dickinson, Ramaswani Harindranath and Olga Linné (eds), *Approaches to Audiences: A Reader* (London and New York: Arnold, 1998), 195.
7   See John Cook, *Dennis Potter: A Life on Screen* (Manchester: Manchester University Press, 1998), 30.
8   John Caughie, *Television Drama: Realism, Modernism and British Culture* (Oxford: Oxford University Press, 2000), 167. What Caughie means by this is that it is possible to connect Potter's drama to a grand modernist tradition of artists and practitioners who believed that any representation of a psychological 'reality' needed, by its very nature, to break up and distort the conventional and habitual forms of representation to reveal the 'inner consciousness' of the human mind. As such, modernist writers and artists were obsessed with trying to capture the sheer complexity of life as it is actually experienced in the subjective moment rather than from an objective exterior. As Peter Childs points out, in *The Wasteland* T. S. Eliot declares that mental life is composed of 'memory' and 'desire' – 'the past and the future organised in the individual mind in the present' (Childs, *Modernism* (London and New York: Routledge, 2000), 50.)
9   Whilst working as a Fleet Street journalist during the winter of 1961–62 Potter was suddenly struck by this illness which would plague him for the rest of his life. For many years the condition would turn the dramatist into a virtual recluse, perhaps contributing to his 'interior' vision of 'reality'. For more details about the writer's life see Humphrey Carpenter, *Dennis Potter: The Authorised Biography* (London: Faber & Faber, 1998).
10 Quoted in Graham Fuller, *Potter on Potter* (London: Faber & Faber, 1993), 93.
11 Glen Creeber, *Serial Television: Big Drama on the Small Screen* (London: BFI, 2004), 5–6.
12 Quoted in Fuller, *Potter on Potter*, 95.
13 On the station platform is a war-time poster asking travellers: 'Is Your Journey Really Necessary?'. Of course, this is an ironic comment on Marlow's sad situation, embarking on a tragic journey with his mother that will eventually lead to deep psychological scars and perhaps could have been easily avoided.
14 Quoted in Fuller, *Potter on Potter*, 87.
15 See Creeber, *Dennis Potter, Between Two Worlds*, 166–78.
16 K. J. Donnelly, *The Spectre of Sound: Music in Film and Television* (London: BFI, 2005), 172.
17 The notion of intimacy appears to be one that has continued to be explored and theorised by more contemporary critics and academics alike. According to John

Ellis's influential discussion of film and television aesthetics in *Visible Fictions*, first published in 1982, televisual direct address to camera serves to generate a unique and particular kind of 'closeness' between viewer and speaker. For Ellis, while 'the cinema close-up accentuates the difference between screen-figure and attainable human figure by drastically reducing its size, the broadcast television close-up produces a face that approximates to normal size – instead of an effect of distance and unattainability, the television close-up generates an equality and even intimacy' (132). Similarly, Horace Newcomb, in his 1974 study *Television: The Most Popular Art*, claims that 'the iconography of rooms is far more important to television than is that of exterior locations' (247).

18 Dennis Potter, *The Singing Detective* (London: Faber & Faber, 1996), 140.
19 For Freudian interpretations of *The Singing Detective* see Creeber, *Between Two Worlds*; Therese Lichtenstein, 'Syncopated Thriller: Dennis Potter's *The Singing Detective*', *Artforum* (May, 1990), 168–72; and Paul Delany 'Potterland', *Dalhousie Review*, 68: 4 (1988), 511–21. Surprisingly perhaps, one of the first and largest academic accounts of Potter's work, Cook's *Dennis Potter: A Life on Screen*, fails to barely mention Freud (his name not even listed in its index).
20 Following Freud's psychoanalytic theories at the turn of the century, emphasis was increasingly placed on the human mind and a belief in solipsism (that nothing is real except for one's own psyche) was born. Writers such as James Joyce and Virginia Woolf seemed to reflect these beliefs in literature, arguing that it was no longer adequate to present verisimilitude or 'external realism' in art. Instead, these writers attempted to explore, examine and represent underlying or *interior* dreams and desires, dealing in, what William James (the psychologist brother of Henry) coined as a 'stream of consciousness' or 'psychological realism'. Indeed, John Middleton Murray stated in his influential essay *The Break Up of the Novel* that for modernist writers across Europe and America, 'inner consciousness *is* reality' (cited in Childs, 2000: 46).
21 See Carl Gustav Jung, *The Structure and Dynamics of the Psyche*, trans. R. F. C. Hull (London and New York: Routledge, 1970).
22 Peter A. Jordon, 'The Mystery of Chance: Jung and Synchronicity', *Strange Magazine*, 2005, www.strangemag.com/mysteryofchance.html, accessed April 2006.
23 John Izod, *Myth Mind and the Screen: Understanding the Heroes of Our Time* (Cambridge: Cambridge University Press, 2001), 172.
24 John Fiske, *Television Culture* (London and New York: Routledge, 1987), 95.

8

Visions: a Channel 4 experiment 1982–85

John Ellis

Any experiment in broadcast television is forced to come to terms with the overarching structures of television as it is lived at a specific time. The broadcast model has dominated television since its inception. So any work that seeks to further another form of television (that is, not that of broadcasting) is, by definition, an experiment. The structures of broadcasting are those of the schedule, intimately linked to the rituals and habits of the domestic spaces into which broadcasting projects itself. In broadcasting, experiment is perhaps more about the structures of the medium than the creation of specific texts. Indeed, my first experience of television work in the 1980s with Channel 4 led me to believe that any thorough form of experimental programming requires an address to the form of the broadcast flow. There now exist many general accounts of the foundation and early years of this channel, including own. This account is much more specific.

10 November 1982, the second week of the new channel's existence, saw the launch of *Visions*, a novel series about cinema. *Visions* was made by an independent production company, Large Door Ltd, founded for that sole purpose by Simon Hartog, Keith Griffiths (producers) and myself, billed as series editor. Like most other production companies working for the new channel, we believed in its statutory mission, "to encourage innovation and experiment in the form and content of programmes".[1] To write about *Visions* twenty years after the series ended is to explore a now almost forgotten concrete attempt to realise something of these aims. According to the channel controller, Jeremy Isaacs, 'Film culture demanded that we have a serious regular programme about cinema. But *Visions*, the channel's film magazine, though it ran various excellent items, never quite caught on.'[2] This is why.

In 1982, the sole regular TV programme devoted to cinema was *Film 82*, a long-running BBC1 review show hosted by Barry Norman. Arts documentary series like ITV's *South Bank Show*, BBC1's *Omnibus* and BBC2's *Arena* sometimes featured documentaries about cinema. No other TV channels existed in the UK at that point. Although by present standards there were a large number of subtitled films on these channels,³ the coverage of cinema centred on Hollywood, particularly on Film 82. Large Door Ltd was founded to propose to Channel 4 a series which would predominantly centre on other cinemas, covering some of the new releases on the art-cinema circuit, neglected or recently discovered cinemas, and take the occasional critical look at the films in commercial cinemas. This was the period in which Chinese cinema was just becoming known in the West, thanks in part to the work of the critic Tony Rayns, who was heavily involved in the *Visions* project. It was also the period in which the BFI was carrying on a cultural politics of cinema, centred on a circuit of regional film theatres and radical critical and analytic practices fostered principally by its education department. It was also the period in which a radical independent cinema had begun to articulate new film forms, in part financed through the BFI's production fund and Arts Council funded regional arts associations. Over it all loomed the relatively new government of Margaret Thatcher, which at that time took a fairly laisser-faire attitude to culture, though it was later to mount a direct attack on the BBC. The Thatcher government created Channel 4 as an instrument of 'freedom'. It saw the idea of a channel that commissioned from others rather than making its own programmes as a means of bringing market economics into the closed circuit of TV broadcasting. The project, however, had been conceived with quite another conception of 'freedom' in mind: freedom of speech and expression. Both sides can claim significant successes for their conception. Broadcasting has indeed become marketised; and a degree of freedom of expression that was unthinkable in 1980 has now been achieved.

It was, therefore, a strange and exciting moment to launch a bold new TV series on cinema. There was considerable activity to draw upon. The contents of the first few *Visions* programmes demonstrates the breadth of the agenda which we had set ourselves.

- 10 NOVEMBER 1982
  Cinema, Cinema: a montage of film clips acting as a prospectus for the series, assembled by Tony Rayns
  An interview with Paul Schrader on the release of *Cat People*
  Angela Carter reviews Peter Greenaway's Draughtsman's Contract (15-minute review with extensive clips)
- 24 NOVEMBER 1982
  Ivor Montagu interviewed by Stuart Hood on his work with Hitchcock, Eisenstein and communist film politics
  British Exhibition Today: a survey of different forms of cinema activity presented by Susan Barrowclough

- 8 DECEMBER 1982
  Festival des Trois Continents: a report from the third cinema festival held in Nantes in November
  French Film Policy: an interview with culture minister Jack Lang
- 22 DECEMBER 1982
  Special Effects: the development of British special effects from *Fireball XL5* to *Superman*, a documentary presented by Lynda Myles
  ET and Tron: a comparison between two current sci-fi releases by John Ellis
  Gandhi: a review of Richard Attenborough's epic by writer Farrukh Dhondy
- 19 JANUARY 1983
  The Cannon Classics Group: a report gate crashing the annual convention of this distinctly dodgy would-be UK cinema major
  Michael Snow: the doyen of the avant-garde interviewed on the opening of a major retrospective in London.

Already some of the intended features of the series made themselves clear. There is an eclectic range of films from the commercial to the most resolutely non-commercial. Where commercial cinema is addressed, it is done so critically and coolly. Reviews of specific films were presented by unusual and often critical voices. Dustin Hoffman, in London to launch his drag performance in *Tootsie*, took particular exception to the *Visions* review of the film by two gay activists on 27 April 1983, and refused to appear on any Channel 4 talk show. The series tried to address the present moment, but at the same time remain resolutely different.

As the series developed, this difference became more marked in the aesthetic of the items in the programmes. The predominantly documentary or direct address format of these early programmes began to give way to a more idiosyncratic approach: a moody essay on Wenders by Chris Petit; an item on Syberberg's film of Wagner's *Parsifal* that managed to include marionettes; a screening of Jean-Luc Godard's mediation on his own film *Passion*. The final series of *Visions*, a monthly magazine running from October 1984 to July 1985 emphasised this authorial approach. It offered the opportunity to produce a montage essay on the month's releases to filmmakers like Peter Wollen, Neil Jordan, Michael Eaton and Sally Potter. It commissioned short films from Chantal Akerman, Marc Karlin and Keith Griffiths, and bought in another made by Raul Ruiz. The idea of a montage essay was novel and had not been tried before, to our knowledge. The commissioning of shorts on filmrelated subjects from filmmakers was derived from the French series *Cinema, Cinemas*.[4] This series, which also started in 1982, came to provide something of a model, and *Visions* offered a selection from the series on 23 May 1984.

Visions had an underlying seriousness of tone, which was criticised even at the time by the commissioning editor Paul Madden. This was by no means unusual in the early days of Channel 4, which ran a programme called Opinions in which an activist or intellectual read prepared text from an autocue to fill a half-hour slot. Such 'seriousness' resulted from the desire to say something predominating over the need to say it in a way suitable to television.There was a lot that needed saying at that time, as the traditional British left was feeling the impact of the new politics of Thatcherism, as Stuart Hall had named it.[5] Largely impotent in the political arena, and, increasingly after the miners strike of 1984–85, in the streets and workplaces as well, many of the left found a refuge of sorts around Channel 4. "The channel", as it tellingly became known, was conducting an experiment in the rules of TV discourse. It was shifting the then mandatory broadcasting practice of 'balance', and replacing it with programmes that asserted particular points of view rather than constructing a discourse that sought to mediate between points of view. Many of Channel 4's attempts at innovation, like Opinions, took such a form. But they were definitely not experiments in the forms and aesthetics of television itself.

The seriousness of Visions was slightly different. The series rested on the tone of seriousness found in many contemporary analytic discourses about cinema, particularly around journals like Screen, Framework and Afterimage. It compounded this by asserting the importance of what were, to much of the audience, novel forms of cinema. If Visions did have a problem, it lay in a seriousness that assumed rather than presented the pleasures of those forms of cinema. Sometimes it worked, especially if the film clips managed to engage and thrill even when truncated. At other times, it seemed, the combination of clip and critic or director commentary simply failed to communicate the pleasures of the large screen, or indeed militated against them. Criticisms of the series at the time tended to include the word 'wilful' as in 'wilfully obscure' or 'wilfully eccentric'.

Some of the problems of early Channel 4 programmes, shared by Visions, also arose from the restricted costs and restrictive technology of the period. Channel 4's budgets were necessarily strained, and series like Opinions filled slots at prices lower even than bought-in US programming. The first 15 programmes of Visions were made for a budget of just under £500,000, giving an average budget of under £34,000 per programme, which would not buy a huge amount even using today's far cheaper technology. From the outset it was decided that the bulk of this money should be spent on a number of filmed documentaries covering the cinema of the Far East. This produced one of the most successful, or at least most widely exported, programme Cinema in China directed by Ron Orders and presented by Tony

Rayns. Outlining the history of Chinese cinema since the 1920s and including interviews with veterans like Sun Yu, Shen Fu and Xie Jin (shown shooting *The Herdsman*), this programme was still being screened in the USA in the mid-1990s. Reports from remote locations like China, Philippines and Nicaragua were shot on film because tape was not a practical originating format at the time in such places. These programmes were almost all completed on tape, however. The main reason for this was the ability to telecine extracts from films. Unbelievable as it now seems in this era of piracy, the major distributors lent us reels from their upcoming releases so that we could telecine our chosen extracts. This facility was extended even at the Cannes Film Festival, to which were devoted most of the programmes on 25 May 1983 and 29 May 1985. Nowadays, an electronic press pack provides pre-chosen, mandatory clips, a development that began in the UK as the *Visions* series was coming to an end.

Without this access to telecine, the *Visions* approach to cinema would have been impossible. Video also enabled us to record longer interviews, work with chromakey, to shoot quickly, and to put together items like the late Mary Holland's commentary on Edward Bennett's first feature *Ascendancy* (25 May 1983) in less than a week. But this use of video came with certain drawbacks, especially in terms of visual style and cutting rate. Video recording was still on 1-inch reel-to-reel tape which required a crew of at least two and had a limited tolerance for contrasting light levels within the frame. Editing was carried out on what now seems a cumbersome linear system, computer-driven but effectively copying from one tape to another using up to three input machines. When a new input tape was required, one existing one had to be spooled to the beginning, taken off the deck and the new one put up. The output player was then adjusted for the levels of this new tape which was then spooled down to the required shot. This took time. Editing was not quite frame accurate, so the trimming out of pauses or other techniques that required fast cutting and a short shot length were effectively not an option. Complex visual effects were also to be avoided because online editing suites were in short supply in the early 1980s and were being worked on a 24-hour basis. It was common for the previous booking to overrun by several hours. Editing was something of an activity of informed guesswork as offline editing was a rarity. It was out of the reach of most productions until late 1983 when the first VHS offline suites became available. All of this militated against any overt stylishness in early programmes.

Visions did introduce one stylistic trait from the outset, however. This was the framing of its film clips. All were shown in their correct aspect ratio, framed by a white line, a kind of audiovisual quotation mark. This enabled a more adventurous transition between film clip and other material, especially in the more experimental work of the series. However, as with all such devices, it relied on audience familiarity. This was particularly the case with Keith Griffiths's *The Cabinet of Jan Svankmajer*, which introduced the work of this Czech animator to British audiences. Extensive extracts from his films including the complete film *Dimensions of Dialogue* (all displayed within the electronic frame) were combined with comments from six art and film critics, plus animated sequences by the Brothers Quay which provided a meditation on the bricoleur activity of Svankmajer the animator. Anecdotally, it appears that some viewers still missed the distinction between Svankmajer and Quay in the programme.

The framing device was intended to indicate the transition between material derived from cinema and that produced by the programme itself. This was necessary as the series deliberately tried to adopt an aesthetic approach derived from cinema. However, the fact that production deadline pressures required the adoption of videotape as the basic production format often worked against this. Where items needed a fast cutting pace, this was often impossible given the technology and budgets available; where attention to the detail of visual style was called for, the limitations of video at that time often became painfully obvious. However, one aspect of cinema remained at the heart of the series' approach: the attitude of always trying something new, of modest experiment. Each programme was conceived as an adventure, in which there were no standard features to items. This was an attempt to integrate into the texture of the programmes themselves something of the excitement and unpredictability that lay at the heart of our experience of cinema. Outside the mainstream of filmmaking, it seemed, one never quite knew what to expect. *Visions* tried to replicate this experience in its own shape as a series, but this in many ways was the main reason why it never quite worked.

The *Visions* series was ambitious. It used video when few others were doing so for arts programming. It married the journalistic approach of Simon Hartog with the aesthetic ambitions of Keith Griffiths and added an approach that I had derived from involvement with *Screen* magazine. It was an experiment in TV that had a relatively long life. Yet it never quite fulfilled its potential. The fundamental reason for this lay not with the variable quality of different programmes, since that variability is a fact of almost every series ever made. Some editions are better than others for all sorts of reasons: because fewer mistakes are made, because the team works with a single objective, because the programme hits a moment of wider relevance, because everyone around seems to be watching, or because a formal and performance unity are achieved. But as an experiment, the *Visions* series' imperfections were more visible than its achievements for one fundamental reason. It was never scheduled as a series, so it did not have the regularity of pattern that its experiments tended to assume. It was an office joke that the series never had the same starting time twice.

The series was commissioned by Paul Madden at Channel 4 because it was one of the very few proposals in the months before the launch of the new channel that took an overtly topical approach to cinema. There were many proposals for films or series dealing with particular aspects of cinema: director profiles, national cinema surveys and even polemics. But the series that became *Visions* was rare if not unique in trying to address the films that people could go and see at the time when those films were available. The initial proposal envisaged a far closer link to Channel 4's own film screenings, which were extensive in the 1980s and later led to the formation of the Film Four channels, initially as a subscription offering only and from 2006 as a free-to-air digital service.

However, the links with Channel 4's own offerings proved virtually impossible in practice. Early scheduling of films was a short-term hand-to-mouth affair, so it was impossible to link the making of a documentary with a lead time of three or four months to any season of films from a particular country or director (the main classifications at the time) since film seasons were planned just weeks in advance. Editorially, Channel 4 preferred the format of a short 3 or 4 minute introduction by a critic to each film rather than a free-standing documentary. So this aspect of the proposal was hardly ever realised. *Visions* was, therefore, principally concerned with current cinema releases, to which it took a strong editorial line, championing the little known and the difficult, and asking awkward questions of mainstream releases.

From the outset, the series sat uneasily in what began to emerge as Channel 4's scheduling pattern. British schedules in the early 1980s did not have the settled pattern of half-hours they now have. Slots could vary in length, especially on BBC2, whose flagship social documentary series was called *40 Minutes* after its distinctive slot length. Where programmes or bought-in feature films dictated a slot length that did not fit a 30 or 60 minute pattern it was difficult to pad the slot out, as is now often the case. There was a lack of promotional trailers and strict regulatory limitations on the total amount of advertising permitted in an hour. The result, even on Channel 4 which screened commercials, was a variable start time for late evening programmes, especially when scheduled after a feature film as *Visions* often was (the schedulers hoping for a certain amount of audience inheritance). Hence, there was never twice the same start time. Schedulers were also prone to trying isolated experiments without consultation with either producers or commissioning editors. The programme of 27 February 1985, designed for a late slot (examining Hungarian and Nicaraguan cinema) was pulled forward to a 9 p.m. slot. It was not a suitable case for such treatment, whereas the preceding programme on 16 January might have been, since it featured British cinema of 1945 on its 40th anniversary and a quirky view of the pre-cinema machines displayed in the newly opened Deutschesfilmmuseum. Such a change of slot in the middle of the series did not help with winning the familiarity that goes with regularity.

However, regularity and the visibility that it brings eluded *Visions*. The dates of this scheduler's experiment show that *Visions*, now in its third series, had become a monthly magazine series which ran for a year. The second series (May and June 1994) had consisted of a conventional series of six one hour-slot length documentaries, including *The Cabinet of Jan Svankmajer*; a survey of contemporary Italian cinema including a rare interview with Sergio Leone; an investigation of the problems of African cinema seen through the cases of the adjacent countries Madagascar, Mozambique and Zimbabwe; and an extended conversation between two British directors, Wendy Toye and Sally Potter. The first series was also a magazine programme of 15 episodes alternating with an intellectual discussion programme named *Voices*. This was a starkly contrasting format to *Visions* as it was an invariable format of studio discussion between figures like Isaiah Berlin, Bruno Bettelheim, Octavio Paz, George Steiner, Susan Sontag and John Berger, produced by the late Udi Eichler.[6] The alternation at least provided a slender sense of regularity for each programme, but also a level of confusion, this being an altogether unfamiliar channel in what had become a very settled broadcasting ecology. The production company of each series received letters intended for the other, even on occasions from Channel 4 itself.

Channel 4 was the first new channel to be launched in British TV since BBC2 almost twenty years before. No one involved realised how much was required to change the audience's long-established viewing habits. Those of us producing programmes tended to assume that the startling nature of what we tried to offer would be a sufficient attraction, and this approach was to a large extent shared by the channel's senior executives. Early schedules offered a bewildering variety of programming, many of them one-offs or short series, with very few fixed points other than a nightly news at 7 p.m. In contrast, when the next terrestrial launch took place in March 1997, Channel 5 prioritised the attempt to establish the regularity of its schedule with its potential audience, boasting that "we'll show you a film every night at 9".[7] By that time, the UK was a multi-channel environment and TV programmes had become definitively subservient to scheduling patterns.

The *Visions* series in some ways anticipated this development. This was partly because it had a journalistic, time-tied aspect to its address. The magazine programmes of series 1 and 3 included items that were entirely addressed to the week or month of transmission. The series also grew to depend on a belief that a few of its devices and approaches were familiar to viewers, particularly the device of framing of film clips, but also a distinctive approach that included the lack of any presenter, the refusal of homogeneity in style within one edition, and the challenging nature of some of its material. If *Visions* had a consistent identity, it lay in a lack of consistency, a sense that it was never certain what would come next. But in television, to be consistent in a lack of consistency requires an underlying regularity of appearance on the screen that the series never attained. As linguistics teaches us, difference and creativity are possible only on the basis of a deeper framework of familiarity and regularity.

This was why *Visions*, in Jeremy Isaacs words, "never quite caught on" even as an experiment in television. It was neither because its experiments were too bold for television, nor because its material was too esoteric. The series was morally acceptable in its content, failing to outrage or offend in the surrealist sense, despite the derivation of the production company's name from the Bunuel/Dali film *L'Age D'Or*. The one and only brush with censorship took place in a careful and rather conventional programme about censorship in Brazil under the military.[8] Nor did the series fail to 'quite catch on' because there were too few decent items in the series: items were widely screened in film festivals and sold to broadcasters, with a co-production arrangement for the final series being made with the new Canal+ in France. It was simply because *Visions* never had the scheduling regularity to enable it to become a recognised micro-brand despite its 32 episodes.

What does this reveal about experiment in television? It shows that programmes matter only marginally. There is still a place for the occasional high profile innovative event that can command wide publicity, a one-off like Peter Watkins' *Culloden* (BBC, 1964) or Peter Kosminsky's *The Government Inspector* (Channel 4, 2005). But beyond such isolated events, experiment in TV requires bulk and regularity. An experimental series needs to establish its ground rules. It needs to use habits of viewing to shift habits of seeing. Perhaps the model I have in mind is a truly industrial one: the experiments that an established series such as *ER* can undertake in primetime, telling a story in reverse, or in real time, or as a live broadcast,[9] each being a deliberate variation from an established pattern. Other examples might be Paul Abbott's BBC1 drama series *Clocking Off* (BBC1, 2000–3), with each episode featuring the story of an individual, all branching off from a common workplace; or the *CSI* (CBS, 2000–) series which has introduced the untrue flashback into the vocabulary of TV; or the format of the *Fast Show* (BBC2, 1994–2000) which transformed the baggy sub-genre of the sketch show into a densely self-referential form. There a fewer examples from the area of factual programming, however, perhaps as such programmes do not provide the same satisfactions of narrative completion that drama and comedy can bring. Examples in the factual area tend to be portmanteau arts series like Channel 4's *Without Walls* (1990–97) or ITV's

South Bank Show (1978–), which consist of single arts documentaries with few common characteristics from week to week. Occasional experiments in visual style or factual address can take place within the double safety of these series: the safety of 'the arts' as a category, and the safety of a single item in a long series. The length and regularity of a series, in short, enables experiment to take place and to be noticed as such.

Notes

1. Broadcasting Act 1980 (HMSO, 1980).
2. Jeremy Isaacs, *Storm Over 4: A Personal Account* (Weidenfeld & Nicolson, 1989), 152.
3. Since at the time of writing the main terrestrial channels show no subtitled films, the two or three such films weekly across the channels now seems a cornucopia of delights.
4. *Cinema, Cinemas* was a monthly series on Antenne 2, produced by Claude Ventura, Anne Andreu and Michel Boulut with a regular offering by Andre Labarthe. It ran from 1982 until 1991.
5. Hall originally coined the term in the journal *Marxism Today*, and by 1983 it was the subject of a collection of essays, *The Politics of Thatcherism* , eds S. Hall and M. Jacques (London: Lawrence & Wishart, 1983).
6. *Voices* ran to 42 editions and was initially presented by Michael Ignatieff. It reprised Eichler's earlier series for Thames TV, *Something to Say*, with Bryan Magee from the 1970s.
7. According to the launch presentation broadcast on 30 March 1997.
8. The programme 'Brazil, Cinema Sex and the Generals' directed by Simon Hartog was pulled from the schedules on the afternoon of planned transmission, 19 June 1985. Accounts can be found in: Isaacs, *Storm Over 4*, 118–19; and an account by Julian Petley in various contributions to Derek Jones (ed.), *Censorship: A World Encyclopedia* (London: Fitzroy Dearborn, 2001).
9. The live broadcast of *ER* is the subject of Jeremy G. Butler 'VR in the *ER*: *ER*'s use of e-media', *Screen*, 42: 4 (Winter 2001).

9

Experimenting on air: UK artists' film on television

A. L. Rees

With the birth of Channel 4, artists' film and video began to appear more frequently on British television than ever before. From the early 80s and through into the next decade, complex films such as *Videovoid* (David Larcher, 1991, tx.1992 C4) and *Chronos Fragmented* (Malcolm Le Grice, tx.1995 C4) were shown – and paid for – by major channels. Shorter work, from the UK and internationally, was first bought in and then newly commissioned by TV. Sometimes short really meant short, as in the one-minute films made for the BBC's Late Show, to pioneer a now-global format for film and video competitions and festivals.[1]

This expansion was due both to the internal constitution of the new channel and forces external to it. First of all, Channel 4 was a commercial television station, the first to be in competition with the BBC since the arrival of ITV in 1955. Next, under Labour governments in the 1970s, independent filmmakers (and others) had lobbied for a fourth terrestrial 'cultural' channel that would recognise the values and social agendas of previously 'disenfranchised' or minority groups. Finally, the new channel was born under the Conservative government elected in 1979 under the leadership of Margaret Thatcher. When Channel 4 was born in 1982, during the first years of this long-lived Tory government bent on private consumerism and market values, it was an explosive mixture: a channel charged with a mission to 'innovate and experiment' (by a 1980 Act of Parliament), supported largely by the left, was to be funded by TV advertising. As these elements clashed, they intersected with changing media and arts practices, as new ideas in film and video making were picked up by funding agencies in the state and in TV itself.[2]

One result was that the independent, advertising-led, companies and the BBC took on more of each other's traditional properties, especially in the cultural sphere. Younger producers, attuned to pop and conceptual art since the 1960s, made headway into the more conservative and corporate worlds of broadcast television. Channel 4's Rod Stoneman saw in the early 1980s 'the movement of some sections of a dissident cultural intelligentsia into television (several from the Screen/BFI penumbra), carrying the values of late sixties radicalism into the broadcasting of the Thatcher years'[3] By the 1990s the context was quite different, with Channel 4's independent film budget of £10m in 1990, later reaching £50m, and with 1000 hours of broadcasting achieved in its first ten years.[4] It was inevitable that the term 'independent' became professionalised and capitalised in this way.

Subtending this generation-based flow of ideas from fringe to mainstream were other economic factors. The first was the slow attrition of the broadcasting trades unions' control over crewing conventions and procedures. Traditionally wary of 'non-professionals' (including unpredictable artists and collectives), when the unions at last relaxed the rules for artists and other independents, they both reflected and encouraged a more flexible production style. The definition of professionalism expanded at both ends, as technicians moved beyond the frontiers of a skills base established in the age of film, just as artists entered new worlds of technology and public access. Simon Blanchard, writing just before Channel 4 opened, cited such a new collaborative vision from a 1979 pamphlet by the Independent Filmmakers' Association: 'creative work with technicians and technologies "should not be limited to 'special effects' in, say, music programmes, but should be encouraged across the whole spectrum of TV"'.[5]

However, the first inklings of collaboration between art and technology in the context of television had, in fact, emerged more than a decade before the arrival of Channel 4. The earliest artists' experimental films to appear on UK television were inspired by the desire to create a televisual art appropriate for the electronic medium. They were primarily abstract explorations of 'special effects', and came out of an 'arts lab' approach to technology that recalled the utopian technics of 1920s modernism. Lutz Becker, best known today as a filmmaker and curator of constructivist art and cinema, met the electronics engineer Ben Palmer at the BBC Television Centre in 1966 and decided 'to collaborate in the search for a method to generate electronic moving images. My hope at the time was that I could develop some kind of a visual equivalent to electronic music.' Using feedback loops, they produced the title sequence for the TV series *Doctor Who* (BBC, 1963–), but also enlisted lab support from real scientists at Imperial College (Professors Colin Cherry and Dennis Gabor) to research visual language. From 1967, at the Slade School of Fine Art under Thorold Dickinson, Becker made geometric and calligraphic experimental films with electronic sound that exploited these 'new visual effects'. One such, *Horizon* (1968), with music by Joy Hall and with colour added in the optical printer, gained its title after being broadcast in 1969 as part of the BBC documentary *Horizon: Will Art Last?*[6]

From the Computer Arts Society (founded 1968) came similar ventures. George Borzykowski and Stan Hayward, who worked with animator Bob Godfrey, were interested in the electronic experiments of the Whitney brothers in the USA. Using computer equipment at Imperial College, in 1969 Hayward produced a one-minute animated film, *Square*, no mean feat at the time. That same year, the Computer Arts Society, with Gustav Metzger among its members and with links to leading art schools, put on a show of interactive installation art at the Royal College of Art. But these first fruits of the alliance between artists and technologists, underpinned by the shift of art schools into the new polytechnics during the 1960s, were limited by the resources of the time. Even by 1974, and around the corner from Imperial at the Royal College of Art's video workshop, Peter Donebauer's pioneering abstract electronic images (*Entering*, 1974), shown on BBC2's *Second House* and produced by Mark Kidel, had to be transmitted live by an outside broadcast van because that was the only option before studio recording.[7]

This first wave of new media art for television presciently sought an interface between the computer and electronic technologies, with origins in constructivism and abstract art rather than cinema, and with art schools like the Slade and the RCA acting as their nurseries.[8] Recently energised by a series of sweeping reforms, and shaken by student demands, sit-ins and calls for more relevance to the times, the UK art schools were a hothouse for radical new media and cultural theory. For Malcolm Le Grice, they were turning into 'one of the components of cultural intervention' rather than simply a preparation for it.[9] Many of the artist filmmakers who made up the structural avant-garde in the UK were art school graduates from this period, as were a considerable number of the social-political independent filmmakers who were among the new voices of the 1970s. The RCA Film and Television School included both camps and more. Headed by Stuart Hood, it housed such diverse and 'argufying' tutors as Noel Burch, Jorge Dana, Peter Gidal, Lutz Becker and Raymond Durgnat.

The appearance of independent and artists' film on television, and hints of more to come, was, therefore neither unproblematic nor unquestioned. It prompted a meeting of film activists in 1974 to discuss and perhaps influence the future of the new arrival, targeting the BFI, the Arts Council and the BBC as potential sources of funding. Held at the RCA, the event illustrates not only a contemporary consciousness of television as a potential exhibition site for this 'marginal' sector, but also, in a growing self-consciousness and confidence, the marks of an incipient 'movement'. It also marks a shift from the earlier association of broadcast art with primarily electronic experimentation to a wider range of media, including video and film. Its organisers, mainly from the Other Cinema and the London Film Makers Co-op, later played wide if differing roles in events to come, and were associated with a more 'film-specific' and politically critical approach to the medium.[10]

The London Film Makers Co-op was in the process of becoming the main focus for artists' film-making at the time. Identified, in the first instance, with materialist film and anti-commercialism, the LFMC had in fact partly grown from an Arts Lab approach to the fusion of art and technics. When it moved in 1969 to Robert Street from its original base in Covent Garden, the Arts Lab renamed itself the Institute for Research in Art and Technology. IRAT housed the LFMC's production equipment, notably the printer-processor practically hand-built by Le Grice. This legacy indicates the extent to which the division between film and electronic media was porous at this time. While Hayward was making *Square*, Le Grice, a Slade graduate then very active in the London Film Makers' Cooperative, was laboriously producing the computer-generated 'target' shape for his film *Threshold* (1970), a process that took over a year for a few seconds of footage. IRAT also housed the TVX video resource, later Fantasy Factory, run by John Hopkins and Sue Hall, pioneers of the lightweight technology or Portapak culture that led early video art in the US and Europe in its first decade and that also inspired community video. David Curtis, who like Le Grice had studied painting at the Slade, joined the LFMC soon after its founding in 1966, and was its leading programmer throughout its Art Lab stages from 1967.

As in other respects, 1968 was a key year that saw significant events in the development both of artists' film and the electronic arts. On the arts front, Jasia Reichardt curated the Cybernetic Serendipity show of computer imaging and electronic art at the ICA. On the film front, American critic P. Adams Sitney visited the UK with a selection of US experimental films, an early inkling of the powerful influence of the North American underground that was confirmed by his better-known film tour in 1974. Curtis circulated his first thoughts on 'Subsidies to Independent Filmmakers', the start of a long and tortuous campaign that at first rejected the notion of funding individuals and favoured the group or workshop instead. That collectivist idea, although much tempered and then combined with individual awards, survived far into the Thatcherite era. In particular, it subtended the ways in which film and video art for TV was made and shown.

As the independent sector grew in numbers, confidence and articulation, the question of funding came increasingly to the fore and gradually, new institutional relations were developed that would provide a future foundation for the relation between the independents and television. The rise of independent film began to permeate the funding bodies such as the British Film Institute and the Arts Council, as they responded to new waves of activity in social-documentary and artist-led filmmaking. From the late 1960s, as these groups sought a higher profile, the institutions, in turn, brought in new staff to reflect changes in film practice and production. Among these was the

Arts Council's first Film Officer in 1970, fine art graduate Rodney Wilson. His main brief was to develop arts documentaries (in fact, he was to radically change the genre) but the Arts Council also funded films made by artists as well as about them, with a sub-committee from 1972 for that purpose.

In a major move, a 1973 Arts Council Committee report (by, among others, Richard Attenborough, Humphrey Burton, Karel Reisz and Colin Young) supported 'applicants wishing to make non-narrative films ... we recommend that the Arts Council should embrace and encourage film-making as a fine art activity'.[11] This unequivocal statement might have been the end of the matter, but instead it heralded thirty years of argument about that very issue of film as a 'fine art activity'. Importantly, it awarded £25,000 for the first year, and waived institutional copyright so that the films could circulate both freely and widely on the underground and college circuits. This support for 'film-making as a fine art activity' also led to David Curtis's appointment, in 1977, as assistant film officer.

Meanwhile, Wilson was nurturing a new generation of documentary film-makers, at a time when, as Ian Christie, puts it, 'documentaries were refusing to lie down and be documentaries.'[12] In the wake of Ken Russell's radical experiments of the 1960s, and then of John Berger's *Ways of Seeing* (1972, BBC), the arts documentary shed its staid and reverential format to mix drama and politics in Ed Bennett's *Hogarth* (1977) or widen to two-screens in James Scott's film about the pop artist Claes Oldenburg, *The Great Ice Cream Robbery* (1971). Scott was also a member of the LFMC and of the social-political Berwick Street Collective, whose other two members, Marc Karlin and Humphrey Trevelyan, had formerly been part of the Cinema Action campaign group. Bennett had studied film at the RCA with Noel Burch, and like his peers was more attuned to theory than to art, reflecting the impact of *Screen* and semiotic theory on the coming generation.

Over in Soho, on the other side of London's West End from the Arts Council in Piccadilly, the story at the BFI was rather similar. The Experimental Film Fund had been set up in the 1950s to encourage young talents that included the Free Cinema group and Ken Russell. By the late 1960s, as the Production Board, it also made small but useful awards to film-makers far from industry goals, such as Jeff Keen, David Hall and Tony Sinden. In 1973, the year of the Arts Council report, Peter Sainsbury succeeded Mamoun Hassan as production officer at the BFI. Sainsbury, who led the board for the next dozen years, had links to both the experimental and the political film, and was committed to materially innovative cinema. He had founded the alternative distribution company The Other Cinema in 1970, with Nick Hart-Williams, and with Simon Field co-edited *Afterimage*, a journal that promoted the international and political Third Cinema and the underground or avant-garde film.

As with the Arts Council, BFI funding was moving into the new aesthetic built on film theory and theorised practice. In these ways, throughout the 1970s, a changing film sector pushed towards new patterns of funding to achieve its core ideas. Increased funding led to increased productivity, generating a constituency of 'independent film-makers' to whom Channel 4 would turn in its mission to encourage 'innovation and experiment'. The Production Board, which included vocal artists such as Peter Gidal and Malcolm Le Grice, favoured directing funding to collectives and groups. A board member from 1972–76, Le Grice successfully argued for equipment awards to the LFMC, the Berwick Street Collective and the London Women's Film Group. These groups spread the skills and technology to make films beyond the narrow production base of the time. Funding of workshops rather than scripts also encouraged filmmakers to experiment with ideas and material. At this point, some workshops with an artisanal or street-level origin in the 1960s were graduating to production-house conditions in the 1970s. Large Door, for example, a leading independent company, brought together Simon Hartog, formerly an LFMC activist and founder, with media theorist John Ellis and documentarist Keith Griffiths.

In 1974, the Independent Filmmakers' Association (IFA) was founded. Bringing together advocates of the political independent cinema and the LFMC avant-garde, the IFA acted as both a forum for the exchange of ideas and as an advocate for the interests of independent film-makers. In 1975 the BFI (having spurned Curtis's and Le Grice's earlier advances) began under the new regime to fund the LFMC. The BFI essentially paid for the 'plant', a succession of converted industrial spaces in north London, while the BFI and the Arts Council both funded the 'product' in the form of individual films, videos and touring schemes. Another group, London Video Arts (later London Electronic Arts), specifically promoted video. By 1978, David Hall, whose role and status among video makers was comparable to Le Grice's among film makers, had successfully got the Arts Council to fund LVA, in part on the grounds that filmmakers at the Co-op were supported by the BFI.

There were evidently complex links between the independent film sector, the arts sector and the artists' organisations that moved between them. On the one hand, the avant-garde was linked to the wider aspiration for a radical cinema that was the base of the new vision at the BFI Production Board. On the other, it was part of a broader arts scene that was slowly opening itself to such new media as film and video. But in this respect there were differences and paradoxes, determined less by the raw material involved (film-stock, videotape) than by some surprisingly complex cultural twists. These were to affect and influence not only the ways in which artists first crept onto the mass TV screen, but the very reasons and purposes for doing so.

Despite limited forays into television, the main goals of film and video activists from 1975–85 were the distribution of prints and tapes to clubs, cultural groups, workshops, colleges and a few sympathetic London and regional cinemas. There were important and, writing in 2006, emblematic inroads to galleries, such as the Festival of Expanded Cinema at the ICA (1976), and the Video Show at the Serpentine Gallery (1975) organised by Stuart Hood, Sue Grayson and David Hall to showcase new work by both LVA and LFMC makers. The main forms of disseminating film and video art were the very opposite of TV. Arts Council documentaries were toured round the country in vans equipped with projectors. Then the Arts Council introduced 'Filmmakers on Tour', to show and debate film and video 'live' in colleges, clubs and Regional Film Theatres. In few art forms was there such a strong and interrogative exchange between artist, audience and work. Over 160 artists took part in the scheme from 1975 to 1989, and personal presentation remains a norm among artist filmmakers today. This pattern was set by the model of cinema and auditorium, crossed with some aspects of the face-to-face encounter of the gallery. Galleries themselves were largely unmoved by these new developments in the 1970s and beyond, until the very different circumstances of the 1990s impelled a dramatic change. Artists' film, as Curtis first observed in 1975, shifted away from the arts scene, which did not embrace it with enthusiasm, and closer to the fringe of the cinema.[13]

Through the Independent Filmmakers' Association, the avant-garde, like its historical predecessors before the Second World War, allied with the social and radical documentary sector and when Channel 4 came on air in 1982, the newly appointed commissioning editors for Independent Film and Video, Alan Fountain and Rod Stoneman, were both IFA members. (Fountain had from 1977 worked as Film Officer of East Midlands Arts. Stoneman had formerly worked at the regional funding body South West Arts with regional film officer Chris Rodrigues and LFMC activist Mike Leggett.) Fountain and Stoneman invented the *Eleventh Hour* series, showing alternative and political film and aiming to irritate and challenge, from the radical fringe, the norms of cinema. Like other departments, Independent Film both 'bought in' existing work, but more excitingly commissioned new projects. Commissioning was a new process for independents and artists, very different from getting a grant, and – while they were not 'producers' in television terms – the department's editors had a more interventionist or guiding role in overseeing the productions than did public-sector grants award panels or committees. They hoped for work that was explicitly made for television – rather than simply being shown on TV – and that took account of its differences from cinema viewing with committed audiences. That transition took time, and some independents never made it, or reverted to more standard documentary formats. But the commissioning model later spread to the Arts Council when it teamed up with television, running parallel to the systems of funding experimental film and video by grants and awards.

David Hall set a different and influential (if short-lived) example that challenged programming itself. In 1971 he made a series of *TV Interruptions*, commissioned by the Scottish Arts Council for the Edinburgh Festival and broadcast (unannounced) by the BBC during August and September. A selection of seven of them was later issued as *7 TV Pieces*. It followed the example of producer Gerry Schum in Germany, whose *Television Gallery* (tx.1968-70, SWF/ARD) slipped artists' films into the regular schedule, including some by Richard Long, Gilbert and George and other new stars of the era's Britart. Over nine days Keith Arnatt showed still photographs in which he slowly disappears into a hole in the ground. 'I think it was a reference to land art – there was a lot of hole-digging going on at the time', he later said in a 1993 TV feature on video art, 'I think I interrupted a lot of programmes'.[14]

Hall's *TV Pieces* were shot on 16mm film, partly because of union rules about broadcast video standards, but were conceived and made for television. They explained nothing of their presence on the TV screen, were uncredited and were deeply enigmatic. Each was the length of a three-minute roll of black and white film. In one, a television burns in time lapse against a landscape of scudding clouds. In another, the screen seems to fill with water – the goldfish bowl analogy – and then empties at an oblique and unsuspected angle. In a third, a TV in a hostel or common room is shot in rapid bursts over the course of an evening. A fourth is an objectivist lyric poem, cutting from a windowed sky to a gnomon-like tree in a courtyard to a field of shadowed clouds, while the sound of the wind persists throughout. A particularly complex piece shows a busy Edinburgh street from four camera positions, each enclosed in or by a TV frame. Hall's short series is an anthology of counter-television strategies, unanchored by a programmer or voiceover, quietly asserting a frame of values that opens a hole in TV space and then refuses to fill it with any other explanatory content.

But the main hopes of independent filmmakers in the early 1980s were put into Channel 4, with its sympathetic commissioning editors and its parliamentary charter to 'encourage innovation and experiment in the form and content of programmes'. While some saw here a new form of state or corporate control, or licence, the reality was less apocalyptic. And, as commissioning editor Rod Stoneman commented much later, the 'cardinal' term for Channel 4 was innovation rather than experiment as such.[15] A main achievement was the Workshop Declaration of 1984, by which the Association of Cinema and Television Technicians[16] agreed to exempt productions by 'franchised' independent workshops from the usual but increasingly byzantine procedures that were mainly aimed at maintaining crewing quotas and wages, which were unsustainable in the independent sector. It was a significant reform of the much-criticised restrictive practices, in the media and elsewhere, which the Tory government elected in 1979 was about to smash along with unionism itself. At the time, it was an advance for filmmakers who stood outside the media organisations and their rigid structures, either union or management.

The opening of Channel 4 was also an opportunity for Rodney Wilson at the Arts Council to get more TV airtime for his new-style arts documentaries. Facing a 50 per cent budget cut in 1981, Wilson offered the channel's film purchaser Derek Hill the rights to the Arts Council's back catalogue. Hill was an underground film promoter whose New Cinema Club from 1970 and Short Film Service were decidedly anti-censorship, still a hot and desirable topic for the new channel to explore. As it was less than clear whether the initial commissioning by the channel would provide enough programming for its airtime in the first few years, Hill had a £3 million budget to buy up transmittable material for the new station. Wilson also negotiated an agreement with Channel 4 Chief Executive[17] Jeremy Isaacs to co-produce an ongoing slate of new documentaries, with 50 per cent match funding for his films, achieving for the first time a direct rather than secondary route to TV exhibition for Arts Council productions. Programmes Director Liz Forgan terminated the agreement in 1989, but by then Wilson had the experience to benefit from the Broadcasting Act of 1990 which gave 25 per cent of BBC commissions to independents. On the strength of these co-produced single documentaries, he initiated two new 'crossover' series, *Dance for Camera* (1991–2003) and *Sound on Film* (from 1995).

The funding of artists' films for television was equally complex, starting with a relatively conventional commission by Rod Stoneman for *Profiles* (tx. 1983, Channel 4) of avant-garde filmmakers, with David Curtis as series editor and Margaret Williams as director. Each programme, based on interviews, was followed by a selection of the artists' work. The subjects were veterans Jeff Keen, Margaret Tait and Malcolm Le Grice, and four women artists associated with the Circles distribution group led by Felicity Sparrow. Of these Tina Keane was one of the first to see that TV could spread 'a political statement in an art context'. Video and performance, once televised, opened a 'window to another world'. In her lyrical *Shadow of a Journey* (1980), a boat and Keane's own shadow mingle with light-play on water to accompany, on the soundtrack, a Gaelic song and memories of the Highland Clearances. More *Profiles* were mooted, but none were made. Instead, and more adventurously, projects for television broadcast were directly commissioned from artists.

Up to this point, experimental film had gained little from the new Independent Film and Video department. The channel's first investments had been in the franchised workshops and in the political avant-gardes led by Cinema Action, the Berwick Street Collective and Amber Films, with some smaller equipment grants to groups like LVA and Fantasy Factory. There were eventually 15 workshops, funded up to 90 per cent of their costs by the channel. By contrast, Wilson and Curtis faced severe cuts in their Arts Council budget (in keeping with Thatcherite policy towards funding of the arts in general) and it was one of these (a 30 per cent reduction in 1985) that impelled Curtis to 'grasp the nettle of television'. He approached Channel 4 with the ideas that led to the Eleventh Hour Awards for commissions by artists, heralding the many schemes that followed.[18] While the workshops and political independents were 'struggling to find appropriate forms' (Rod Stoneman)[19] with which to communicate to new audiences, both challenging television language and being challenged by it, Fountain let Stoneman plunge into new and unknown territory by commissioning experimental artists' films for television broadcast. There were open submissions, with no stipulation of themes or length. The channel contributed three-quarters of the budget and had rights to two transmissions. The artists retained copyright.

While Stoneman and Curtis set up their new model, working directly with artists, another format was in the making with Stoneman's 1985 'packaged' selection of three programmes for the *Eleventh Hour* slot, produced by Triple Vision (Terry Flaxton) and fronted by media theorist Sean Cubitt (*Video 1/2/3*, tx. 1985 Channel 4). These included a mixture of reflective personal videos by Ian Breakwell and Catherine Elwes with brash and cut-up 'Scratch Video' from George Barber and the Duvet Brothers. It was followed by the more ambitious six-part series *Ghosts in the Machine*, from 1986, produced by John Wyver in Arts broadcasting, a different branch of Channel 4 from Stoneman's Independent Film and Video department. Wyver had seen a festival of US video art while visiting Los Angeles for Channel 4 in 1983 and was struck by its vitality. *Ghosts*, commissioned by Mike Boland, had a brighter and more attractive style than the more sombre productions of the UK independents, although Wyver's later business partner Keith Griffiths (then a rival at Large Door) had strong links to the IFA's social agenda.[20]

Ghosts was TV-oriented from the start, with snazzy inter titles and slogans (but no presenters), and was watched by a new generation reared on video rather than film. It was also more oriented to North America, showing Bill Viola, Gary Hill, Max Almy, Peter Campus, Joan Jonas, John Sanbourn and William Wegman, but included few of their UK counterparts from either the pioneering black-and-white reel-to-reel 1970s or the more colourful 1980s. After *Ghosts* was lavishly praised by Chris Dunkley in the *Financial Times*,

Channel 4 executives Jeremy Isaacs and Michael Jackson backed Wyver to make a second series, which would include some newly commissioned work from the UK and abroad. This provided another broadcast outlet for work funded by the Arts Council or part-funded with Channel 4. *Ghosts 2,* in 1988, showed sixteen new works, half of them international (including *Steps* by Zbigniew Rybczynski) and the other half from the UK, co-funded with the Arts Council. Over twenty hours of material were broadcast. But when Michael Grade replaced Isaacs in 1988, the programme was suddenly switched from an adventurous Friday-night slot at 10.30 p.m. to a remoter, if more underground, early Monday at midnight.[21]

For a brief spell in 1986–87, *Ghosts* was flanked by NeTwork 21 pirate television, organised by Bruno de Florence and Thomas Mutke, formerly at the LFMC, by then at the Fridge in Brixton. NeTwork 21 showed Barber, John Maybury, Derek Jarman and Genesis P. Orridge. These legendary broadcasts were confined to London and seen by few, although they inspired the format of Janet Street-Porter's 'youth' TV programmes. And in any case, a larger number of viewers were exposed to similar underground material in the mid-1980s under Michael Kustow's adventurous régime as Arts Editor of Channel 4. For example Jane Thorburn produced the *Alter-Image* series (tx. 1983) which featured Brion Gysin and William Burroughs, *Psychic TV* (also with G. P. Orridge), the Biff cartoonists Mick Kidd and Chris Garratt (also from the LFMC) and Dougie Fields. Kustow and his successor Waldemar Januszak also encouraged new media experiments by the painter Tom Phillips, working with Peter Greenaway on *TV Dante* (tx. 1987 and 1990, Channel 4) and Greenaway's outstanding programmes *Four American Composers* (tx. 1983 Channel 4), on Meredith Monk, John Cage, Robert Ashley and Philip Glass. At the same time the BBC's *Video Paintbox* (tx. 1985) invited David Hockney, Howard Hodgkin and Richard Hamilton to play with computer imaging on screen.

The BBC connection was especially productive for the Arts Council when its officers persuaded Alex Graham, formerly of the ICA, and Michael Jackson, to support a different kind of film for television. One-minute films by experimental rather than prestigious artists featured as part of *The Late Show* for BBC2 from 1990 to 94. A total of 45 new works varied from the poetic and lyrical to the humorous one-liner; Tony Hill puns on the cycle of history, transforming a wheel from horse-carriage to car and spinning bicycle (*A Short History of the Wheel,* tx. 1994); William Raban charts the course of a day around the 'sundial' of the Canary Wharf Tower *(Sundial,* tx. 1994); Judith Goddard brings a painting to life against a changing London background (*Luminous Portrait,* tx. 1991). The BBC also funded and screened with the Arts Council a new wave of 10-minute experimental videos (*Expanding Pictures,* tx. 1997) by a new generation of artists, such as

Gillian Wearing, Sam Taylor-Wood, Station House Opera, John Wood and Paul Harrison, Bobby Baker and Mark Wallinger.

The 1-minute film had been pioneered by Fluxus artists and by Peter Kubelka and Stan Brakhage. At the same time as it intensifies the viewing experience, the format also comes close to the rapid-flow rate of image consumption in TV as a whole. But the major funders also wanted to support longer productions, an ambition first seen in Sainsbury's attempt at the BFI Production Board to build a British Art Cinema.[22] This included the diverse realisms of Terence Davies and Mike Leigh, the counter-cinema film essays of Peter Wollen and Laura Mulvey and the first films of Sally Potter, who went from the Arts Council-funded *Thriller* (1979) to her BFI-funded first feature *The Gold Diggers* (1983). An unexpected success was Peter Greenaway's *The Draughtsman's Contract* (tx. 1982), the first BFI film to be co-financed with Channel 4. Originally a dissident structuralist, and another ex-art student, Greenaway exemplified the cross-over culture that broke down the differences between the funding institutions, with cinema supposedly the responsibility of the BFI and visual art of the Arts Council. This mirrored the open structures by which, for example, arch-experimentalist Le Grice made his longer semi-narrative films through the BFI, while Channel 4 funded the more relaxed and shorter *Sketches for a Sensual Philosophy* (tx. 1988 Channel 4). Like Derek Jarman, the other best known independent filmmaker of the period, Greenaway was both prolific and unconfined by a single medium. Like Jarman and Le Grice, he moved easily between drawing, music, high- and low-grade video and all the available film formats to produce his 'expanded cinema'.

In contrast, the Production Board's Young Director's Scheme (1987–98) looked like a step backwards when Ben Gibson, who had recently taken over as head of production from Colin MacCabe, revealed that it would fund 'some atmospheric conventional narratives with unusual subjects'. But he also affirmed that subcultures and race were on the subject agenda, and that the scheme would be 'a mechanism through which the BFI can engage with experimental, abstract film and the avant-gardes', along with Super-8 and video makers.[23] The maximum budget for a production was £25,000, and its output included David Larcher's *Granny's Is* (1990, tx. Channel 4) as well as many shorter works shown on Channel 4's *The Dazzling Image* series (tx. 1990 and 1992). Curtis's enthusiasm for animation as a creative and experimental art, with Claire Kitson and Keith Griffiths, led to the first of the animate! schemes between the Arts Council and Channel 4.[24]

The largest Arts Council/Channel 4 collaborations spanned a decade until the late 1990s. The model was set by Wilson, Curtis and Wyver in the first instance of linkage between a TV channel, the Arts Council and an independent production company to fund British artists' film and video for direct television output. The second series of *Ghosts* (broadcast in 1988) was initiated by a call for submissions by artists to make new work for TV broadcast. Some of the pilots, dubbed 'Art for Television', were developed into the eight new UK pieces finally shown by *Ghosts*. The separate Eleventh Hour Awards also began with commissions in 1988 and broadcasts two years later, this time with the participation of Stoneman, Wyver and Curtis.

After 1991, with four extensive programmes to its credit, these awards were succeeded by the four series of work funded by Experimenta (1991–95) and by producer Jane Thorburn's *The Dazzling Image* (1990 and 1992, with new BFI-funded work by Cerith Wynn Evans, Isaac Julien, Sandra Lahire, David Larcher and Cordelia Swann). *Experimenta* encouraged 'long form' work with budgets of up to £50,000 per film. But it also funded innovative shorter work by new talents like Andrew Kotting, Chris Newby and John Maybury, all of whom were later to make longer films for screen and television, as did experimental animators like Simon Pummell, Kayla Parker and Clio Barnard. While the funding schemes were generating innovative films and videos by contemporary artists, Curtis, Wyver and Stoneman devised a wholly new venture – *Midnight Underground*, a double-whammy of a title for an avant-garde film series. The first six programmes in 1993 mainly showed 'underground classics' and were especially important as avant-garde archiving and propaganda. The series included rarely screened films by Kenneth Anger, Stan Brakhage, Ernie Gehr, Bruce Conner, the Quays, Bruce Baillie, Le Grice, Dwoskin and many others. With brief introductions by Benjamin Wooley, the series introduced an eclectic and lively mix of international avant-garde films, mixing the surreal with the structural and the lyrical.

Midnight Underground was an astute anthology of both legendary and little-known works, directed at and reaching wide audiences in the UK for the first time. It bears out Curtis's view that 'artists' film and video has been held back by the fact that no one gets to see it, not because there isn't an audience for it'.[25] The first series remains a storehouse of key works. It led Mark Webber to name his first film and music events 'Little Stabs at Happiness' (at the ICA, 1998–99), after the 1963 Ken Jacobs film shown on *Midnight Underground*. The second series in 1997 was a different venture, programmed by Stoneman to showcase new films commissioned by the channel from the Experimenta scheme and the BFI Production Board.

But the major funding schemes of the Arts Council and the BFI with TV programmers were only part of the story of getting new media arts and film on television. The first Video Positive Festival, 1987 (organised by Eddie Berg and Stephen Littman) was held at three major Liverpool arts venues. With commercial and art sponsorship it featured new multi-monitor and installation video by David Hall, Judith Goddard, Kate Meynell, Stephen

Partridge, Simon Robertshaw, Dan Reeves, Chris Rowland, Mona Hatoum and many others. Terry Flaxton's Granada TV programme on this new wave in UK video was aptly called *Celebration: In the Belly of the Beast* (tx. 1987). More colourful and lavish than its 1970s predecessors, this wave permeated 'straight' TV and advertising as some of its ideas were picked up and fine-tuned by ever-watchful industry eyes. By 1994, it seemed an accepted fact that this linkage between fringe and core was part of the media fabric. The Arts Council 'Hi Tech' scheme that year similarly gave placements to artists in professional production studios (including Susan Collins, John Maybury and Simon Pummel).

What of the 'interventions' strategy of David Hall, the notion that artists could interrupt the visual flow rather than add new slots or scheduled programmes? This almost vanished, although much of its spirit was caught by ventures like *Dadarama* (tx. 1984), produced for Channel 4 by Hall's early collaborator, Anna Ridley. Like Hall and his now prominent ex-students, such as composer David Cunningham and video artist Stephen Partridge, Ridley approached TV from a quite different angle, in a context of live and performance art rather than cinema, and above all of video rather than celluloid. Post-modern from the start, her Annalogue productions side-stepped film language to focus on the electronic image. This began a decade earlier with the *Arena: Video Art Special* programme (tx. 1976, BBC2), conceived by Ridley and produced by Mark Kidel. A survey of the field internationally, it featured Hall's *This is a Television Receiver*, in which the newsreader Richard Baker recites a text about his own material construction as a TV image. Successively reshot and degraded, the cool delivery of the presenter is reduced to a grotesque distortion of the human form and voice: analytical art with a Dada streak.

In 1984 Ridley produced several programmes for *Artists' Work for Television* on Channel 4, with the emphasis firmly on 'for TV'. These included the 21 parts of Ian Breakwell's *Continuous Diary* and *Dadarama*, featuring new work by Rosemary Butcher, David Cunningham, John Latham and Stephen Partridge. Her example perhaps inspired *Video 1/2/3* (tx. 1985, Channel 4), produced by Terry Flaxton's Triple Vision, but this also featured the new Scratch Videos that had enthused the International Television Festival in Edinburgh a month before the broadcasts. Scratch Videos were assembled from off-air recordings or old films and set to new soundtracks, reinventing the montage tactics of Americans Bruce Conner and Dara Birnbaum. The movement was short-lived but very effective. It was also the most explicitly political video art in ten years. The Duvet Brothers' *Blue Monday* (1984), set to music by New Order, satirised the Thatcher government with intercuts of slogans and clips from 1930s documentaries, alongside news footage of the epic confrontation between police and strikers at the new Wapping base of Rupert Murdoch's News International. Gorilla Tapes from Luton chopped up TV news and US army propaganda films to make sarcastic anti-war agit-prop. Fast, blatant and heralding the remix culture to come, Scratch Video offended video purists. At the same time, the techniques, and some of the makers themselves, were instantly recuperated by the television industry. The effect on advertising and music videos was immediate and lasting throughout the decade.

In 1990, Ridley with Stephen Partridge and Jane Rigby of Fields and Frames, made a new series of *TV Interventions* (tx. 1990, Channel 4). Unlike the Hall originals, which were retransmitted as part of the series, these were credited and scheduled, with new work by Hall, Partridge, Littman, David Mach, Bruce McLean and Pratibha Parmar. In the following year, BBC2 Scotland picked up the idea through Partridge's Television Workshop at Duncan of Jordanstone College of Art, with video artists Doug Aubrey, Judith Goddard and Kate Meynell contributing (*Not Necessarily*, tx. 1991, BBC2 Scotland). Two years later, Hall, again produced by Ridley, made the last of his interventions – six one-minute 'interruptions' for MTV, repeated throughout the year. These intense short pieces succeed in bringing moments of stasis and reflection to the mega-mix flow of music television.

The cash-crop culture finally caught up with the visual arts sector in the second half of the nineties. Stuart Cosgrove took over as Head of Independent Commissioning at Channel 4 in 1995, advocating 'innovation and change' but significantly dropping the word 'experimental' that had featured in the channel's charter. Effectively, he rejected the social and aesthetic activism of the first independent commissioners in favour of the new populism, and continued to do so more widely when he was made Head of Arts and Entertainment.[26] A new generation of media-savvy 'young British artists', who used video as just another item in the tool-kit (as John Baldessari and others had predicted twenty years earlier) were also setting a new pace, re-targeting the gallery rather than television as their output medium. Media artists outside this axis lost their specific locale when the LUX Centre, opened in 1997 after the merger of the LFMC and LEA, suddenly closed in 2002, a victim of rising costs in the part of East London it had helped to renew (Hoxton Square, also home to Jay Jopling's White Cube). It retrenched to a smaller venue and cheaper premises where it operates today, distributing and promoting new film and media art as part of a current UK wave of experimental time-based art.

The Lux was not the only victim of late 1990s closedown. The Production Board was 'frozen' in 1998, and then shunted in 1999 into the new Film Council, but stripped of its cultural remit. Meanwhile Wilson's Arts Council Department of Film, Video and Broadcasting was axed, and the artists' film and video section transferred to the Visual Arts Department in 1999. In 2000 the Arts Council reallocated film funding to its regional associations. The quota of twelve or so artists' films a year resourced by a regional successor such as Film London is a far cry from the TV-funded heyday.[27] The Arts Council continues to fund some artists' films as part of exhibition and touring programmes, but individual artists now compete for local funds with other independents, from community groups to would-be cinema or TV directors. A film or digital video artist today is just as likely to look for 'research' funds in the education sector as in the arts organisations. This is where the loss of specific funding bites most, because it breaks the link between film and video production and exhibition, including television.

Stoneman recalls wanting artists to ask 'how can I articulate or renew or play with the specific space of television?'[28] In a paper for the Arts Council Committee in 1992 Curtis worried that 'the work we fund tends to be more homogenous than it should be. Our patronage, with and without TV partners, is based on an "open" invitation of proposals for works. In the absence of any specific guidelines, there are all sorts of ways in which applicants are bound to tailor their proposals to what they perceive as our expectations.'[29] Similar concerns were expressed at the 1994 conference on 'Artists and Broadcast', held at the National Film Theatre, where artists and producers debated these perceived norms of television.[30] John Wyver later admitted that, as a producer of artists' films in the 1980s, 'we said it's got to be a certain length, it's got to be acceptable for television.'[31] However, at the conference he argued that TV was a multiple and not 'specific' space, and that video art in particular should dissolve itself into this new environment rather than seek outdated kinds of autonomy. His eclectic selection of new work for the bi-annual festival of new media, held at the Institute for Contemporary Arts, programmed rock videos alongside art video and demonstrated this meltdown theory.[32]

Wyver's provocative views were challenged during the next, and as it turned out, final, years of the major projects of the 1990s. Michael O'Pray, whose touring 'Umbrella' programmes had in fact introduced Scratch and rock videos to many new viewers, alongside 'regular' artists' film and video, defended the personal and complex voice in the experimental tradition.[33] As visual media encroached on every aspect of daily life, from TV screens to surveillance cameras, he called for work that did not compromise, that was personal but not sensationalist, and that aimed to trouble rather than to reinforce the stable identity of image and object, word and picture, self and other. He noted that visual regimes do overlap, citing the way that surveillance cameras unwittingly imitate the stark imaging of the structural film, and arguing that this was all the more reason to preserve and redefine the differences. The same logic today might apply to the now familiar, if spurious, link sometimes made between Reality TV and Warhol's long-take observational films.

The most memorable films for or on TV were by firm-minded artists who had already established their ideas and styles, such as Larcher, Le Grice, Jayne Parker, Derek Jarman. While their films were played without introductions, selections of shorter works were often 'packaged' and introduced, too often with a 'do not adjust your sets' warning, in an attempt to reach viewers totally unfamiliar with the work. Spike Milligan, Anthony Clare, Ken Livingstone, Tilda Swinton and Susie Orbach presented the second series of *The Dazzling Image* in 1992. Changes in TV viewing habits, channel-hopping in particular, increasingly undermined these attempts to cross the barrier between the viewer and what was thought to be 'difficult' work.

In retrospect, the mid-1980s to the late 1990s look like golden years for televising artists' film and video, but it did not always seem so at the time. What now figures as a regeneration of the avant-garde, especially in video and digital media, for some was a falling away from the classic days of underground and then structural film, which had put the UK on the vanguard map. The crossing of frontiers confused old boundaries, and the unbarring of television was part of the effect. At the same time, LFMC filmmakers such as Larcher, Le Grice, Lis Rhodes and William Raban were among the first to move from 16 mm film to newer media and an expanded frame of vision. The ACE/BFI/Channel 4 schemes, many of them also overlapping, funded an astonishing array of new work. The Eleventh Hour Awards introduced Nina Danino, Andrew Stones, John Smith, Vivienne Dick and Sandra Lahire to TV. Experimenta led to major work by John Maybury (*Remembrance of Things Fast*, 1991), David Larcher (*Videovoid*, 1991), Stephen Dwoskin (*Trying to Kiss the Moon*, 1994), Jayne Parker (*Crystal Aquarium*, 1994), William Raban (*Island Race*, 1994) and Lis Rhodes (*Letters Never Written*, 1995). The BFI, which had funded some key structural and political films in the 1970s, in this period produced and televised films by Chris Petit, Derek Jarman, the Brothers Quay, Cerith Wynn Evans, Jayne Parker, Margaret Tait, John Maybury, Patrick Keiller and Isaac Julien.

The main impulse behind the funding strategies was to get the work where it had not yet been seen. Viewing figures may have been 'small in terms of television ratings but huge in terms of the audiences which that work had never reached before', said Stoneman – a view shared by Curtis, Le Grice and most of the producers.[34] Small is of course relative. The final series of *Midnight Underground* had audiences of around 50,000 after it was moved to 'the dark zones of post-midnight transmission' (William Raban),[35] compared to the original *Eleventh Hour* slot of half a million. Despite this, both figures exceed the equivalent numbers for gallery video, however high its profile. The story of the film and video avant-garde on TV is also only part of a wider history. Some leading figures such as Chris Welsby, Nicky Hamlyn and Guy Sherwin have refined their work with little TV exposure, while for others such as Paul Bush or George Snow it was central to their developing wizardry in the edit suite. While television spread the word, or image, and importantly allowed new work to be made, it was not all-determining. The films of the single most influential and highly regarded filmmaker and theorist from the LFMC orbit, Peter Gidal, have never been shown on UK television at all.

Overall, film art for and on television in the UK in the 1980s and 1990s was extraordinarily various. It was engineered by 'fringe' departments at the BFI, the Arts Council, Channel 4 and the BBC, who were more often collaborators rather than rivals, as in the broadcast of Jarman's *Blue* by Channel 4 and BBC Radio 3 in 1993. It gave opportunities for established makers to expand, and for newcomers to show alongside them. There was perhaps too much anxiety about screening the most difficult work from this sector (this was left for a younger generation to rediscover outside TV in the last few years). Instead, it doggedly sought broader audiences within the television mainstream flow, rather than through a specialist satellite or digital outlet, as long as that wider option remained possible. It heralded new forms of audiovisual experiment and ushered the avant-garde towards a new media environment, in television's unique space for artists between cinema and gallery.

Notes

1 Data, dates and figures are mainly taken from materials held at the British Film and Video Artists' Study Collection based at Central St Martins, University of the Arts, London, and originally part of the AHRB Research Centre for British Film and Television History. See website www.studycollection.ac.uk, especially Research Papers, Michael Mazière, 'Institutional Support for Artists' Film and Television in England, 1966–2003'. The informative 'History', 'Chronology', 'Interviews' and 'Appendices' in this (unpaginated) report are supplemented by the following collections of historical source-material and contemporary essays: Julia Knight (ed.), *Diverse Practices: A Critical Reader on British Video Art* (Luton: University of Luton Press, 1996); Michael O'Pray (ed.), *The British Avant-Garde Film 1926 to 1995: an anthology of writings* (Luton: University of Luton Press, 1996); Margaret Dickinson (ed.), *Rogue Reels: Oppositional Film in Britain, 1945–90* (London: British Film Institute,1999). See also David Curtis, *A History of Artists' Film and Video in Britain, 1897–2004* (London: British Film Institute, 2006).

2 The decision to allow no production facilities to Channel 4, so that it had to buy in or commission all its output, was another of the conditions that allowed new forms of film art to appear on TV through collaborations between Channel 4 , the Arts Council of Great Britain (from 1993 the Arts Council of England) and the BFI.

3 Rod Stoneman, 'Sins of Commission', originally in *Screen*, 33: 2 (1992), reprinted in M. Dickinson (ed.), *Rogue Reels Oppositional Film in Britain, 1945–90* (London: BFI, 1999), 177. In 'Thoughts on the BBC' (*London Review of*

Books, 27: 13, 7 July 2005, 16–20), David Edgar described 'the salutary tale of Channel 4. Founded in 1982, it arose out of the 1997 report of the Annan Committee, which had in turn been influenced by left-wing critics, theorists and programme makers, who saw the new channel, with its pluralist structure, experimental ambitions and minority remit, as an ideal site for a new alliance, in which the provocative would make common cause against the paternalistic BBC. For a while it worked. It was the decision to allow the channel to sell its own advertising which inevitably led to the decline of the democratic in favour of the demographic'. (18)

4 Stoneman interview, Report, Appendix 4. Also see 'TV Artists and Schemes', List 3, and 'TV Chronology', List 5.
5 Simon Blanchard, 'Where do new channels come from?', in S. Blanchard and D. Morley (eds), *What's This Channel Fo(u)r?* (London: Comedia, 1982), 17.
6 Lutz Becker letter to author, 2005. *Horizon* is featured in Gene Youngblood, *Expanded Cinema* (New York: Dutton, 1970), 334–6.
7 See Richard Wright, 'More Power: the pioneers of British Computer Animation and their legacy', in Julia Knight (ed.), *Diverse Practices: A Critical Reader on British Video Art* (Luton: University of Luton Press), 147–70, and Peter Donebauer, 'A personal journey through a new medium', in Knight (ed.), *Diverse Practices*, 87–98. Also see Chris Meigh-Andrews, *A History of Video Art: the Development of Form and Function* (Oxford: Berg, 2006).
8 Ironically, as a former filmmaker in Grierson's GPO Film Unit, Sir William Coldstream, Head of the Slade (and member of the Arts Council) turned down Curtis's and Le Grice's request for BFI funding of artists' films when they visited him in his role as BFI Chairman during the 1960s. Apart from the many Slade-trained fine artists who became filmmakers and activists, Coldstream's Slade also housed the Film Studies Unit, under Thorold Dickinson and James Leahy, from which graduated not only Lutz Becker but also a later generation that included Rod Stoneman, Deke Dusinberre, Simon Field and Annette Kuhn. For the history of the Film Unit, see Bruce Laughton, *William Coldstream* (New Haven and London: Yale University Press, 2004).
9 Malcolm Le Grice interview, Report.
10 Stephen Dwoskin, Peter Gidal, Simon Hartog, Nick Hart-Williams, Marc Karlin, Malcolm Le Grice, Laura Mulvey, James Scott. 'People coming from outside London who need beds should contact The Other Cinema', stated the advertisement in *Film & Television Technician*, November 1974, reprinted in Dickinson (ed.), *Rogue Reels*, 125.
11 Arts Council Committee Report cited in Report, Section 3, Chronology (1973 entry).
12 Ian Christie interview, Report, appendix 2.
13 David Curtis, 'English Avant-Garde Film, an early chronology', *Studio International*, 190:978 (November/December 1975), reprinted in O'Pray (ed.), *British Avant-Garde Film*, pp.101–19.
14 Keith Arnatt in 'The Happening History of Video Art', *The Late Show* (BBC2, December 1993), produced by John Wyver, directed by George Barber.
15 Stoneman interview, Report.

16 The ACTT later merged with the BBC's in-house union to form BECTU.
17 From 1981 to 1987.
18 Curtis interview, Report.
19 Stoneman, 'Sins of Commission', in Dickinson (ed.), *Rogue Reels,* 182.
20 Their production company Illuminations still specialises in art for television, including the annual Turner Prize award presentations. Griffiths has directed many television programmes about the avant-garde, including Robert Breer (*The Five-and-Dime Animator,* 1985), Len Lye (*Doodlin'*, 1987) and *Abstract Cinema* (1992), and Wyver is currently documenting the leading UK avant-garde filmmakers for DVD release by the BFI.
21 Ironically enough, the *Eleventh Hour,* 'established [1983] in the tundra of the schedule at 11 p.m. on a Monday night' (Stoneman in O'Pray (ed.), *British Avant-Garde Film,* 290), was dropped as a distinct slot in that same year of 1988.
22 Ian Christie interview, Report.
23 Ben Gibson interview, Report. PB statement cited in Report, Section 3, 'Chronology' (1987 entry).
24 Animate! is the only current survivor of these artists' funding schemes, producing to date over 40 films.
25 Curtis interview.
26 In an interview with *Vertigo* magazine, cited in Report Section 5, Cosgrove stated that there were 'a hell of a lot of other ways of resisting the state' than 'a fairly narrowly defined notion of political resistance, defined by the trajectory of largely Marxist materialist, left-liberal politics'.
27 London Artists' Film and Video Awards documentation, 2005 (also see www.filmlondon.org.uk). The Arts Council Film and Video panel funded over a thousand individual awards to artists between 1973 and 2000.
28 Stoneman interview.
29 David Curtis, 'Notes on Film Production', ACGB Artists' Film and Video Committee Policy Meeting, 28 2 1992, Report, Appendix document D2.
30 Artists and Broadcast round table discussion, National Film Theatre, in Knight (ed.), *Diverse Practices,* 99–102.
31 Wyver, interview (speaking of the 1988 pilot series *Art for Television,* for *Ghosts*).
32 John Wyver, 'The necessity of doing away with "video art"', originally a talk at the Video Positive Festival 1991, published in LVA Video Access Catalogue, 1991, reprinted in Knight (ed.), *Diverse Practices,* 315–20.
33 Michael O'Pray, 'The impossibility of doing away with "video art"', in Knight (ed.), *Diverse Practices,* 321–34.
34 Stoneman interview. Also see Malcolm Le Grice interview: 'The realistic audience of success is, does it actually get it into the arena and do people see it?'
35 William Raban, 'Expanded Practice in Television – Defending the Right to Difference', *Vertigo,* 1: 8 (Summer 1998), 42–4; an informative and lucid review of TV funding for artists' films by a leading avant-garde filmmaker.

10

Experimental music video and television

K. J. Donnelly

The music video as an aspect of experimental or avant-garde television has received surprisingly little attention in the frequent and wide ranging discussions on the topic. This is particularly surprising since many of the techniques of the avant-garde became evident (and some filmmakers worked) in music video and profoundly altered the way that pop music appeared on television. Considerations of television still suffer from ocular-centric assumptions that prioritise the image despite the fact that television has always been an audio-visual medium, often having a close relationship with its cousin, the radio. However, until the advent of NICAM (near instant companded audio multiplex) stereo broadcasts in the late 1980s, television in Britain suffered from poor sound quality that hindered the development of its sonic aspect. Furthermore, television had only embraced these new techniques around its edges, often aiming for audio-visual economy and dominated by convention, whether the talking head of news presentation or the naturalism of television drama.

Music television is a broad area encompassing not only programmes devoted to popular music but also the ways in which music is presented on television. These are not the same, as popular music is often presented on programmes not specifically devoted to music, such as talk shows or children's programmes. This chapter focuses on the presentation of pop music on television, specifically the pop promo, rather than the dedicated music television programme. It thus focuses on experimentation with a 'televisual unit', whose migratory malleability has led to the development of specialist channels (MTV being the first), appearance on VHS and DVD compilations, as well as increasingly important 'content' on the internet and mobile technologies. In this sense, the pop promo is a particularly important component within a digitised media environment. Yet, if this chapter is not necessarily about music television, many of the videos it discusses appeared on a range of music television programmes on British television: from the populist *Top of the Pops* (BBC1, 1964–2006) to the more 'serious' *The Old Grey Whistle Test* (BBC2, 1971–87); from the mixed appeal (and video-only format) of *The Chart Show* (Channel 4/ITV, 1986–98) to the more specialist, lo-fi aesthetic of *Snub TV* (BBC2, 1988–90). This chapter attempts to trace the development of the pop promo (which developed out of music television) and focus on some of its more experimental moments. In particular, it focuses on its links with the avant-garde and the implications of translating avant-gardist strategies into such a format.

By and large, the historical avant-garde was primarily concerned with the development of new thought, and new political and social structures through innovative cultural forms and style. With the decline of the political left in the last couple of decades of the twentieth century, this political brief gave way, in much audio-visual work, to new techniques that were developed as a means in themselves rather than as a means to an end. In the 1980s, as significant space opened up for pop songs, avant-garde practice emerged on television as their visual accompaniment. The immediate context, however, was not welcoming. A fear of alienating audiences led to an audio-visual conservatism, rather than a sense of technical development. Pop videos were not only aimed at a youth audience that was already (in theory at least) alienated from large areas of television output, but also needed to grab attention quickly in a crowded marketplace, while also expressing something of the 'individuality' of the musical artist in question. Once MTV had become a dedicated channel in 1981 (1987 in Europe), and needed pop promos to fill its homogeneous space, a new opportunity for audio-visual culture opened up and, indeed, became the 'cutting edge' of audio-visual culture at the time. Since then, 'music television' has expanded into a galaxy of dedicated channels. It should be noted that pop video and music television are not synonymous and that there is a fringe of pop videos that rarely or never appear on broadcast television.

As popular music is a multi-million dollar industry, it is perhaps no surprise to find that it is one of the most conservative areas of culture, hostile to the presence of the avant-garde in its domain. Yet since the advent of the counterculture in the 1960s, it has developed its own 'avant-garde' fringe while otherwise embodying Adorno and Horkheimer's concept of a standardised culture industry.[1] In this chapter, the term 'avant-garde' is used to mean a certain approach that foregrounds cutting edge techniques in relation to both the image and sound. Pop video has a heterogeneous and inconsistent cultural presence: it belongs to the mainstream and also mixes the mainstream with more avant-garde tendencies. It is certainly not hard to find pop promos whose banality perfectly reflects the lack of adventure in mainstream pop music. On the other hand, there are pop promos that transcend a direct visual translation of the song, integrating a variety of visual devices that create an extraordinary accompaniment to the music. Just as the advent of counterculture generated a cultural underground in the late 1960s, pop music itself has had a persistent 'underground', a shifting marginal zone of music that regularly thought of itself as something more than simply sonic product for consumption. It is, unsurprisingly, in this sub-generic area of popular music that the avant-garde tendency in pop promos can predominantly be found.

The avant-garde impetus in pop promos manifests itself as a self-conscious parading of audio-visual technique, in a manner that traditionally has been associated with the filmmaking avant-garde. However, the techniques lose their initial political and cultural context and in most cases become merely an attraction in themselves, simply allowing for the differentiation of products in a crowded and competitive market. In order to identify avant-garde tendencies in pop promos, we should not only think of a promo as simply an advertisement for a commercial recording, but also as an object in itself, with its own integrity.

Promo history

The music video developed from hybrid and heterogeneous roots: some within television itself, some developing out of the needs of the music industry. In the first instance, British television tended to include only the most mainstream popular music and British pop shows on television have by and large been an outgrowth of the traditional popular music entertainment format, such as *Top of the Pops* and even more up-to-date shows in the 1970s such as *Lift Off With Ayshea* (Granada, 1969–74) and *Marc* (Granada, 1977). One of the first British music shows to vary this blueprint was *The Old Grey Whistle Test* (BBC2, 1971–87).[2] It was self-consciously serious and, although primarily based on live performances by musicians in the studio, album tracks were also played in the programme. These tracks posed a problem for the producers: how should they accompany music, with no access to the group and little budget? They solved the problem through the use of old black and white animated films, such as *Felix the Cat* cartoons or 3D animation by Ladislaw Starewicz, which were run simultaneously with the song, irrespective of notable synch points or dynamic matching. While there was a strange discontinuity between modern sound and antique images, the aesthetic effect was often quite polished despite the random basis of the tie between music and visuals, and illustrated the malleability of image and sound, and the relative autonomy, in certain circumstances, of one from the other.

The idea of the 'pop promo' had its origins in the short films made by television programmes to accompany prerecorded songs. This strategy had advantages for both sides: the group need not be present during the programme, nor, indeed, be paid as much as they would for a live performance. Quickly, the musicians themselves and other organisations realised the worth of these films to promote a specific release. One of the earliest was by The Kinks for their song *Dead End Street* in 1966, while over the next couple of years, Pink Floyd had promotional films made for them by the Central Office of Information and Pathé News. The Beatles made their own films in an attempt to fill a punishing schedule of television appearances, and, from 1966, these became the only way to see the group in action. The previous year, they made a number of promos with Joe McGrath for songs including *Daytripper, We Can Work It Out* and *I Feel Fine*.[3] In 1967, they made promos with Swedish director Peter Goldmann, which ranged from simple representations of live performances to startling stylistic devices such as images running backwards, most notably Paul McCartney jumping 'up to' a tree in *Strawberry Fields Forever*.[4]

The Beatles's *Magical Mystery Tour* (1967) should be seen as an experimental (and extended) pop promo for television, rather than, misleadingly, as a musical film. Its production was partly inspired by Paul McCartney's interest in experimental film and the *cinéma-vérité* sequences in *Magical Mystery Tour* which were similar to the style being used at the time by American filmmakers such as the Maysles brothers.[5] It certainly was an uncharacteristically bold move for the BBC. It got a negative reception and, despite its colourful nature, was first broadcast by the BBC in black and white (26 December 1967).[6] *Magical Mystery Tour* was certainly an expensive promo, made with big money and television station backing. Later pop promo developments were made on a smaller scale, and often facilitated through technological developments. Paul McCartney went on to make a number of short 'avant-garde films',[7] while John Lennon made films with Yoko Ono that still have an avant-garde status more than thirty years later. *Magical Mystery Tour* should be seen in the context of late 1960s arts crossfertilisation, which inspired the founding of The Beatles's Apple films, and allowed *Yellow Submarine* (1968) to find a popular context for radical visual design.

During the 1970s, rock music became more 'serious' and certainly more serious about itself. This was reflected in television programmes like *The Old Grey Whistle Test* and rock opera films like *Tommy* (1975) and *Lisztomania* (1975). Rock 'dinosaurs' sought to aggrandise themselves through the cinema screen's epic capabilities rather than the limited vision and sound available on the television set. However, this is not to suggest that television programmes embraced more serious 'rock' at the expense of more easily-consumed 'pop'. Rock programmes were often premised upon group performances, while the use of film clips allowed more leeway for avant-gardism on screen, yet the vast majority of programmes were visually as banal as their songs were prosaic. In 1975, Queen's promo for *Bohemian Rhapsody* was an important element in the massive success of the single. Interestingly, the success of the video arguably set the group on a course away from being a progressive rock band to being a far more commercially-oriented pop band in the next decade.

Progressive rock self-indulgence was shunted aside by the crudity, directness and lack of pretension in the wave of punk rock that overtook Britain in the late 1970s and found some outlet on television. After the break-up of the Sex Pistols and the dissipation of punk, John Lydon (the erstwhile Johnny Rotten) formed Public Image Limited (PiL). They led the way in terms of product format. Their second album *Metal Box* (1979) was an aluminium film can containing 12-inch 45 RPM 'dubplate' records, which had a better audio response than a normal $33^{1}/_{3}$ record. This group was in the forefront of what Greil Marcus called 'Britain's postpunk pop avant-garde'.[8] In 1981, they rhetorically declared that they were no longer a pop group in the traditional sense, but a 'communication corporation' who would be involved in video making and film soundtracks.[9] In fact, they did little in this direction, although their artistic aspirations led to a bizarre riot-inducing performance behind a screen at a New York nightclub in 1981. The group projected video onto a screen while hiding themselves behind it, clearly upsetting an audience happier with a conventional concert performance. PiL also made a notable appearance on *The Old Grey Whistle Test* in 1980. Their performance of *Careering*, which involved tuneless singing, a lack of conventional song form, highly repetitive bass and drums backing and seemingly random guitar and synthesiser noises led presenter Annie Nightingale to conclude their appearance by noting that it was one of the most remarkable performance ever seen on the programme.

Despite PiL's intentions, they never realised the audio-visual potential of their rhetoric, although in the late 1970s and early 1980s, they certainly brought some avant-garde musical techniques into the popular domain, including the performance of *Death Disco* to a bemused audience on *Top of the Pops* in 1979. The predominantly teenage audience was no doubt shocked by the surface sheen of mainstream pop conventionality being tarnished not only by PiL's punk appearance, but also by the tuneless song that included an out-of-tune guitar quotation from Tchaikovsky's *Swan Lake*. Remaining at the cutting edge, in 1986 they released a pop promo called 'Video' as an accompaniment to a single called 'Single and an LP called 'Album'.[10]

The first dedicated outlet for pop promos was MTV, which started broadcasting in the USA in 1981 and Europe six years later. In its early incarnation, MTV was quite experimental, allowing a flow of videos without any

Experimental music video and television   171

mediating presenter, although it later gave way to more conventional programmes and scheduling. However, pop promos at this time might be characterised as what Raymond Williams called an 'emergent form',[11] preparing to become dominant in the near future. When MTV first started it had trouble filling its schedules as there were barely enough pop promos in existence to allow for significant variation. They developed in response to this already-existing and needy audio-visual broadcasting space, which allowed an incredible scope and leeway for operation in terms of style.

The early years of pop video were plagued by a crude 'literalism' as the image attempted as far as possible to double the words of the song and, as most pop promos are conceived as illustrative of the songs, this impetus has never gone away, although it has become far less pronounced. There was also at this time an increasing use of Quantel Paintbox visual effects. Pop promos came to be the place to see such cutting-edge technological capabilities, although they quickly became over-used. A good illustration of its possibilities were shown by Baltimora's *Tarzan Boy* (1985), which was created with multiplied images and blue backgrounds. It resembled certain avant-garde films, such as the abstract animated films by Len Lye and Norman McLaren that used saturated colour to obscure rather than enhance the image. *Tarzan Boy* also used the principle of simultaneity, rendering the singer one of a number of competing elements and undermining any sense that the image simply expressed the production of the music. The aesthetic possibilities of Paintbox were showcased in a BBC television series called *Painting in Light* in 1986, which allowed artists such as Richard Hamilton and David Hockney to demonstrate its capabilities. The irony was that its capabilities were already more than evident in mainstream music video.

Promos and their makers

With respect to pop promos, the avant-garde impetus manifests itself as a foregrounding of audio-visual technique. This is more common than might be expected, due to the desire for differentiation in a competitive marketplace. Thus techniques become an attraction in themselves rather than a subversion of the norms of mainstream audio-visual culture or a means to a conceptual end. According to some, the use of specific and cutting-edge film techniques for their own sakes marks a travesty of avant-garde sentiments. For others, it underlines the collapse of avant-garde culture into a postmodern play of aesthetics that have lost their original meanings and contexts.

Pop promos quickly began to develop a strong stylistic tendency to use montage, involving fast cutting, jump cuts, and collapsing spatial cohesion with discontinuities along the lines of other audio-visual traditions, such as action movies or avant-garde film. They also adopted dramatic camera movement, probably derived from the film musical, that became the 'pop promo style' of mainstream Hollywood films in the 1980s. There was also a tendency to lapse into a series of visual clichés, such as slow motion shots of flying doves, images using saturated colour and shot with special lenses, or fairly crude Quantel paintbox effects. A 'pop surrealism' proliferated: a radical juxtaposition of seemingly disparate and illogical images. Influences came not only from surrealist art but from abstract filmmakers such as Norman McLaren and Len Lye, in the riot of kinesis, colour and movement reflecting the dynamics of the music that the visuals complemented. The influence of the avant-garde can be divined in a persistent rejection and negation of the characteristic transparency of mainstream television (and film), premised upon an illusionistic world on screen without a foregrounded visual style. However, similar stylistic characteristics were noticeably present in television commercials, arguably pop video's close cousin. Examples of 'pop surrealism' include David Bowie's *Ashes to Ashes* (1980), which reached number one in the British charts, and included strident colour adapted and solarised with Quantel Paintbox, and bizarre and obscure imagery, including Bowie and others in white pierrot costumes walking in front of a mechanical digger. Similarly, Ultravox's *Vienna* (1981), which was directed by Australian Russell Mulcahy, included footage of tarantulas walking on people's faces and children playing as a string quartet, mixed in with nostalgic images of neo-classical buildings in Vienna. Both of these examples illustrate the surreal imagery evident in contemporary mainstream videos, in heavy rotation on prime-time shows, such as *Top of the Pop*, that featured top ten music.

Two of the most influential figures in the production of pop videos in Britain in the 1980s and 1990s were Kevin Godley and Lol Creme. Both had been very successful as part of the top international pop group 10cc in the 1970s. After they had developed a device called the 'Gizmo' with which to bow an electric guitar and make interesting sounds, they took a break from 10cc to produce a demonstration record. The record took on a life of its own and became the sprawling concept triple-album *Consequences* (1978). While their work with 10cc had exhibited as much irony and pop literacy as might be possible in a top chart act, this concept album showed an altogether more experimental side to the duo. *Consequences* was notoriously unsuccessful and for years was spoken of as a limit case of artist and industry excess. Godley and Creme persisted with their musical career as a duo and moved fairly rapidly into producing their own promo videos for singles. The first to bring them to prominence as video makers was for the single *Cry* (1985), where a succession of close-ups of faces merged together while lip-synched to the words of the song. This was startling to audiences at the time, as these were precise fades in and out to give smooth transitions, before the advent of digital morphing, a 'trick' that became overused in the 1990s. *Cry* showed how close the aesthetics of pop promos could be to that of small-scale experimental films. The song itself was very conventional but the video elevated it to another plane, imbuing a much stronger sense of the song words through the series of facial expressions across a wide range of male and female archetypes.

As pop video makers they worked in the mainstream but also with more challenging material, for instance, U2's *Even Better than the Real Thing* (1992). The video had a prominent place in U2's rebranding with its postmodern concern with information overload and the contradictions of politics and pop music. The spine of the video is imagery of U2 performing the song with the camera mounted on a large wheel that allows it to travel in a circuit above the group and below their feet on a glass floor, thus avoiding a succession of angles on the action. The effect is highly disorientating, particularly with fast cutting, flash frames and the interpolation of footage of U2 tribute band Doppelganger, who, in the mêlée of the fast-paced action and images, appear to be the real U2. For the guitar solo section of the song, the promo changes mode to show a rapid selection of TV news images in smaller frames within the screen. In stylistic terms, *Even Better than the Real Thing* is a remarkable visual accompaniment to U2's song, utilising a vast range of stylistic techniques in pursuit of informational overload.

Blondie's *Eat to the Beat* (1979) was publicised as the 'first video album', released as an object with images as well as a music disc. In the next decade, the British group The The released the album *Infected* (1986), with purpose-made videos, as a 'video album', which was broadcast in its entirety on Channel 4, although in a late-night format and at a time when the channel was self-consciously offering more minority interest programming. Apparently an aesthetic unity, it was in fact a succession of videos directed by different people, including Mark Romanek and Tim Pope, who regularly worked with The Cure. Three songs, *Mercy Beat*, *Heartland*, and *Infected* were directed by Peter Christopherson, an important figure in the British avant-garde music scene, as a member first of Throbbing Gristle and then Coil. He had worked with Derek Jarman on a number of occasions including the collaboration with Coil on the music for the television film *The Angelic Conversation* (1985), while Jarman had also filmed Throbbing Gristle in *T.G.: Psychic Rally in Heaven* (1981). Christopherson made some avant-garde inspired videos for American group Nine Inch Nails, whose collection he directed, and included Edison's short reality film *Electrocution of an Elephant* (1903).[12]

Arguably, the most interesting pop promos, with the most impetus from the avant-garde, were in 'independent' music that was hardly related to 'top

10' pop music culture. Some examples illustrate the direct influence from the cinema's avant-garde and artistic wing. Clock DVA produced a video for their recording *The Hacker* (1992), which is premised upon rapid cutting, to match the rapid continuous quaver rhythm of the music. This yields a highly stylised effect that, on the one hand, removes the emphasis from the fairly banal black and white images while, on the other, renders the whole into something resembling a piece of 'Op Art'. Indeed, this video is very difficult to watch, and presumably impossible to watch for those suffering from epilepsy. The promo for Propaganda's *Dr Mabuse* (1984) was directed by Anton Corbijn using some stylistic tropes taken from European art cinema. Shot in black and white, featuring gothic castles and monks with dramatic shadows crossing the screen, it copied the visual style and iconography of German Expressionism. And, in clear reference to the effect performed by Jean Marais in Jean Cocteau's *Orpheé* (1949), singer Claudia Bruecken goes into and through a mirror. Its title and theme were derived from the series of films directed by Fritz Lang. Corbijn was a stills photographer who specialised in portraits of pop personalities, and the video exhibits a strong aesthetic sense, in addition to the references to film history. The House of Love's *Destroy the Heart* (1987) employed a camera panning continuously on its axis, as had Laura Mulvey and Peter Wollen's avant-garde film *Riddles of the Sphinx* (1977). For Mulvey and Wollen, this technique sidestepped the limits of conventional space and time creation in the cinema. For the House of Love, this technique undermined the format's dominant sense of frontal on-stage performance and, further, undermined the idea of choreography for the camera, as the group were shown in undramatic poses rather than mugging for the camera as was and is the norm of pop video.

Art and the pop promo

During the 1980s, there was a significant cross-over between British art cinema and pop videos. One of the most significant British art film directors, Derek Jarman, had already used popular music in his feature films. *The Tempest* (1979) concluded with a song sequence of *Stormy Weather* that parodied traditional musicals. *Jubilee* (1977) had exploited developments in punk rock and used a number of punk musicians in acting roles as well as showing music being performed, most notably Siouxsie and the Banshees playing in a studio (although it was actually Siouxsie singing with Adam and the Ants). Jarman went on to make a pop promo for the Smiths, called *The Queen is Dead* (1986) after their album, accompanying a few songs with blown up 80 mm footage. This technique, that Jarman had been working with for a number of years, made for vague images but an unusual texture. Although the promo was clearly not made to be played in heavy rotation on music television as the image quality worked against the promo's commercial potential, some of it was, bizarrely screened on the most mainstream (and most conservative) of British pop programmes, *Top of the Pops*. Jarman also made the video for The Pet Shop Boys' *It's A Sin* (1987), which on the surface looked like it used the same set and costumes as his feature film *Caravaggio* (1986). He also made the promos for that group's *Violence* (1986) and *Rent* (1987), and Suede's *The Next Life* (1993).

One of Jarman's assistants on his feature films was John Maybury, who, particularly in the wake of Jarman's death, was expected by many to take on Jarman's mantle as the leading progenitor of British art cinema. Instead, he made a career in the 1980s as a pop promo maker, having worked with Jarman and the Pet Shop Boys (on *It's a Sin*). Maybury went on to make many promos, including *Each and Everyone* (1984), *Native Land, Mine* (1984) and *These Early Days* (1984) for Everything but the Girl; *Dreams* (1992) for The Cranberries; *Buffalo Stance* (1989), *Kisses on the Wind* (1989) and *Money Love* (1992) for Neneh Cherry, and most notably, *Nothing Compares 2 U* for Sinead O'Connor (1990). This last promo doubtless played an important part in the song's success on both sides of the Atlantic, and earned popular acclaim for Maybury. He was still a teenager when he worked on Jarman's *Jubilee*, later working on Jarman's *The Last of England* (1987) and *War Requiem* (1988), where he directed a sequence. Along with Cerith Wynn Evans, Maybury was the leading light of the 'New Romantic' wave in British art and filmmaking, which was highly exotic and inspired by filmmakers such as Jean Cocteau and Kenneth Anger. This movement made an impact in 1981 at the exhibition 'A Certain Sensibility' at the Institute for Contemporary Art in London. Maybury often used super 8 film and video for his short films, which include *Is Like a Melody* (1981) and *Pagan Idolatory* (1984). He later went on to make feature films and, despite the amount of money available to pop promo makers, Maybury appears now to have forsaken that world for the more art cinema-based career that had looked likely in the early 1980s. At the same time, another of the New Romantics went into making pop videos: John Scarlett-Davies also worked with Jarman and Scratch Video (an influential political video collage group) in the 1980s. His pop video work was certainly more mainstream, and included *Wood Beez (Pray like Aretha Franklin)*, *Absolute* and *The Word Girl* for Scritti Politti, *Who Needs Love (Like That)* and *Heavenly Action* for Erasure and *Good Morning Britain* for Aztec Camera.

American-born twin brothers Stephen and Timothy Quay, often known as 'the Brothers Quay', became notable British-based avant-garde filmmakers in the late 1970s and 1980s, making television advertisements and pop videos as well as more esoteric, personal films. They made part of Peter Gabriel's acclaimed video for *Sledgehammer* (1986), other sections being made by Stephen R. Johnson, and Nick Park, who later went on to make animated films such as *Creature Comforts* (1989) and the *Wallace and Gromit* series. The Quay brothers also made pop videos for His Name is Alive (*Are We Still Married?* [1991] and *Can't Go Wrong Without You* [1993]) and Sparklehorse (*Dog Door/Heloise* [2001]). In both of these cases, their work dovetailed with less mainstream pop music and they produced promos that were not out of keeping with the highly singular style of their other films.

The most high profile pop video collaboration between the art world and the pop promo world is, perhaps, Blur's *Country House* (1995) directed by fine artist Damien Hirst. One of the group known as Young British Artists that came to national notoriety in the 1990s, Hirst also belonged to a conceptual pop group Fat Les with comedian Keith Allen and Blur's bass guitarist Alex James. Director Chris Cunningham made startling promos for Aphex Twin, *Come to Daddy* (1997) and *Windowlicker* (1999). Both used CGI technology to highly dramatic, and in the case of the second promo comic, effect. Along with other pop video directors Michel Gondry and Spike Jonze, Cunningham is now seen as a 'respectable' filmmaker, having released a DVD that brings together his promos, packaged as short films rather than 'merely' as pop videos (as *The Work of Director Chris Cunningham*). Indeed, these releases mark a clear recognition of the art of some contemporary pop promos.

U2's succession of pop promos demonstrates how far some mainstream rock groups have endeavoured to connect with more esoteric filmmaking (and other) practices. In addition to Godley, a succession of highly interesting filmmakers have made promos for U2 and have stayed on the cutting-edge of audio-visual culture. These include Wim Wenders, Anton Corbijn, Jake Scott, director of the film *Plunkett and Maclaine* (1999), novelist William S. Burroughs, film director Mark Pellington, Jonas Akerlund, film director Neil Jordan and film director and artist Donald Cammell.[13] The interface between pop/rock groups and filmmakers not only demonstrates an alliance between those who choose to work in esoteric and personal areas but also shows how many artists, in the loosest sense of the term, saw potential in pop promos from which they gained creative status beyond simply advertising a pop record.

Conclusion

While some theorists of music video have embraced the notion of its radical potential,[14] others have conceived music television channels merely as 'image radio'.[15] While some pop promos have gained critical status from the involvement of 'respectable' film directors, in many cases creative and challenging work has all too readily been ignored. It is not hard, however, to see references to, or similarities with, certain aspects of a fine art based avant-garde in pop videos (for example, Franz Ferdinand's *Take Me Out* (2004) that included visual montage aspects that were clearly influenced by some of Kurt Schwitters's 'Merzbild' work). If the avant-garde has fallen into decline since the mid-twentieth century, in its place has developed a post-modern culture of blank quotation and an aesthetic devoid of purpose that has lost touch with an original context and thus a primary or intrinsic meaning. According to Fredric Jameson: 'In a world in which stylistic innovation is no longer possible, all that is left is to imitate dead styles, to speak though the masks and with the voices of the styles in the imaginary museum.'[16]

This famous passage was doubtless at least partly inspired by the proliferation of pop promos in the early 1980s, and their most visible culture of visual pastiche. Pop promos have created a space in which avant-garde aesthetics are co-opted for commercial purposes. This cuts both ways. Although, on the one hand, the traditions of avant-garde subversion and challenge to the norms of mainstream audio-visual culture are diverted, on the other, this mainstream culture has to try to integrate material that has traditionally been kept well outside its solidly demarcated boundaries. It can clearly be argued that the avant-garde has been institutionalised and tamed and pop video is now an established format that, despite pressure to differentiate product, tends by and large toward docile, even banal audio-visual styles and ideas. 'Generic' pop videos are heavily standardised, with repeated elements de rigeur as iconic accompaniments to their associated genre of music. Prime examples are heavy metal videos, which overwhelming embrace a format that is based on showing a group performing on stage, and rap videos, many of which show a rapper frontally gesturing towards the camera while accompanied by seemingly adoring female 'groupies'. Of course, not every video in these genres follows this blueprint, but it is striking how many do. The possibilities that still remain 'outside' generic production are, all too often, devoted to the musician's public image or 'creative' pretensions.

New developments in pop promo style owe much to technological advances, such as cheaper filming equipment and video imaging effects, or to institutional innovations, most notably the advent of MTV, and a host of other channels, such as The Box and VH1 and VH2. We stand at a point where platforms of dissemination and modes of production are changing, becoming more accessible and immediate. The way television has been broadcast through radio waves, the way it has been decoded and the way that television sets work, have all undergone radical changes in recent years. 'Internet television' is considered to be a certainty for the future, as the logical conclusion of the process of 'convergence' on to a single consumption platform. Pop video as a medium has been at the cutting edge of these developments. In terms of the past, MTV was one of the first television channels to be used widely in public spaces. In terms of the future, not only has pop video been endemic on the internet for some years but also some of its more experimental aspects have already translocated there. A key example is 'mashup pop promos': the amateur practice of adding images to music. This new form begins to question the hierarchy of music and image, with one of the most prominent instances being music added to television images of the 9/11 attack on the World Trade Center. These 'unofficial' pop promos have lost the requirement to act as an advertisement for a piece of music, and thus point to a new, less polished future for the promo in a shifting televisual landscape.

Notes

1. Theodor Adorno and Max Horkheimer, 'The Culture Industry: Enlightenment as Mass Deception', in Simon During (ed.), *The Cultural Studies Reader* (London: Routledge, 1993), 30.
2. In later years, music shows were less willing to attempt innovation, apart perhaps from *The Tube* (Tyne Tees, 1983–87).
3. Robert Neaverson, *The Beatles Movies* (London: Cassell, 1997), 120.
4. Ibid., 4.
5. The Maysles already had worked with the group on the documentary *Yeah Yeah Yeah: New York Meets The Beatles* (1964).
6. Many have disdainfully pointed out that the BBC broadcast this colourful film first in black and white rather than colour. Yet this was due to the fact that the BBC was changing from a 405 line system to a 625 line system. BBC1 was still using the 405 line system and could not, therefore, be received in colour. *Magical Mystery Tour* was broadcast for a mass audience on BBC1. Its second broadcast was on the 625 line BBC2, where it went out in colour but to a very small number of people who owned colour 625 line television sets.
7. Ian Peel, *The Unknown Paul McCartney: McCartney and the Avant Garde* (London: Reynolds and Hearn, 2002).
8. Greil Marcus, *In the Fascist Bathroom: Writings on Punk, 1977–92* (London: Penguin, 1992), 108.
9. Gavin Martin, 'Company Lore and Public Disorder', *New Musical Express* (14 March 1981), 31.
10. Rather than having filmmakers produce a documentary (or 'rockumentary') or concert film, some musicians in the wake of punk rock decided to make their own films. This was enabled by the increased availability of video equipment. Good examples were The Cure, who made a short film called *Carnage Visors* in 1981, and Bauhaus, who made an elliptical narrative film in 1982.
11. Raymond Williams, *Marxism and Literature* (Oxford: Oxford University Press, 1977), 131–2.
12. His pop promo work runs from mainstream acts (Erasure's *A Little Respect*,

Level 42's *To be With You Again* and Van Halen's *Can't Stop Loving You*) to more esoteric, left field popular music (Nine Inch Nails's *Wish*, and *March of the Pigs*, Ministry's *New World Order*, and *Just One Fix*, Rage Against the Machine's *Freedom* and Front 242's *Rhythm of Time*). This exhibits the full spectrum of the pop promo video from mainstream pop teenagers Hanson to austere industrial groups whose music is aimed at anything but chart success.

13 Godley made *Even Better than the Real Thing* (1992), *One* (1992), *Numb* (1993) and *Stuck in a Moment* (2001). Wenders made *Night and Day* (1990), *Stay* (1993) and *The Ground Beneath Her Feet* (2000). Corbijn made *Pride* (third version, 1984), *Please* (1997) and *The Hands That Built America* (2002). Jake Scott made *Staring at the Sun* (1997), William Burroughs made *Last Night on Earth* (1997), Mark Pellington made *One* (second version, 1992), Jonas Akerlund made *Walk On* (second version, 2001) and *Beautiful Day* (2000), Neil Jordan made *Red Hill Mining Town* (1987) and Donald Cammell made *Pride* (1984).

14 E. Ann Kaplan, *Rocking Around the Clock: Music Television, Post Modernism and Consumer Culture* (London: Routledge, 1987).

15 Andrew Goodwin, *Dancing in the Distraction Factory: Music Television and Popular Culture* (Minneapolis: University of Minnesota Press, 1992); Michel Chion, *AudioVision: Sound on Screen* (New York: Columbia University Press, 1994).

16 Fredric Jameson, 'Postmodernism and the Consumer Society', in Hal Foster (ed.), *Postmodern Culture* (London: Pluto, 1985), 112.

11

'Yes, it's war!': Chris Morris and comedy's representational strategies

Brett Mills

When dancing, lost in techno trance, arms flailing, gawky Bez. Then find you snagged on frowns and slowly it dawns, you're jazzing to the bleep-tone of a life-support machine that marks the steady fading of your day-old baby daughter. And when midnight sirens lead to blue-flash road mash, stretchers, covered heads and slippy red macadam and finds you creeping 'neath the blankets to snuggle close to a mangle bird, hoping soon you too will be freezer-drawered. Then welcome. Mmm ... uu [sic] chemotherapy wig. Welcome. In jam. (Distorted) Jam. (Pitch lowered) Jam. (Piercingly distorted) Jam. (Extremely distorted) Jam. (Very slow, mechanised) Jaaaaam.

This is the opening voice-over for the first episode of *Jam* (Channel 4, 2000), the most blatant of Chris Morris's assaults on the representational strategies traditionally employed by British television comedy. It violates a number of conventions which have been accepted about television comedy for some time, not least in its insistence in finding humour in subjects such as premature babies and victims of car crashes. The dense use of language, sometimes poetic, sometimes near-unintelligible, refuses to make deciphering – and enjoying – the jokes a simple task. And the whole is shot using a variety of techniques – jump cuts, bleached images, extreme lighting, an intermingling of grotesque and naturalistic performance, slowed-down and speeded-up sequences – which do not often find a home in entertainment programming. In all, the sequence is a useful summation of Morris's repeated refusal to make comedy which looks like it should, and, therefore, often refuses to offer the audience the kinds of pleasures most commonly associated with humour.

The experimentalism in Morris's work is only meaningful because it reacts against, and plays around with, the generic expectations of comedy aesthetics. There are a set of traditions which have informed the ways in which comedy and entertainment programming have been shot, promoted and understood, and these have remained fairly unchanged since the beginning of television. The aesthetics of comedy have provided producers and performers with the means to demonstrate the comic intent of their programming. In addition, these aesthetics have also helped maintain the distinctions between non-comic and comic media, which is vital to comedy's pleasures as well as, more importantly, upholding the worth and necessity of serious, factual forms. Morris's experimentation with the look and content of comedy programming has led to many complaints and public debates, along with, in many cases, sheer confusion. That it should do so is testament to the rigid stability which has for decades informed the aesthetics of entertainment, and the fear engendered in certain groups of the viewing public should a comedy programme dare to experiment with its look and content. And such consequences are no accident. A quick summary of Morris's career, coupled with information from the relatively few interviews he consents to give, shows that this experimentalism constitutes a sustained attack on the conventional ways in which comedy is presented and the uses to which it is put.

Chris Morris – a life

Chris Morris has spent his career irritating those who work within broadcasting as much as the audiences who consume his programming. After graduating from Bristol University, Morris joined BBC local radio in Cambridgeshire and, later, Bristol. His first recorded 'stunt' – in which he already demonstrated his desire to experiment with the relationship between comedy content and media forms by undermining established conventions and removing the barrier between seriousness and comedy – came when he released helium into a radio studio in which a live news broadcast was being performed. He was quickly sacked.[1]

He came to further prominence after moving first to BBC GLR in London, and then to BBC Radio 1, with whom he maintained a relationship on and off for a number of years. Perhaps, though, 'maintained' is the wrong word: a sketch broadcast on Christmas Day 1990 about a musical collaboration between the Pet Shop Boys and 'moors muderer' Myra Hindley led to his sacking. When he later returned to Radio 1 legal problems and public censure followed sequences which implied the death of MP Michael Heseltine. It is significant that, despite his controversial antics, the offers of other jobs have repeatedly followed his sackings.

Morris's later work in television has always demonstrated its roots in radio, with a number of his series being adaptations of earlier radio programmes. Thus Morris first came to serious television prominence with *The Day Today* (BBC2, 1994), which was an on-screen version of the earlier BBC Radio 4 series *On the Hour* (1991–92). Both programmes were pitch-perfect parodies of news programming, replete with a sports reporter (Steve Coogan as Alan Partridge, who later became a comedy star in his own series), regional reports, and vox pops with real members of the public. At the centre of it all was Morris himself, performing a phenomenally accurate impersonation of a number of the BBC's most famous reporters and news presenters, such as Jeremy Paxman and Michael Buerk. Morris's later television series *Jam* (Channel 4, 2000), was a television version of the late-night BBC Radio 1 comedy series *Blue Jam* (1997–99). Both series were sketch shows in which much of the material, including death, illness and sex, was presented in a dreamlike, hallucinogenic style, with sequences slowed down and often filmed as though through dense fog. This visual style was taken to its extreme in Morris's 'remixing' of *Jam* as *Jaaaaam* (Channel 4, 2000), in which the technical trickery was so extreme as to render the programme virtually unintelligible. Yet it will be *Brass Eye* (Channel 4, 1997; 2001) for which Morris will be most obviously remembered, primarily because of the public outrage which the series engendered.

Brass Eye's first series was a parody of all manner of contemporary current affairs programming, from hard-hitting investigative reporting to the empathising of audience talk shows such as *The Oprah Winfrey Show* (Harpo, 1986–). Each episode took a different theme, such as sex, science, or crime, and in recreating the language and ideologies adopted by most factual programming, demonstrated the limited ways that such topics are conventionally presented. It was, therefore, unsurprising that with the rise of tabloid concern over child sex abuse and paedophilia in Britain in the late 1990s, Morris would return to his *Brass Eye* format and produce a one-off special about paedophilia. Broadcast in 2001, it became the most complained-about television programme in British history. Morris's most recent series was the sitcom *Nathan Barley* (Channel 4, 2005–), co-written with Charlie Brooker, about the self-obsessed London media scene and those who work within it.

Morris has made his career out of his persistent investigation into the conventions of broadcast media, particularly those of factual programming. In parodying news programmes and current affairs series he has repeatedly refused to accept the distinction commonly held between factual and fictional media which, while constantly critiqued, is nevertheless routinely upheld by broadcasters, audiences and regulators. He has similarly refused to accept the conventions of what can and cannot be joked about, particularly in a social arena such as television. In examining whether Morris's output can be deemed 'experimental', both its form and its content need to be explored. More fundamentally, it is helpful to interrogate broadcasters' assumptions about television's forms, and its social functions, for it is these which his programmes have repeatedly refused to accept as sacrosanct.

Comic form and comedy aesthetics

The production of comedy has changed little since the inception of television, with both the production system and the resulting programmes noticeably similar to those from over fifty years ago. These similarities can be seen in a number of ways: some are to do with personnel, some to do with performance, and some to do with aesthetics. What links them all is that comedy programming has, on the whole, failed to escape the theatrical roots that formed the assumptions upon which most television is founded, and from which the medium has spent the intervening years attempting to move away. Comedy and entertainment drew many of its stars from vaudeville and music hall, as the new medium attempted to capitalise on the public awareness of entertainers who had spent many years honing their craft in front of live audiences. The first major entertainment and comedy stars of television were people like Jack Benny and Milton Berle in America, and Tony Hancock in Britain. Noticeably, many of these performers came to television from theatre via radio, which is still the case in many contemporary British comedy programmes, such as *Little Britain* (BBC1, BBC2, 2003–) and *The League of Gentlemen* (BBC2, 1999–2002). The recurring television success of performers with theatrical training, whose eventual, rather than primary, home is the broadcast medium, has significant consequences for the ways in which comedy has been repeatedly shot and performed.

These formal properties are most obviously expressed in a particular shooting style associated with comedy, known as the 'three-headed monster'.[2] Developed for *I Love Lucy* (CBS, 1951–57) by Lucille Ball, Desi Arnaz and the cinematographer Karl Freund, this consists of a three-camera set-up: one camera captures a medium two-shot between the participants in a piece of comic dialogue, and a separate camera is trained on close-ups of each of them. This enables editors to cut rapidly from the comic utterance that one character has made to the bemused reaction of the other, thus getting two laughs from a single joke. This shooting style also frames the performers in a much wider way than is the case for drama, creating a literal distance between the action and the audience and discouraging an emotional engagement that may hamper the comedy's success. It also helps capture any physical business a performer may employ to enhance a comic moment's funniness. The three-headed monster has remained the dominant way in which comedy in Britain and America has been shot for over fifty years, and is employed to great comic effect in contemporary series such as *Will and Grace* (NBC, 1998–) and *My Family* (BBC1, 2000–).

Yet this shooting style, through the repetition of its use, has become more than the most appropriate way to capture the comic skills of a particular performer. It has also come to be a signal for comedy itself. It creates a particular comic look, which means that any programme can be recognised as having comic intent, even if not all of its moments are clearly funny. The shooting style for comedy has, therefore, become one of is generic markers, signalling the ways in which audiences are intended to respond to it, as well as being a tool to ensure that comedy performance is captured successfully. It has often been agued that comedy – whether media or social – requires such 'metacues'[3] or 'para-linguistic markers',[4] which constitute the mode's 'metacommunication'.[5] More importantly in terms of experimentation, however, such markers have served to distinguish comedy programming from the serious matter of news, current affairs and other factual programming as quickly and clearly as possible. The separation of comedy from factual forms represents the assumption that comedy is, within broadcasting, separate from forms such as news and drama, which are 'serious'[6] because of their relationship to 'the real'.[7]

It is this aesthetic distinction which Morris (and some other programmes discussed below), has repeatedly attempted to demolish. More importantly, his series often adopt the aesthetics of other forms, in order to demonstrate how easy it is to appropriate and recreate them. The pleasure in such comedy becomes a mixture of admiration at the accuracy of the recreation coupled with enjoyment in their being exaggerated and perverted. For example, *The Day Today*'s opening titles are an over-urgent mix of a sequence of spheres, each one representing a different part of the news's remit, such as sport, economics, crime, government and the royal family. Dotted throughout the programme are graphics illustrating concepts which are relevant to the fake news stories being presented, such as the Space Shuttle on its stunt mission to jump over a row of other shuttles, or techniques used by police to combat the plague of 'bombdogs' destroying large parts of central London. The fact that these graphics have the visual style and expensive polished sheen of news programming is both part of the programme's pleasure as well as a demonstration that such 'truthfulness' can easily be recreated. In order to ensure authenticity, they were made by the creators of the contemporary ITN News graphics, Russell Hilliard and Richard Norley, who 'welcomed the opportunity to stretch their style'.[8] In this way, the graphics experiment with audiences' relationship with the factual implications of media representations, demonstrating the graphics' status as electronic trickery rather than an objective representation of actual events.

Morris, though, parodies factual programming for political and social purposes in addition to comic intentions. The pleasures to be gained from these series are partly to do with recognising the 'source archaeology',[9] but more to do with the consequences of that recreation. Morris's ability to create a comedy programme which uses the representational strategies of other, distinct, serious forms demonstrates two things. Firstly, that the surface appearance and formal properties of both comedy programming and serious, factual programming are little more than conventions, and not necessary consequences of the content they contain (even if the institutional structures which produce such programming, and the expectations brought to them by audiences, might suggest otherwise). Secondly, this experiment demonstrates that abandoning traditional comedy conventions does not result in programmes which are not comic, opening up a whole set of possibilities not only for comedy's aesthetics but also for its content and, therefore, its social and political power.

Morris's work also experiments with, and responds to, changes in the ways in which the public make sense of video images, and the role such imagery now plays in social and private life. That is, the expansion of CCTV coverage in Britain suddenly made available a wealth of footage of real-life events such as street brawls and car chases which could be collated in programmes such as *Police, Camera, Action* (ITV, 1994–2002). At the same time, the growing availability of cheap home video cameras meant that people falling over or dogs running into patio doors could be the basis for programmes like *You've Been Framed!* (ITV, 1990–) and *The Planet's Funniest Animals* (ITV, 1999–), as well as becoming important recorders of unexpected news events such as the planes crashing into the World Trade Center in New York[10] or the Asian tsunami of Christmas 2004. While this footage was often of poorer quality than was the norm for television, it quickly became a standard part of news broadcasting, and accepted as 'evidence'[11] by audiences. Indeed, the grainy, hand-held, poor colour quality of such footage was often a powerful indicator of its veracity.[12] In these ways, the public became accustomed not only to seeing public and private activities which had previously been impossible to capture and broadcast, but those images had become part of the process through which televisual representations of the real world became defined, which consequently upholds the distinction between them and images of fiction. *The Day Today*, *Brass Eye* and *Jam* all include sequences made to look as if they were captured on CCTV or camcorder, and these are employed as evidence of the claims which most of the media make for them. Yet here, such an aesthetic becomes merely that, a set of visual signifiers which connote, but do not demonstrate, reality.

Yet, probably the most famous – and certainly most contentious – technique used by Morris in order to demonstrate the fallacy behind the authority of factual media was his interviews with 'real' people who were unaware of the real nature of his programming, and proved themselves willing to say and do pretty much anything in order to 'get on the box'. In *Brass Eye* this technique was made possible by Morris setting up fictitious campaigns in which he enlisted the great and the good to lend their support, reading out nonsense facts that could be used in protest videos to raise awareness of, in one case, an elephant being kept in a cage so small that it's trunk was stuck up its own anus, and, in another, the dangers of 'heavy electricity', supposedly reducing the members of various African tribes to the size of midgets. In the paedophilia special Phil Collins proudly stated his support for a campaign called 'nonce sense', while DJ Doctor Fox nailed a crab to a table stating it had the same DNA as a paedophile. The list of people fooled in this way ran from television has-beens, through major stars, to members of the government; indeed, Morris managed to get a question asked in the Houses of Parliament about the fictitious drug 'cake' by the MP David Amess, who had lent his support to the campaign arguing for its criminalisation.

Alongside the technique of enlisting celebrities to contribute to campaign videos, Morris has also carried out studio-based interviews, usually adopting alternative personae such as Daviv Voffov, in which interviewees are subjected to a barrage of nonsense questions, until they eventually agree with the absurd proposals Morris presents to them. Thus agony aunt Claire Rayner railed against the use of dogs as a filter for smoking drugs and, in *The Day Today*, 1980s pop star Kim Wilde expressed disgust at the police clamping London's homeless population. In many interviews Morris presented the interviewees with a circular board split neatly into 'right' and 'wrong', and asked them to turn an arrow to point to what they thought about the issue under discussion; the vast majority quickly turned the arrow to 'wrong'. The fact that no grey area existed on the board, and the vehemence with which the majority of opinions were expressed, demonstrated the simplistic nature of much current affairs programming, in which the presentation of an immovable stance in response to an issue is deemed more important – or simply more newsworthy – than the acceptance of contradictory positions or the acknowledgement of the need for debate.

All of this dupery is experimental in two ways. Perhaps most important is its wilful playing around with the conventions of television. By logically extrapolating the medium's usual presentation of difficult contemporary issues into a requirement to adopt an unshakeable position, humour is found in nothing more than exaggeration. Furthermore, in carrying out such interviews, the programme refuses to adhere to the cult of celebrity, in which certain people's views are allowed to find a space on television only because they are famous for something, even if their fame has nothing to do with the issue under discussion.[13] It also deflates the assumption that celebrity support for causes and campaigns has any meaning, because their expression of informed concern is rendered as a commodity which can be attached to any issue, even ones that are not only invented, but which one would expect those celebrities to recognise as such, were it not for the fact that their primary concern was their belief in the social value of their fame. And in demonstrating how easy it is to get MPs on board, and to get questions raised by government, it becomes apparent not only do they often have little sense of what they are talking about, but also how easily their concerns are swayed by lobbying. As the Broadcasting Standards Commission's inquiry into the programme found, public figures are willing to speak 'with apparent authority about matters they do not understand'.[14] In all, Morris's use of interviews renders apparent the symbiotic relationship between television and those who appear on it, redrawing the vast majority of factual television meaningless in a single stroke.

In terms of aesthetics this is also experimental for an audience who were given few cues as to how to read and react to this stuff. That is, Morris's impressive recreation of the conventions of factual programming, as well as his downplaying of those of comedy, made it difficult for audiences used to having the comic intent of humour clearly signalled to them, through decades of recurring representational strategies, to know not only which bits were intended as funny, but whether the programme was meant to be funny at all. Thus it was perfectly possible for audience members to be fooled, for a time at least, into thinking this was 'real' factual television. Such confusion was highlighted by the scheduling of *The Day Today*, which ran on BBC2 at exactly the same time that the real evening news was on BBC1; anyone accidentally flicking to wrong channel at that time could easily have spent some time quite worried about what was going on in the world.

In doing so, these programmes contribute to a significant trend in recent media, and particularly British television comedy: the fake documentary. 'Comedy vérité'[15] series such as *Marion and Geoff* (BBC2, 2001–2), *People Like Us* (BBC Radio 4, 1995–97; BBC2, 1999–2002), *The Office* (BBC2, 2001–3), and *Human Remains* (BBC2, 2001) have all abandoned the conventional characteristics of broadcast comedy, and instead adopt the look of a range of 'neo-vérité'[16] popular factual programming, particularly docusoaps, which swept British broadcasting in the 1990s. The rise of the docusoap led to much hand-wringing not only about the purpose of factual programming in public service broadcasting but also, and more importantly, about the veracity of factual forms.[17] Docusoaps have been criticised for their deliberate choice of extreme personalities as subjects, their heavy editing, their preoccupation with exciting narrative, and voice-overs which refuse to allow for alternative readings.[18] In all, the criticisms worry about the use of factual forms for entertainment purposes, and the lack of supposed objectivity which has always underpinned factual programming.

This is taken even further by Morris's programmes, all of which take as their comedy subject those factual conventions, finding humour in the relationship between the filmed and the filmers, and the pomposity of those who work in factual departments. This is most clearly demonstrated in one episode of *The Day Today* where Morris, having engineered a declaration of conflict between an Australia and Hong Kong who only minutes previously had signed a peace deal, exultantly declares 'Yes, it's war!', as the set behind him mutates into a rolling news-station and the news staff run around self-importantly.

The manipulation of factual television's aesthetics through humour has another consequence, however; the concomitant destruction of comedy's aesthetics. In this way *Jam* (and its remix, *Jaaaaam*) can be seen as experimenting with the aesthetics of comedy, which constitute another assault on the assumption that factual and fictional television must have distinct and distinctive identities. So, rather than comically aping the format of other genres, *Jam*'s visual style is unlike anything else seen on television, and instead sometimes appears more akin to the extreme fringes of art cinema. It consists of a variety of sketches, usually unrelated, and with a surprisingly small number of recurring characters. Unlike *Little Britain* whose voice-over and introductory sequences attempt to place the characters in particular locations, viewers are given no such guidance by *Jam*, and are instead presented with a dislocated series of comic moments. Sketches often end with no clear punchline, and the movement from one sketch to another is usually accomplished through a fade accompanied by ambient music, which belongs to neither sketch alone, as if the sequences are bleeding into one another and the whole becomes an undistinguished mass. The visual aesthetic of the series helps reinforce this lack of specificity. In many sketches the picture is digitally treated, speeding up or slowing down the action, altering colours and picture clarity to make it difficult to see what is on the screen, and using a range of dance and trance music so that the whole is imbued with an ambient atmosphere. While a viewer might be fooled into thinking *The Day Today* is a real news programme, it is difficult to conceive what a channel-surfer might make of *Jam* if they happened to stumble across it. Most significantly, Morris abandons the bright, clear visual style which has been the mainstay of television comedy for decades, in a stroke removing one of the clearest cues television comedy has recurrently adopted.

For example, one sketch involves a husband and wife arguing in their kitchen because the woman has found out that the man has slept with another woman. She berates and physically abuses him and, in content, the sketch appears like any number of sequences which make up the regular fodder for soap opera. The punchline of the sketch is that the man reveals that the woman should not be afraid that he is going to leave her because he doesn't fancy the other woman, and their sexual encounter was one of rape rather than any form of romantic intimacy. The woman forgives him, and they reconcile their differences. While the content of this sequence is itself shocking, the ways in which audiences are intended to respond to it are problematised by the way it looks. The viewer is positioned outside the house, seeing the conversation through the windows of the large patio doors to the kitchen, and which act as a frame. The viewer is, then, positioned as a voyeur, given a view which suggests that they are spying on a private moment. Of course, comedy, as well as the majority of fictional programming, allows viewers access to private moments, but audiences are rarely required to acknowledge this intrusion as necessary to their pleasure. Here, the unease that accompanies a comic sketch, which employs rape as its punchline, is intensified by the implication that, as viewers, we are willing to intrude upon the private moments of others in order to get comic pleasure, which is a necessary aspect of the comic encounter, but one which, as viewers, we are rarely ordered to take stock of.

Access to the private worlds of others is repeatedly demonstrated throughout *Jam*, and is most obviously shown in those sequences which purport to be taken from CCTV cameras. An example of this would be the sequences in which the television presenter and parliamentarian Robert Kilroy-Silk is shown running amok naked in a shopping centre, scaring shoppers, urinating on his own image on a television, and eventually curling up and sleeping in a supermarket freezer. Clearly, some of the pleasure here can be attributed to the absurdity of the sequence, and the 'gross-out'[19] nature of the comedy. However, much of the sequence is shot as if it is taken from the shopping centre's CCTV footage, with Kilroy-Silk often an indistinct blob seen at a distance on grainy stock. The effect is one which raises questions about whether such a private act as a nervous breakdown, even if it takes place in a public arena such as a shopping centre, should be seen as suitable material for broadcast.

Yet the rape sequence's aesthetics are more complex than merely looking like a voyeur's video diary. The picture has been electronically treated so that it is a negative image, albeit with a blue tint and, therefore, has little relationship to the realism that is implied by its framing. Ambient music plays over the sequence, as if it were some kind of music video. In that sense, the scene does not look like something normally witnessed in a comedy programme; indeed, it does not look like anything which we would easily recognise as television. The aesthetic of experimentalism is displayed proudly, producing a visual image which is at once arresting and distancing.

However, it is very easy to overstate this experimentalism, for *Jam* still remains bound by the majority of the conventional representational strategies of comedy. That is, while the music and digital trickery may not conform to the traditions of comedy, the shooting-style is a disguised version of conventional comedy aesthetics. In its use of a two-shot, which frames the characters in mid-shot and places the audiences at one side of the action, the rape sequence has, at its core, the 'three-headed monster' shooting style common to so much comedy. If the audience has commonly been placed as the theatrical fourth wall in comedy, the same remains true here; the only difference is that we get to see the wall – the patio doors through which we view the action. This aesthetic can be seen throughout *Jam*, where visual trickery is a supplement to the traditional comedy aesthetic, rather than a reworking or abandonment of it. In many sketches, characters often sit or stand in unrealistic lines, acting out through an imaginary fourth wall just like the theatrical structuring of sitcom shot in front of studio audiences. The digital manipulation of the images in *Jam* goes some way to covering up the use of these conventions, and certainly removes much of the bright glossiness which is usually associated with them. However, Morris's reliance on a camouflaged version of the ways in which the majority of comedy programmes are shot demonstrates that humour's metacues may well be inescapable, and that any form of comic experimentalism must, in the end, adhere to the dominant representational strategies in order to be understood as comedy at all.

Comic content/comic form

Brass Eye's intermingling of experimental aesthetics with the traditional comedy shooting style demonstrates the necessity for such material to be ultimately understood as comedy for it to remain acceptable within broadcasting regulations and audience expectations. That is, the notion that a woman would forgive her partner's infidelity because it was rape, or that Robert Kilroy-Silk would run naked around a shopping centre, are unpalatable – or even libellous – within the context of factual broadcasting, but are allowable – just – if they are jokes, albeit ones with a satirical intent. In this sense, Morris must rely on the distinctions between factual and fictional programming for his work to be justified, even at the same time as questioning the aesthetics which uphold those distinctions. The interplay of factual and fictional aesthetics are, then, symbolic of his work's content, which can make serious points only through comedy, even though that comedy is itself justified through its serious intent. Here, then, this is also experimentation with comic content, and it is the contentiousness of the particular arguments that Morris intends to express that require a redrawing of the aesthetics of comedy. In doing so, it highlights the complex role comedy plays within broadcasting, particularly in a country with a public service ethos which has a 'relentless drive to *explain*'.[20]

Indeed, the regulation of broadcast comedy demonstrates the confused position humour holds in contemporary society, and how such regulation attempts to deal with the conflicts between the social nature of humour and the public service expectations for broadcasting. The now-defunct Broadcasting Standards Commission noted that comedy has a 'special freedom',[21] allowing it to engage with concepts in ways which would be offensive if presented seriously; indeed, it also argued that this is one of the fundamental roles of comedy, presenting it less as a liberty and more of a duty. On the other hand, regulations repeatedly list those topics which it is difficult to deal with comically without causing offence, such as disability and death. This sets up a highly contradictory understanding of comedy, in which its freedom is upheld and cherished, while at the same time its inability to present certain issues is underlined. It is this contradiction which is at the heart of Channel 4's comedy output, for it is a public service broadcaster whose remit to produce innovative programming for minority audiences can land it in trouble when mass audiences see things not intended for them, as its ex-Chief Executive Michael Jackson notes.[22]

The ethical stance that broadcasting should, as much as possible, seek to minimise offence demonstrates the socially cohesive nature central to the public service broadcasting ethos. In interviews Morris has stated that the *Brass Eye* paedophile special was meant to be offensive;[23] indeed, that was the point. He states that cultural assumptions about children, the ways in which they mature into adults, and their 'innate' innocence, has led to simplistic ideas concerning the relationship between adults and children (which could be seen as feeding into the justification of vigilante attacks on those convicted of child abuse). By using the format of factual programming Morris clearly intends to examine the role media plays in constructing that phenomenon, but he also talks about his relationship with his own child, stating that it is far more problematic one than it is usually socially acceptable to acknowledge. The aim behind his programming, then, is indeed to shock, if only in order to force a more complex debate back onto the agenda, and to stimulate the public into thinking about their own children in a more sophisticated manner. Here, offence, upset and outrage become, for Morris, valid and necessary responses to his programmes. Such aims have been central to comedy at various points in its history, and Morris seems to be pushing taboo-breaking as far as he possibly can. Through testing the 'limits' of comic material he, therefore, explores questions of social hypocrisy that have been core to a tradition of satire. In this sense, he is working within an established, conventional mode, but also experimenting with that mode, pushing such conventions into new configurations.

Morris thus explores serious issues in terms of content, but also does so in a formally experimental manner. In this sense, his work can be placed in a tradition of television comedy that has been feted for its formal innovation, such as *Monty Python's Flying Circus* (BBC1 & 2, 1969–74), Spike Milligan's *Q* (BBC2, 1969–80) and *The Young Ones* (BBC 2, 1982–84). Nevertheless, such experimentalism may also serve to justify content that is less concerned with exploring serious issues. A large proportion of Morris's sketches, for example, seem to generate laughter for less socially 'serious' purposes than has been mentioned. These would include enjoyment in the repeated use of nonsense language, offensive words, and jokes about death, the body, sex and genitalia. Morris reads the introduction of one episode of *Brass Eye* while engaging in energetic and vocal sex, his cry of ejaculation emitted as the programme begins proper; in the paedophile special a re-enactment of the activities of one child abuser includes a potato emitting sperm; in *Jam* a doctor's solution to pretty much every male ailment is for the patient to drop their trousers and jump up and down so he can watch their penis rhythmically flapping around.

Influence and legacy

And what are the consequences of such experimentalism? By demonstrating that comedy need not conform to the traditional aesthetics which have defined it for decades, it is tempting to think that Morris may have paved the way for a new golden age in comedy in which a raft of programmes employ a variety of representational strategies depending on their content, intentions and audiences. It is possible to see other series drawing on the aesthetics of Morris's work. *Green Wing* (Channel 4, 2005–), for example, has a complex visual style, most noticeably in its use of speeded-up and sloweddown sequences, and is shot in a manner which attempts to distinguish itself from traditional comedy programming; indeed, the entire marketing of the programme rests on its experimentalism. The series, however, has no obvious critical intention, demonstrating that the novel aesthetic form which Morris pioneered can be appropriated purely as visual trickery, detached from the social purposes which were their original aim. This can also be seen in *Broken News* (BBC2, 2005), which, like *The Day Today*, is a parody of the multiplicity of rolling news channels which the public now has access to, and which cuts from one channel to another in rapid succession to produce a series of disjoined and decontextualised sections of reports whose cumulative consequence is confusion and nonsense. However, there is little here to suggest that the series' aesthetic is intended as a critique of news content and the difficulties of living in an information society; indeed, interviews with the writer/producer John Morton show that he attempted to distance the series as much as possible from *The Day Today*, and certainly did not intend it to have any kind of social purpose.

Comedy programming, therefore, remains much as it ever was, despite Morris's repeated interventions into its aesthetics, content and social purpose. Those series which have experimented with such controversial content, such as *Monkey Dust* (BBC3, 2003–), *Nighty Night* (BBC3, 2004–) and *Ideal* (BBC3, 2005–), have done so in a traditional sitcom aesthetic, albeit without a laugh track. Those series which have attempted to look unlike traditional comedy, such as *15 Storeys High* (BBC3, 2002), *Doubletake* (BBC2, 2002–3), *The Mighty Boosh* (BBC3, 2004–), *The League of Gentlemen* and *The Smoking Room* (BBC3, 2004–) remain, in content, very traditional series whose comic intent is unproblematised. And the social purpose of comedy continues to be one of entertainment rather than critique; the BBC's heavy investment in comedy, in particular through BBC3, has allowed a variety of writers and performers to get their work broadcast, but there is little to suggest that any of this comedy might have any political or critical purpose. Indeed, the two most popular comedies of the twenty-first century on British television are *My Family* (BBC 1, 2000–) and *Little Britain*, which are also the most traditional, and which display their conventionality explicitly. Television comedy, then, remains much as it ever was, as if Morris's experimentalism is the allowed exception to the rule; it also demonstrates how such experimentalism can, with the minimum of fuss, be absorbed into the mainstream. This can also be seen in Morris's own work, where he has turned to writing much more conventional forms such as the sitcom *Nathan Barley*, or his willingness to do an absurd comic turn in the extremely traditional comedy series *The IT Crowd* (Channel 4, 2006–). It seems that Morris's war on the aesthetics, content and social purpose of comedy is over, and the future of critical experimentalism in television humour looks uncertain.

Notes

1 Andy Beckett, 'Prank Master', *The Independent on Sunday*, Sunday Review (21 August 1994), 12.
2 Gerard Jones, *Honey, I'm Home! Sitcoms: Selling the American Dream* (New York: St Martin's Press, 1992), 66.
3 John Allen Paulos, *Mathematics and Humor* (Chicago: University of Chicago Press, 1980), 92.
4 Jerry Palmer, *The Logic of the Absurd: On Film and Television Comedy* (London: British Film Institute, 1987), 23.
5 Richard Schechner, *Performance Studies: an Introduction* (London and New York: Routledge, 2002), 92.
6 John Caughie, *Television Drama: Realism, Modernism and British Culture* (Oxford: Oxford University Press, 2000).
7 John Corner, *Television Form and Public Address* (London: Edward Arnold, 1995), 175.
8 Mark Lewisohn, *The Radio Times Guide to TV Comedy, 2nd edn* (London: BBC Worldwide, 2003), 534.
9 Dan Harries, *Film Parody* (London: British Film Institute, 2000), 4.
10 Justin Lewis, 'September 11, 2001', in Glen Creeber (ed.), *Fifty Key Television*

Programmes (London: Edward Arnold, 2004), 174–7.
11 Karen Lury, *Interpreting Television* (London: Hodder Arnold, 2005), 18.
12 Dai Vaughan, *For Documentary: Twelve Essays* (Berkeley and Los Angeles: University of California Press, 1999), 120.
13 Jessica Evans and David Hesmondhalgh (eds), *Understanding Media: Inside Celebrity* (Maidenhead: Open University Press, 2005).
14 Quoted in Jessica Hodgson, 'ITN Newsreader loses Brass Eye Case', *The Guardian*, Media Section (March 5, 2002), http://media.guardian.co.uk/print/0,,4367747-105236,00.htm, accessed April 2006.
15 Brett Mills, 'Comedy Vérité: Contemporary Sitcom Form', *Screen*, 45: 1 (Spring 2004), 63–78.
16 John Corner, *The Art of Record: a Critical Introduction to Documentary* (New York and Manchester: Manchester University Press, 1996), 50.
17 Brian Winston, *Lies, Damn Lies, and Documentaries* (London: British Film Institute, 2000).
18 Stella Bruzzi, *New Documentary: a Critical Introduction* (London and New York: Routledge, 2000), 76.
19 Geoff King, *Film Comedy* (London: Wallflower Press, 2002), 63.
20 Sue Thornham and Tony Purvis, *Television Drama: Theories and Identities* (Basingstoke: Palgrave Macmillan, 2005), 72, italics in original.
21 Broadcasting Standards Commission, *Codes of Guidance* (London: Broadcasting Standards Commission), 16.
22 Michael Jackson, 'The Fourth Way', *The Observer* (29 July 2001), 29.
23 John Dugdale, 'Taped up for Auntie', *The Guardian*, G2 Section (25 July 1994), 16–17; Bruce Dessau, 'The Prank Manager', *Time Out* (29 January 1997), 20–1; Euan Ferguson, 'Why Chris Morris had to Make Brass Eye', *The Observer* (5 August 2001), 13.

Bibliography

Adorno, T. and Horkheimer, M., 'The Culture Industry: Enlightenment as Mass Deception', in Simon During (ed.), *The Cultural Studies Reader* (London: Routledge, 1993).
Anonymous, 'Eye Witness', *TV Times*, 3 June 1960.
Anonymous, 'ITV Chronicle, 1955–65', *Contrast*, 4: 4 (Autumn 1965).
Bakhtin, M., *Rabelais and his World* (Bloomington and Indianapolis: Indiana University Press, 1984).
Bakhtin, M., *The Dialogic Imagination* (Austin: University of Texas, 1981).
Banham, R., 'The Message is a Monkee' [*sic*], *New Society* (23 February 1967).
Barry, M., 'Reaction: replies to Troy Kennedy Martin's attack on naturalistic television drama', *Encore*, 49 (May–June 1964).
Bateman, A., 'Alan King Clocks Up its First Twenty Five Years', *Film and Television Technician* (December/January 1986/87).
Baxter, J., *An Appalling Talent: Ken Russell* (London: Michael Joseph, 1973).
Beckett, A., 'Prank Master', *The Independent on Sunday*, Sunday Review (21 August 1994).
Bignell, J., Lacey, S. and Macmurraugh-Kavanagh, M. K. (eds), *British Television Drama: Past, Present and Future* (Basingstoke: Palgrave, 2000).
Black, P., 'Foreword', *Contrast*, 1: 1 (Autumn 1961).
Black, P., *The Mirror in the Corner: People's Television* (London: Hutchinson and Co., 1972).
Blanchard, S., 'Where Do new Channels Come From?', in S. Blanchard and D. Morley (eds), *What's This Channel Fo(u)r?* (London: Comedia, 1982).
Booker, C., *The Neophiliacs: The Revolution in English Life in the Fifties and the Sixties* (London: Pimlico, 1992 [1969]).
Bordwell, D. and Thompson, K., *Film Art: An Introduction*, 4th edn (New York: McGraw-Hill, 1993).
Brandt, G., *British Television Drama* (Cambridge: Cambridge University Press, 1981).

Brecht, B., 'The Modern Theatre is Epic Theatre', in *Brecht on Theatre*, trans. John Willett (London: Eyre Methuen, 1964).

Briggs, A., *The BBC: The First Fifty Years* (Oxford: Oxford University Press, 1985).

Briggs, A., *The History of Broadcasting in the United Kingdom, Volume Five: Competition* (Oxford and New York: Oxford University Press, 1995).

Bruzzi, S., *New Documentary: a Critical Introduction* (London and New York: Routledge, 2000).

Buscombe, E. (ed.), *British Television: A Reader* (Oxford: Oxford University Press, 2000).

Butler, J. G., 'VR in the *ER*: *ER*'s use of e-media', *Screen*, 42: 4 (Winter 2001).

Carpenter, H., *Dennis Potter: The Authorized Biography* (London, Faber & Faber, 1998).

Caughie, J., 'Rhetoric, Pleasure and "Art Television" – *Dreams of Leaving*', *Screen*, 22: 2 (1982).

Caughie, J., *Television Drama: Realism, Modernism and British Culture* (Oxford: Oxford University Press, 2000).

Chayevsky, P., *Television Plays* (New York: Simon & Schuster, 1955).

Childs, P., *Modernism* (London and New York, Routledge, 2000).

Chion, M., *AudioVision: Sound on Screen* (New York: Columbia University Press, 1994).

Christie, I., 'Forms 1890–1930: the Shifting Boundaries of Art and Industry', in Michael Temple and Michael Witt (eds), *The French Cinema Book* (London: BFI, 2004).

Clarke, M., *Teaching Popular Television* (London: Heinemann Educational Books, 1987).

Clarke, P., *Hope and Glory: Britain 1900–2000* (London: Penguin History, 1997).

Coleman, R. R. M., *African American Viewers and the Black Situation Comedy* (New York: Garland, 2000).

Cook, J. R., *Dennis Potter: A Life on Screen* (Manchester: Manchester University Press, 1998).

Cook, J. R., '"Between Grierson and Barnum": Sydney Newman and the Development of the Single Television Play at the BBC, 1963–7', *Journal of British Cinema and Television*, 1: 2 (2004).

Cooke, L., 'Interview with Troy Kennedy Martin', *Movie*, 33 (Winter, 1989).

Cooke, L., *British Television Drama: A History* (London: BFI, 2003).

Corner, J. (ed.), *Popular Television in Britain: Studies in Cultural History* (London: BFI, 1991).

Corner, J. (ed.), *Documentary and the Mass Media* (London: Edward Arnold, 1986).

Corner, J., *Television Form and Public Address* (London: Edward Arnold, 1995).

Corner, J., *The Art of Record: a Critical Introduction to Documentary* (Manchester: Manchester University Press, 1996).
Craig, S., 'Have Story, Need ... QUANTEL!', *Time Out* (31 October–6 November 1980).
Creeber, G., *Dennis Potter: Between Two Worlds, A Critical Reappraisal* (Basingstoke: Macmillan, 1998).
Creeber, G., *Serial Television: Big Drama on the Small Screen* (London: BFI, 2004).
Creeber, G., 'The Single Play', in G. Creeber (ed.), *The Television Genre Book* (London: BFI, 2001).
Crisell, A., *An Introductory History of British Broadcasting*, 2nd edn (London and New York: Routledge, 2002).
Day-Lewis, S., 'Drama by slogan – not frankness', *Daily Telegraph* (5 November 1980).
Delany, P., 'Potterland', *Dalhousie Review*, 68: 4 (1988).
Dessau, B., 'The Prank Manager', *Time Out* (29 January, 1997).
Dickason, R., *British Television Advertising: Cultural Identity and Communication* (Luton: University of Luton Press, 2000).
Dickinson, M. (ed.), *Rogue Reels: Oppositional Film in Britain, 1945–90* (London: BFI, 1999).
Dienst, R., *Still Life in Real Time: Theory After Television* (Durham: Duke University Press, 1994).
Donebauer, P., 'A Personal Journey Through a New Medium', in Julia Knight (ed.), *Diverse Practices: A Critical Reader on British Video Art* (Luton: University of Luton Press, 1996).
Donnelly, K. J., *The Spectre of Sound: Music in Film and Television* (London: BFI, 2005).
Dugdale, J., 'Taped up for Auntie', *The Guardian*, G2 Section (25 July 1994).
Edgar, D., 'Thoughts on the BBC', *London Review of Books*, 27: 13 (7 July 2005).
Eisenstein, S., *The Film Sense* (London: Faber & Faber, 1970 [1943]).
Ellis, J., *Visible Fictions* (London and New York: Routledge, 1982).
Ellis, J., *Seeing Things: Television in the Age of Uncertainty* (London: I. B. Tauris, 2000).
Evans, J. and Hesmondhalgh, D. (eds), *Understanding Media: Inside Celebrity* (Maidenhead: Open University Press, 2005).
Fairservice, D., *Film Editing: History, Theory and Practice* (Manchester: Manchester University Press, 2001).
Ferguson, E., 'Why Chris Morris had to Make Brass Eye', *The Observer* (5 August 2001).
Fiske, J., 'Television: Polysemy and Popularity', in Roger Dickinson, Ramaswani Harindranath and Olga Linné (eds), *Approaches to Audiences: A Reader* (London and New York: Arnold, 1998).

Fiske, J., *Television Culture* (London and New York: Routledge, 1987).
Fuller, G. (ed.), *Potter on Potter* (London: Faber & Faber, 1993).
Gardiner, J., 'Variations on a Theme of Elgar: Ken Russell, the Great War, and the television 'life' of a composer', *Historical Journal of Film, Radio and Television*, 23: 3 (August 2003).
Gardner, C. and Wyver, J., 'The Single Play from Reithian Reverence to Cost-Accounting and Censorship', *Screen*, 24: 4–5 (1983).
Gardner, C. and Wyver, J., 'The Single Play: An Afterword', *Screen*, 24: 4–5 (1983).
Gilbert, S., 'Comedy, with Chips', *Radio Times* (1–7 November 1980).
Goodwin, A., *Dancing in the Distraction Factory: Music Television and Popular Culture* (Minneapolis: University of Minnesota Press, 1992).
Goodwin, A., Kerr, P. and MacDonald, I. (eds), *Drama-Documentary: BFI Dossier Number 19* (London: BFI, 1983).
Gray, F., *Women and Laughter* (Basingstoke: Macmillan, 1994).
Grote, D., *The End of Comedy: the Sit-Com and the Comedic Tradition* (Hamden: Archon, 1983).
Hall, S. and Jacques, M. (eds), *The Politics of Thatcherism* (London: Lawrence & Wishart, 1983).
Harries, D., *Film Parody* (London: British Film Institute, 2000).
Hartley, J., *Communication, Cultural and Media Studies: The Key Concepts* (London and New York: Routledge, 2002).
Hayward, P. (ed.), *Picture This: Media Representations of Visual Art and Artists* (London: John Libbey and Co. Ltd, 1988).
Hayward, S., *French National Cinema* (London and New York: Routledge, 2005).
Herbert, C., 'Comedy: The World of Pleasure', *Genre*, 17: 4 (1984).
Hewison, R., *Culture and Consensus: England, Art and Politics Since 1940* (London: Methuen, 1997).
Hill, J., *Sex, Class and Realism: British Cinema 1956–1963* (London: BFI, 1986).
Hodgson, J., 'ITN Newsreader loses Brass Eye Case', *The Guardian*, Media Section (5 March, 2002), http://media.guardian.co.uk/print/0,,4367747 –105236,00.html, accessed April 2006.
Housham, D., 'Primetime', *Are We Having Fun Yet? The Sight and Sound Comedy Supplement*, 4: 3 (1994).
Hunningher, J., '*The Singing Detective*: Who Done It?', in George W. Brandt (ed.), *British Television Drama in the 1980s* (Cambridge: Cambridge University Press, 1993).
Hynd, S., 'Adventure in Drama for Vance', *TV Times* (6 June 1956).
Isaacs, J., *Storm Over 4: A Personal Account* (London: Weidenfeld & Nicholson, 1989).
Izod, J., *Myth Mind and the Screen: Understanding the Heroes of Our Time*

(Cambridge: Cambridge University Press, 2001).
Jackson, M., 'The Fourth Way', *The Observer* (29 July 2001).
Jacobs, J., 'Early Television in Great Britain', in M. Hilmes (ed.), *The Television History Book* (London: BFI, 2003).
Jacobs, J., *The Intimate Screen: Early British Television Drama* (Oxford: Oxford University Press, 2000).
Jameson, F., 'Postmodernism and the Consumer Society', in Hal Foster (ed.), *Postmodern Culture* (London: Pluto, 1985).
Jhally, S. and Lewis J., *Enlightened Racism: The Cosby Show, Audiences, and the Myth of the American Dream* (Boulder: Westview Press, 1992).
Jones, D. (ed.), *Censorship: A World Encyclopedia* (London: Fitzroy Dearborn 2001).
Jones, G., *Honey, I'm Home! Sitcoms: Selling the American Dream* (New York: St Martin's Press, 1992).
Jordan, P. A., 'The Mystery of Chance: Jung and Synchronicity', *Strange Magazine,* www.strangemag.com/mysteryofchance.html, accessed April 2006.
Jung, C., *The Structure and Dynamics of the Psyche*, trans. R. F. C. Hull (London and New York: Routledge, 1997).
Kaplan, E. A., *Rocking Around the Clock: Music Television, Post Modernism and Consumer Culture* (London: Routledge, 1987).
Kennedy Martin, T., 'Nats Go Home: First Statement of a New Drama for Television', *Encore*, 48 (March–April, 1964).
Kennedy Martin, T., 'Sharpening the Edge of TV Drama', *The Listener* (28 August 1986).
King, G., *Film Comedy* (London: Wallflower Press, 2002).
Kretzmer, H., 'The Taste of Sour Red', *Daily Mail* (5 November 1980).
Kroker, A., 'Digital Humanism: The Processed World of Marshall McLuhan', *CTheory.net* (May 1995), www.ctheory.net/text_file.asp?pick=70, accessed April 2006.
Laing, S., 'Banging in Some Reality: The Original "Z Cars"', in John Corner (ed.), *Popular Television in Britain: Studies in Cultural History* (London: BFI, 1991).
Lane, S., untitled review, *Morning Star* (5 November, 1980).
Laughton, B., *William Coldstream* (New Haven and London: Yale University Press, 2004).
Leslie, C., 'Playbill', *TV Times* (15 November 1957).
Lewis, J., 'September 11, 2001', in Glen Creeber (ed.), *Fifty Key Television Programmes* (London: Edward Arnold, 2004).
Lewis, P., 'Z Cars', *Contrast* (Summer, 1962).
Lewisohn, M., *The Radio Times Guide to TV Comedy*, 2nd edn (London: BBC Worldwide, 2002).

Lichtenstein, T., 'Syncopated Thriller: Dennis Potter's *The Singing Detective*', *Artforum* (May 1990).
Loach, K., 'Film versus Tape in Television Drama', *Journal of the Society for Film and Television Arts*, 23 (Spring 1966).
Lury, K., *Interpreting Television* (London: Hodder Arnold, 2005).
MacCabe, C., 'Realism and the Cinema: Notes on some Brechtian theses', *Screen*, 15: 2 (Summer, 1974).
McGrath, J., 'TV Drama: The Case Against Naturalism', *Sight & Sound*, 46: 2 (Spring 1977).
McGrath, J., *A Good Night Out* (London: Nick Hern Books, 1996 [1981]).
McGrath, J., *Naked Thoughts That Roam About* (London: Nick Hern Books, 2002).
McLuhan, M., *Understanding Media: The Extensions of Man* (London: Sphere, 1967).
Macmurraugh-Kavanagh, M. K., 'The BBC and the Birth of "The Wednesday Play", 1962–66: institutional containment versus "agitational contemporaneity"', *Historical Journal of Film, Radio, and Television*, 17: 3 (1997).
Mann, T., *Mario and the Magician and Other Stories* (London: Minerva, 1996).
Marcus, G., *In the Fascist Bathroom: Writings on Punk, 1977–92* (London: Penguin, 1992).
Martin, G., 'Company Lore and Public Disorder', *New Musical Express* (14 March 1981).
Marwick, A., *The Sixties* (Oxford: Oxford University Press, 1998).
Mathers, P., 'Brecht in Britain: From the Theatre to Television', *Screen*, 16: 4 (Winter, 1975/76).
Meigh-Andrews, C., *A History of Video Art: the Development of Form and Function* (Oxford: Berg, 2006).
Mellencamp, P. (ed.), *Logics of Television: Essays in Cultural Criticism* (London: BFI, 1990).
Mercer, D., *Collected TV Plays: Volume 1* (London: John Calder, 1981 [1964]).
Mercer, D., *Three Generations: A Trilogy of Plays* (London: John Calder, 1964).
Michelson, E., 'Film and the Radical Aspiration', *Film Culture*, 42 (Fall 1966).
Mills, B., 'Comedy Vérité: Contemporary Sitcom Form', *Screen*, 45: 1 (Spring 2004).
Moore-Gilbert, B., 'Introduction', in Bart Moore-Gilbert (ed.), *The Arts in the 70s: Cultural Closure?* (London: Routledge, 1994).
Neaverson, R., *The Beatles Movies* (London: Cassell, 1997).
Newcomb, H., *TV: The Most Popular Art* (New York, Anchor Press, 1974).
Newman, S., 'Drama', *Journal of the Society for Film and Television Arts*, 15 (Spring, 1964).

Newman, S., 'Producing a Television Play', in ABC Television Ltd, *The Armchair Theatre: How to Write, Design, Direct, Act and Enjoy Television Plays* (London: Weidenfeld & Nicolson, 1959).

Nichols, B., 'Getting to Know You ...': Knowledge, Power and the Body', in M. Renov (ed.), *Theorising Documentary* (London: Routledge, 1993).

O'Pray, M. (ed.), *British Avant-Garde Film The British Avant-Garde Film 1926–1995* (Luton: University of Luton Press, 1996).

Palmer, J., *The Logic of the Absurd: On Film and Television Comedy* (London: British Film Institute, 1987).

Paulos, J. A., *Mathematics and Humor* (Chicago: University of Chicago Press, 1980).

Peel, I., *The Unknown Paul McCartney: McCartney and the Avant Garde* (London: Reynolds and Hearn, 2002).

Petley, J., 'Factual fictions and fictional fallacies: Ken Loach's documentary dramas', in G. McKnight (ed.), *Agent of Challenge and Defiance: The Films of Ken Loach* (Trowbridge: Flicks, 1997).

Potter, D., *The Singing Detective* (London: Faber & Faber, 1986).

Purser, P., 'Landscape of TV Drama', *Contrast*, 1: 1, (Autumn 1961).

Raban, W., 'Expanded Practice in Television – Defending the Right to Difference', *Vertigo*, 1: 8 (Summer 1998).

Ray, R., 'Impressionism, Surrealism, and Film Theory: Path Dependence, or how a Tradition in Film Theory Gets Lost', in John Hill and Pamela Church Gibson (eds), *The Oxford Guide to Film Studies* (Oxford: Oxford University Press, 1998).

Riggs, K. E., *Mature Audiences: Television in the Lives of Elders* (New Brunswick, New Jersey and London: Rutgers University Press, 1998).

Robinson, D., 'Editorial', *Contrast*, 4: 1 (Winter 1964/65).

Russell Taylor, J., 'Television of the Month: Drama', *The Listener* (13 August 1964).

Russell Taylor, J., 'The Quarter: BBC Drama', *Contrast* (Autumn 1964).

Russell, K., *A British Picture: An Autobiography* (London: Heinemann, 1989).

Schechner, R., *Performance Studies: an Introduction* (London and New York: Routledge, 2002).

Sendall, B., *Independent Television in Britain, Volume One: Origin and Foundation, 1946–62* (London and Basingstoke: Macmillan, 1982).

Sendall, B., *Independent Television in Britain, Volume Two: Expansion and Change, 1958–1968* (London and Basingstoke: Macmillan, 1983).

Sexton, J., '"Televérité" hits Britain: Documentary, Drama and the growth of 16 mm Filmmaking in British Television', *Screen*, 24: 4 (Winter 2003).

Shubik, I., 'Television Drama Series: A Producer's View', in J. Bignell, S. Lacey and M. MacMurraugh Kavanagh (eds), *British Television Drama: Past, Present and Future* (London: Palgrave, 2000).

Shubik, I., *Play for Today: The Evolution of Television Drama* 2nd ed. (Manchester: Manchester University Press, 2000).

Silverstone, R., *Television and Everyday Life* (London: Routledge, 1994).

Sitwell, E., *English Eccentrics* (Harmondsworth: Penguin Books, 1973).

Spalding, F., *British Art Since 1900* (London: Thames & Hudson, 1986).

Spigel, L., 'High Culture in Low Places: Television and Modern Art, 1950–1970', in L. Spigel, *Welcome to the Dreamhouse: Popular Media and Postwar Suburbs* (Durham and London: Duke University Press, 2001).

Stoneman, R., 'Sins of Commission', *Screen*, 33: 2 (1992), reprinted in Margaret Dickinson (ed.), *Rogue Reels: Oppositional Film in Britain, 1945–90* (London: BFI, 1999).

Swinson, A., *Writing for Television Today* (London: Adam & Charles Black, 1965).

Taylor, D., 'David Mercer and Television Drama', appendix to David Mercer, *Collected TV Plays: Volume 1* (London: John Calder, 1981 [1964]).

Taylor, D., 'The Gorboduc Stage', *Contrast*, 3: 3 (1964).

Taylor, J. R., 'Armchair Theatre', in *Anatomy of a Television Play* (London: Weidenfeld & Nicolson, 1962).

Thomas, H., 'The Audience is the Thing', in ABC Television Ltd, *The Armchair Theatre: How to Write, Design, Direct, Act and Enjoy Television Plays* (London: Weidenfeld & Nicolson, 1959).

Thomas, H., *With an Independent Air* (London: Weidenfeld & Nicolson, 1977).

Thornham, S. and Purvis, T., *Television Drama: Theories and Identities* (Basingstoke: Palgrave Macmillan, 2005).

Tutty, E., '*New Tempo*: the Search for an Alternative Arts Programming Aesthetic' (MA Dissertation: Birkbeck/BFI, 1997).

Vaughan, D., *For Documentary: Twelve Essays* (Berkeley and Los Angeles: University of California Press, 1999).

Walker, J., *Arts TV: A History of Arts Television in Britain* (London: John Libbey/Arts Council of Great Britain, 1993).

Wheatley, H., 'Putting the *Mystery* back into *Armchair Theatre*', *Journal of British Cinema and Television*, 1: 2 (2004).

Wheldon, H. (ed.), *Monitor: An Anthology* (London: MacDonald, 1962).

White, H., 'Historiography and Historiophoty', *American Historical Review*, 93: 5 (December 1988).

White, L., *Armchair Theatre: The Lost Years* (Tiverton: Kelly Publications, 2003).

Williams, R., *Drama from Ibsen to Brecht* (Harmondsworth: Pelican Books, 1973).

Williams, R., *Marxism and Literature* (Oxford: Oxford University Press, 1977).

Willis, T., *Evening All: Fifty Years Over a Hot Typewriter* (London: Macmillan, 1991).

Winston, B., *Claiming the Real: The Documentary Film Revisited* (London: BFI, 1995).

Winston, B., *Technologies of Seeing: Photography, Cinematography and Television* (London: BFI, 1996).

Winston, B., *Lies, Damn Lies, and Documentaries* (London: BFI, 2000).

Wright, R., 'More Power: the Pioneers of British Computer Animation and their Legacy', in Julia Knight (ed.), *Diverse Practices: A Critical Reader on British Video Art* (Luton: University of Luton Press).

Wyver, J., "The necessity of doing away with "video art"', in Julia Knight (ed.), *Diverse Practices: A Critical Reader on British Video Art* (Luton: University of Luton Press).

Wyver, J., 'Representing Art or Reproducing Culture? Tradition and Innovation in British Television's Coverage of the Arts (1950–87)', in Philip Hayward (ed.), *Picture This: Media Representations of Visual Art and Artists* (London: John Libbey Press/Arts Council of Great Britain 1988).

Youngblood, G., *Expanded Cinema* (New York: Dutton, 1970).

Index

7:84 Theatre Company 107–12, 115
10cc (pop group) 172
16 mm film, use of 11–12, 64, 89–94, 97–8, 159
40 Minutes 142

Abbott, Paul 38, 144
ABC Television 32–5, 44–5, 91
Actors' Studio 54
adaptations, literary 19–20, 26, 50
Adorno, Theodor 167
Adrian, Max 79
Adventures of Frank, The 9, 106–7, 110–17
advertising 95, 98
aesthetics of television programmes 1–13, 27, 61, 102, 141, 181, 185, 188–92
After the Funeral 37–8
Afterimage (journal) 150
Afternoon of a Nymph 21
Akerlund, Jonas 176
Akerman, Chantal 138
Allan King Associates (AKA) 89, 92, 98
Allen, Jim 110
Allen, Keith 176
Alter-Image (television series) 156
Amess, David 186
Amiel, John 120
Angelic Conversion, The 173

Anger, Kenneth 175
Annan Report (1977) 4
anthology series 31–7, 45
Aphex Twin 176
Armchair Mystery Theatre 7, 32, 36, 40–5
Armchair Theatre 6–7, 21, 25, 31–45, 49
Arnaz, Desi 183
art schools 147–8
Artists' Work for Television 159
Arts Council 137, 148–63
arts programming on television 89–91, 97–103, 145
Ascending 140
Association of Cinema and Television Technicians 153–4
Attenborough, Richard 150
Aubrey, Doug 160
avant-garde movements 13, 24, 40–1, 76, 80, 83, 86, 102, 148–58, 162, 166–74, 177
Avengers, The 103
Aztec Cinema 175

Baker, Richard 159
'balance' in broadcasting 139
Baldessari, John 160
Ball, Lucille 183
Baltimora 171
Banham, Reyner 98

Barber, George 155
Barnard, Clio 158
Barr, Charles 20
Barry, Michael 18–22, 25–8, 48
Baudelaire, Charles 76
Baverstock, Donald 51
Bayerischer Rundfunk 98
Beatles, The 169
Becker, Lutz 147–8
Béla Bartók 71–85
Bennett, Edward 140
Benny, Jack 183
Berg, Eddie 155
Berle, Milton 183
Berliner Ensemble 8
Big Brother 15
Birnbaum, Dara 156
Birt, John 13–14
Black, Peter 44
Blackmailing of Mr S, The 40–1
Blake, Peter 75, 93
Blanchard, Simon 147
Bleasdale, Alan 110, 117
Blondie 173
Blue 163
Blue Monday 159–60
Blur 176
Bofors Gun 107
Boland, Mike 152
Borzykowski, George 148
Bosher, Derek 93
Bowie, David 172
Boys from the Blackstuff, The 9, 117
Brakhage, Stan 157
Branson, A. 102
Brass Eye 3, 5, 182, 185, 190–3
Brayne, William 92, 98
Breakwell, Ian 155, 156
Brecht, Bertolt (and Brechtian style) 8–10, 53–7, 63–5, 107–8, 112, 114, 116
Briggs, Asa 76
British Broadcasting Corporation (BBC) 6–7, 25–7, 32, 39, 45, 48, 51–2, 60–1, 75, 77, 84, 86, 98–9, 102, 116, 137, 146–54, 160, 169, 181, 193
British Film Institute (BFI) 81–2, 137, 147–9, 157–8, 162–3
Broadbent, Jim 114
Broadcasting Act (1980) 4, 146
Broadcasting Act (1990) 5, 151
Broadcasting Standards Commission 187, 190–1
Broken News 192
Brooker, Charlie 182
Bruecken, Claudia 174
Buerk, Michael 182
Burch, Noel 148
Burroughs, William 156, 176
Burton, Humphrey 150
Bush, Paul 163
Butcher, Rosemary 159

Cabinet of Jan Svank-majer, The 141
Cage, John 95
Caldwell, John Thornton 120–1
Callaghan, James 109
camera techniques 6–8, 12, 20–4, 27, 38–43, 49, 52–4, 90, 95, 97, 171–2, 183–4
Cammell, Donald 176
Canadian Broadcasting Corporation 92, 98
Candide 111
Cannes Film Festival 140
Caravaggio 175
Carey, Tristram 99
Carleton Greene, Hugh 94
Carry On films 123
Carson, Charles 37
Catherine 50–1
Cathy Come Come 12, 64
Caughie, John 6, 8, 11, 21, 32–9, 49, 74–5, 122
Celebration: In the Belly of the Beast 159
Censored Scenes from King Kong 111
censorship 84, 144, 151

Chandler, Raymond 124
Channel 4 4–5, 13–14, 136–9, 142–4, 146–63, 173, 191
Channel 5 143
Chart Show, The 167
Chayevsky, Paddy 36, 54
Cherry, Colin 147
Cherry, Neneh 175
Cheviot, The Stag and the Black Black Oil, The 107–9
Christie, Ian 41
Cinema, Cinemas 138–9
Cinema in China 139–40
cinéma vérité 12, 97, 100, 169
Clare, Anthony 162
Class, The 90
Clock DVA 174
Clocking Off 144
closed-circuit television (CCTV) 185, 189
Cocteau, Jean 175
collaboration in television writing 9–10
Collins, Phil 186
Collins, Reginald 91
Collins, Susan 156
colour separation overlay process 111–12, 114
Colqhoun, Robert 80
comedy on television 180–93
Computer Arts Society 148
Conner, Bruce 158
consensus politics 14
consumer society 6
Contrast magazine 44
Coogan, Steve 182
Cook, John 51, 65, 122
Corbijn, Anton 174, 176
Corner, John 36
Cosgrove, Stuart 160
Cranberries, The 175
Creeber, Glen 125
Creme, Lol 172
Cubitt, Sean 152
Culloden 72, 144

culture, definition of 74, 94
Cunningham, Anne 42
Cunningham, Chris 176
Cunningham, David 159
Cure, The 173
current affairs programmes 12, 186
Curtis, David 150–5, 161–3

Dada 93
Dadarama 159
Dana, Jorge 148
Dance for Camera 154
Dance of the Seven Veils 3, 70–2, 83–6
Danino, Nina 162
David, Hugh 37
Davies, Russell T. 38
Davies, Terence 157
Day-Lewis, Sean 115
Day Today, The 181–8, 192
Dazzling Image, The 157–8, 162
Debussy Film, The 71–85
Delius, Jelka 80
Delius – The Song of Summer 71–84
Delius, Jelka 80
Delius – The Song of Summer 71–84
Delluc, Louis 40
Derbyshire, Delia 99
Destroy the Heart 174
Diary of a Young Man, A 7–10, 24, 48, 51–2, 55–65, 106–9, 113, 116
Dick, Vivienne 162
Dickason, René 95
Dickinson, Thorold 147
Dickson Carr, John 50
digital technology 14, 116
Dimensions of Dialogue 141
direct address, use of 12, 20 121
'distancing' techniques 54, 62, 81, 112, 116, 183
Dr Finlay's Casebook 51
Doctor Fox 186
Doctor Who 147
documentaries 11, 97–100, 149
docu-soaps 187

Donebauer, Peter 148
Donnelly, K.J. 128
Doppelganger 173
Dorne, Sandra 23
Dotty World of James Lloyd, The 90
Douglas Home, Sir Alec 56, 59
Downey, Robert 125
drama documentaries 11
Draughtsman's Contract, The 157
Dromgoole, Patrick 42
Duguid, Peter 48
Dulac, Germaine 40
Dunkley, Chris 155
Durgnat, Raymond 148
Duvet brothers 155, 159
Dwoskin, Stephen 159

Eaton, Michael 138
Edgar, David 110
Edge of Darkness 117
Edwards, Glynn 56
Eichler, Udi 143
Eisenstein, Sergei 53, 55, 64
Electrocution of an Elephant 173
Eleventh Hour 151, 155 158, 162
Elgar 70–3, 77–86, 90, 103
Elliott, Denholm 42
Elwes, Catherine 155
emotional engagement of television audiences 54–5
Encore 49
Englishness 8, 10, 80–1
  see also national identity
Epstein, Jean 40
ER 144
Erasure 175
Establishment, the 8–10, 56
Events While Guarding the Bofors Gun 107
Everything but the Girl 175
Experimenta 158, 159
experimental films 2, 13, 152
Experimental Group (in the BBC) 18–19

expressionism 7, 122, 174
Exton, Clive, 25
Eyre, Richard 110, 116–17

factory-like production of television programmes 35
Fast Show, The 144
Fat Les 176
Fenby, Eric 72, 79, 82
Festival 51
Field, Simon 150
Fields, Dougie 156
Film Council 157
Film 82 136
Film Four 142
film noir 124
fine art 149, 176–7
Finney, Albert 131
First Night 51
Fiske, John 121, 133
Flaxton, Terry 155, 159
'floating signifiers' 130
de Florence, Bruno 156
Fontaine, Dick 92, 98–101
Ford, Mick 114
Forgan, Liz 154
Fountain, Alan 151, 152
Four American Composers 156
Franz Ferdinand 176–7
Fraser, Sir Robert 44
free association 95, 130
Freud, Sigmund 130–1
Freund, Karl 183
Frisch, Max 101–2
Fuller, Graham 123–8
funding for film-making 151–2

Gable, Christopher 79, 84
Gabor, Dennis 147
Gabriel, Peter 175
Gambon, Michael 122
Gance, Abel 40
Gardiner, John 70, 82
Gardner, Carl 14, 32–3

Garnett, Tony 10–11, 48, 51, 63–4
Garratt, Chris 156
Ghosts in the Machine 155–8
Gibson, Ben 157
Gidal, Peter 148–51, 163
Gilbert, Stephen 113
Godard, Jean-Luc 138
Goddard, James 93
Goddard, Judith 156, 160
Godfrey, Bob 148
Godley, Kevin 172, 176
Godwin, Dame Anne 61
Gold, Jack 107
Gold Diggers, The 157
Goldman, Peter 169
Gondry, Michel 176
Goodyear Television Play-house 37
Gordon, Keith 125
Gorilla Tapes 159
Government Inspector, The 144
Grade, Michael 156
Graef, Roger 98
Graham, Alex 156
Grainger, Percy 77
Granny's Is 157
Green Wing 192
Greenaway, Peter 156–7
Griffiths, Keith 136, 138, 141, 151–7
Gropius, Walter 102
Gysin, Brion 156

Hall, David 150, 159–60
Hall, Stuart 94, 139
Hamilton, Richard 156, 171
Hamlyn, Nick 162
Hancock, Tony 183
Harris, John 120
Hartog, Simon 136, 141, 150
Hart-Williams, Nick 150
Hassan, Mamoun 150
Hayward, Stan 148
Hayward, Susan 40–2
heavy metal 177
Henfrey, Janet 129

Henry, Victor 56
L'Herbier, Marcel 40
Heseltine, Michael 181
Hewett, Tim 11
Hewison, Robert 8
Hill, Derek 154
Hill, John 106, 108
Hill, Tony 156
Hilliard, Russell 184
Hindley, Myra 181
Hiroshima Mon Amour 22
Hirst, Damien 176
His Name Alive 176
Hitler, Adolf 85, 111, 129–30
Hockney, David 93, 156, 171
Hodges, Mike 91–2
Hodgkin, Howard 156
Hoffman, Dustin 138
Hoggart, Richard 74
Holland, Mary 140
Hood, Stuart 148
Hopkins, John 107
Horizon (film) 147
Horkheimer, Max 167
Horner, Penelope 22
House of Love, The 174
Houston, Charles 22
Huston, John 98

Imperial College 148
impressionism 40–3
Independent Filmmakers' Association (IFA) 151, 155
independent producers of film and television 4, 14, 98, 136, 146–55
Independent Television (ITV) 6, 144–5
Independent Television Authority (ITA) 44, 91
Institute for Contemporary Arts 175
internet resources 177
involvement of television audiences 62
Isaacs, Jeremy 136, 144, 154, 155
IT Crowd, The 193
Izod, John 131

Jackson, Michael 155, 191
Jacobs, Jason 21
Jacobs, Ken 155
Jam 180–92
James, Alex 176
Jameson, Frederic 177
Januszak, Waldemar 156
Jarman, Derek 156–7, 160–3, 173–5
Jetée, La 58
Joe of England 106, 109, 111
Johnson, Stephen R. 176
Jones, James 100
Jonze, Spike 176
Jordan, Neil 138, 176
Jordan, Peter A. 131
Journal of Bridget Hitler, The 111, 117
Jubilee 174
Julien, Isaac 158
Jung, Carl 131

Karaoke 131
Karlin, Marc 138
Keane, Tina 154
Keen, Jeff 150, 154
Kennedy Martin, Troy 7–9, 17, 24, 27, 48–65, 106–10, 116–17
Kidd, Mick 156
Kidel, Mark 156
Kilroy-Silk, Robert 189–90
King, Allan 89, 92, 98, 100
Kinks, The 169
Kirk, Roland 95
kitchen-sink drama 34–7, 44, 79
Kitson, Claire 154
Kosminsky, Peter 144
Kotcheff, William 37, 39
Kotting, Andrew 158
Kretzmer, Herbert 115
Kubelka, Peter 157
Kustow, Michael 156

Lahire, Sandra 158, 162
Laing, R. D. 96
Lane, Stewart 115

Lang, Fritz 174
Langham Group 7, 17–28, 49–50
Larcher, David 157–8, 162
Large Door Ltd 136–7, 151, 155
Larkins, The 61
Late Show, The 156
Latham, John 159
Lawrence, D. H. 26
Le Grice, Malcolm 148–54, 157, 162
League of Gentlemen, The 183
Leavis, F. R. 8, 74–5
Leggett, Mike 150
Leigh, Mike 110, 157
Leiterman, Richard 92
Lena, O My Lena 21, 26, 37, 39
Lennon, John 169
Leone, Sergio 143
Life and Times of John Huston Esq., The 98
Little Britain 183, 188, 193
Littman, Stephen 155
live broadcasting 11, 15, 27, 49, 90
Livingstone, Ken 162
Loach, Ken 48, 51, 63–5, 108
location filming 27, 38, 51, 64, 90, 97
London Film Makers Co-op (LFMC) 148–52, 156, 160–63
Long Roads, The 117
Look Back in Anger 6
Lucas, William 37
LUX Centre 160
Lydon, John 170
Lye, Len 171–2

McBryde, Robert 80
MacCabe, Colin 157
McCartney, Paul 169
MacColl, Ewan 23
McEnery, Peter 39–40
McGivern, Cecil 26–7
McGrath, Joe 169
McGrath, John 9, 48, 50, 62, 106–15
MacKenzie, John 108
Mackie, Philip 48

McLaren, Norman 171–2
McLuhan, Marshall 92–6
MacTaggart, James 48–51, 58, 60, 111
Madden, Paul 139, 142
Magical Mystery Tour 169
Mailer, Norman 99–102
Malamud, Bernard 50
Mallarmé, Stéphane 76
Man Alive 12
Man and Mirror 41–2
Mann, Thomas 20, 22, 27
Marais, Jean 174
Marcus, Greil 170
Mario 18–27
Marker, Chris 58
Marsh, Jean 57
Marty 54
Maybury, John 153–9, 162, 175
Maysles brothers 101, 169
Meet Mr Lucifer 20
melodrama 40–2
Mercer, David 17, 25
Metzger, Gustav 148
Meynell, Kate 160
Midnight Underground 158, 162
Midweek 115
Milligan, Spike 162, 191
Model, Tad 36
modernism 8–11, 77, 103, 122
Monitor 4, 10, 70–2, 75, 81–2, 86, 89–91, 97, 102
montage, use of 9, 11, 20, 23–4, 41–3, 53–5, 58–9, 63–4, 78, 92, 95, 108, 138, 156, 171, 177
Montagu, Ivor 137
Monty Python's Flying Circus 13, 191
Moore, Henry 90
Moore, Richard 56
Morris, Chris 3, 13–14, 180–2, 185–93
Morris, Michael 103
Morton, John 192
Mrs Patterson 19
MTV 160, 166–7, 170–1, 177–8
Mulcahy, Russell 172

Muller, Robert 42
Mulvey, Laura 157, 174
music industry 13
music on television 73–8, 99, 127–8, 166–5
music videos *see* pop promos
Mutke, Thomas 156
My Family 183, 193
Myers, Mike 93

narrative drama 50–7, 95
Nathan Barley 193
national identity 37, 86; *see also* Englishness
'Nats Go Home' 8, 17, 48–9, 52–5, 63, 106–10
naturalism on television 11, 52–4, 63, 106–14, 117, 123, 166
Nazism 85–6
NeTwork 21 156
New Cinema Club 154
New Tempo 4, 12, 75, 89, 92–9, 102–3
new wave culture 5, 7, 37, 49
Newby, Chris 158
Newman, Sydney 21, 33–7, 40, 48–51, 58–61
News International 157
NICAM stereo 166
Nightingale, Annie 170
Nine Inch Nails 173
Norley, Richard 184
Norman, Barry 136
Normanbrook, Lord 61

O'Connor, Sinead 175
Old Grey Whistle Test, The 167–70
Omnibus 10, 86
On the Edge 18, 24
On the Hour 181–2
Ono, Yoko 169
Opinions 139
Oprah Winfrey Show, The 182
O'Pray, Michael 160–3
Orbach, Susie 162

Orders, Ron 139
Orridge, Genesis P. 153
Osborne, John 49
Other Cinema, The 148–9
Owen, Alun 25, 37
Oz magazine 94

paedophilia 182, 186, 192
Painter's Progress 90
Painting in Light 171
Palmer, Ben 147
Paolozzi, Eduardo 93
Park, Nick 176
Parker, Charles 23, 26
Parker, Jayne 162
Parker, Kayla 158
Parsifal (film) 138
Partridge, Stephen 158–9
Pasco, Richard 42
Paxman, Jeremy 182
Pelissier, Anthony 3, 7, 18–28
Pellington, Mark 176
Pennies from Heaven 128
Peploe, Mark 99, 101
perceptions of the television audience 44
Perrin, Tony 110
Perry Mason 61
Pet Shop Boys, The 175, 181
Petit, Chris 138
Phillips, Tom 156
Phipps, C.V. 102
Pilkington Report (1962) 4, 44, 74, 94
Pink Floyd 169
Pinter, Harold 37
Piper, John 90
Planet's Funniest Animals, The 185
Play for Today 110, 112–13
Playhouse 90 37
pluralism in television 4, 35
Police, Camera, Action 185
'political' drama 64, 117
polysemic nature of television 121–5, 133

Pop Art 10, 90, 93, 98, 102–3
Pop Goes the Easel 10, 75, 90
pop promos 166–78
  and art 174–6
  history of 168–71
  makers of 171–4
Pope, Tim 173
populism 32, 75, 160, 167
Postle, Denis 93, 98, 100
post-modernism 89, 97, 103, 122, 156, 171, 173, 177
Potter, Dennis 9–10, 48, 65, 117, 120–31
Potter, Sally 138, 143, 157
Powell, Jonathan 117
Preston, Trevor 93
Prisoner, The 103
Prisoner and Escort 44
'producerly text' 133
'profile' format for arts programmes 90–1
Profiles 154
Prokofiev 71–2
Propaganda 174
Pryor, Maureen 79
Public Image Limited (PiL) 170
public service broadcasting 4–6, 14, 27, 89–91, 102–3, 187, 190–1
Pummell, Simon 158–9
punk rock 170, 174
Purser, Philip 38

Quantel technology 111–16, 171–2
Quay brothers 141, 175
Queen (rock band) 170

Raban, William 156, 162
Race Relations Act (1965) 81
radicalism, aesthetic and political 8, 94
'Radio Ballads' 24
Radio Times 48
rap videos 177
Ray, Robert 43
Rayner, Claire 186
Rayns, Tony 137–40

'reaction index' 61
Read, John 90
realism on television 8–9, 27, 31–2, 35–40, 43–5, 51, 58, 62, 110, 122
reality television 159
Reed, Oliver 76
regional arts associations 137
Reisz, Karel 150
Reithian ethos 14
Resnais, Alain 55
Rhodes, Lis 162
Riddles of the Sphinx 174
Ridley, Anna 159–60
Rigby, Jane 160
Rigby, Ray 37
Rock Follies 111
Rodrigues, Chris 150
role play 101
Romanek, Mark 173
Romeo and Juliet 19
Rose Affair, The 44
Royal College of Art (RCA) 93, 148
Ruiz, Raul 138
Russell, Ken 3–4, 8, 10, 70–86, 89–90, 103, 107, 149
Rybczynski, Zbigniew 156

Sainsbury, Peter 150
Saki 64
Sandford, Jeremy 110
satire on television 13, 59, 190–1
Saville, Philip 39, 44, 107, 111, 117
Scarlett-Davies, John 175
scheduling of television programmes 4, 15, 141–4
Schlesinger, John 90
Schuman, Howard 111
Schwitter, Kurt 177
Scott, Jake 176
Scratch Video 156–7, 175
Scritti Politti 175
Seeger, Peggy 23
September 11th 2001 attacks 178, 185
Sequin, Ken 93

Serling, Rod 36
sex scenes 26, 61
Shadow of a Journey 154
Shakespeare, William 23
Sharrock, Ivan 92
Shen Fu 140
Sherwin, Guy 162
Short Film Service 154
Silverstone, Roger 2
Simpson, Christian 19
Sinden, Tony 150
Singing Detective, The 5, 10, 117, 120–33
Siouxsie 174
Sitwell, Edith 80
Sketch Club 90
Sketches for a Sensual Philosophy 157
Slade School of Fine Art 147–8
Sleeping Clergyman, The 20, 27
Smith, John 162
Smith, Richard 100
Smith, Roger 50, 107
Smiths, The 174
Snow, George 163
Snow, Michael 137
Snub TV 167
Sound on Film 154
South Bank Show, The 144–5
Spalding, Frances 93
Sparklehorse 176
Sparrow, Felicity 154
specificity of the television medium 2–4, 8, 11–15 27, 36
Spigel, Lynn 97
Square 148
Stampe, Will 57
Stanislavsky, Konstantin 54
Starewicz, Ladislaw 168
State of the Art 102
Steiger, Rod 54
still images 58
Stimulants 94, 96
Stoneman, Rod 147, 152–62
Stones, Andrew 162
Storyboard 50–3

Strasberg, Lee 54
Strauss, Richard 71–2, 83–6
Street-Porter, Janet 156
Studio 4 50
studio system 11, 35
subversive content in television programmes 3–4
Suede 175
Suitable Case for Treatment, A 27
Sun Yu 140
Sunday Night at the London Palladium 32
Suzman, Janet 123
Swann, Cordelia 158
Swinson, Arthur 17
Swinton, Tilda 162
synchronicity 131–2

Tait, Margaret 154
Tamer Tamed, The 19
Taylor, Don 17, 25, 27
Taylor, John Russell 25, 64
technological change 95–7
Tempest, The 174
Tempo 75, 91–2
Tempo International 91–2, 97
Tennant, Emma 100
Tesler, Brian 35–6
Tetetales 50, 53
T.G.: Psychic Rally in Heaven 173
That Was The Week That Was 13, 56
Thatcher, Margaret (and Thatcherism) 5, 109–10, 116–17, 137, 139, 146–7, 155, 159–60
The The 173
'theatrical' approach to tele-vision drama 52–4, 63
This is a Television Receiver 159
Thomas, Howard 35
Thompson, E. P. 74
Thorburn, Jane 156
Thorndike, Sybil 42
Thriller 154
Throbbing Gristle 173

Time is Now, The 19, 23
Time out of Mind 41
Times, The 56
Top of the Pops 111, 113, 167–72, 175
Torrents of Spring 3, 7, 18–27
Toye, Wendy 143
trade unions 147, 153–4
Trodd, Kenith 120
Turgenev, Ivan 20, 26
TV Interventions 160
Twin Peaks 122
Two Scottish Painters 80
Tynan, Kenneth 91

Ultravox 172
United States 36–7, 81, 97
Up the Junction 12, 64
U2 173, 176

Vance, Dennis 33–4
Vasarely, Viktor 99–100
Video 1/2/3 156
Video Paintbox 156
Video Positive festivals 158–9
video technology 7, 49, 111–16, 140–1, 157, 175
Visions 4–5, 13, 136–44
voice-overs 55, 59, 64, 78–9
Voices 143
Voytek 44

Wagon Train 44
Wangler, Christian 92
War Requiem 175
Warhol, Andy 159
Watkins, Peter 72, 144
Wearing, Michael 117
Webber, Mark 158
Wednesday Play, The 11, 65
Weland, Colin 110
Welsby, Chris 162
Wenders, Wim 176
Wheldon, Huw 10, 70–3, 78–9, 82, 86, 90

Where the Difference Begins 25
White, Hayden 73
White, Leonard 32–6, 39–42, 45
Whitehouse, Mary 3, 81
Whitelaw, Billie 39
Who Is? series 12, 89, 98–103
Wilde, Kim 186
Will and Grace 183
Will the Real Norman Mailer Please Stand Up? 99
Williams, Christopher 50
Williams, Frank 56
Williams, Margaret 154
Williams, Raymond 2–3, 57, 74, 94, 122, 171
Willis, Ted 36–7
Wilson, Rodney 150–61
Winfrey, Oprah 182
Winston, Brian 6
Without Walls 144
Witness 41
Wollen, Peter 138, 157, 174
Wood, Charles 44
Wooley, Benjamin 155
Worcester 82
working class life and culture 5–7, 25–7
Workshop Declaration (1984) 149–53
World in Action 11–12, 91–2, 101
writer-led experimentation 37
writer-less drama 25
Wyndham, John 50
Wyngard, Diana 41
Wynn Evans, Cerith 158, 175
Wyver, John 14, 32–3, 90, 155–8, 161

Xie Jin 140

Young, Colin 150
Young British Artists 176
You've Been Framed 185

Z Cars 50–2, 62, 106–7
Zola, Émile 63

EU authorised representative for GPSR:
Easy Access System Europe, Mustamäe tee 50,
10621 Tallinn, Estonia
gpsr.requests@easproject.com